To Kate and Brian

The College Student's Introduction to Christology

William P. Loewe

A Michael Glazier Book

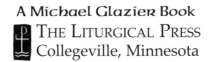

THE LITURGICAL PRESS
Collegeville, Minnesota

About the author: William P. Loewe, Ph.D., is associate professor and former chair of the Department of Religion and Religious Education at The Catholic University of America. His teaching and writing focus on christology, soteriology, and Lonergan studies.

A Michael Glazier Book published by The Liturgical Press

Cover design by David Manahan, O.S.B. Detail, "Supper at Emmaus," Caravaggio, 1573–1610, Italy. Courtesy of Planet Art.

2	3	4	5	6	7	8

Library of Congress Cataloging-in-Publication Data

Loewe, William P., 1941–
     The college student's introduction to Christology / William P. Loewe.
          p.   cm.
     "A Michael Glazier book."
     Includes bibliographical references and index.
     ISBN 0-8146-5018-X
     1. Jesus Christ—Person and offices. 2. Jesus Christ—History of doctrines.
I. Title.
     BT202.L584   1996
     232—dc20
                                                                96-26127
                                                                     CIP

Contents

Chapter One

By Way of Introduction

Recent years have seen a steady stream of new books about Jesus. A quick look through the catalogues put out by religious publishing houses shows that christology, as it is called, has come to form a cottage industry all by itself. Even after two thousand years people are still discovering things to say about Jesus that have not been said before. Sometimes those discoveries make a splash and Jesus gets featured on the cover of *Time* or *Newsweek*.

Among Roman Catholic authors the most recent ferment of scholarship about Jesus to capture the attention of the popular media can be traced back to something that happened about forty-five years ago. At that time the stream of books about Jesus began to shift its course and create a new channel. Something started changing, and the kind of book Catholic scholars were writing about Jesus started taking on a whole new shape.

What that change was about and what goes into the new shape of these scholarly theological books about Jesus, or christologies, is the topic of this book. To state our goal a bit formally, we want to arrive at a grasp of the current stage of Christian, and especially Catholic, theological reflection on the religious significance of Jesus. To achieve this goal we shall need to get a fix on three things. We need to become familiar first of all with the issues that constitute this current stage of reflection, with what people in fact are talking about these days with regard to Jesus. Second, to understand these issues and why people are talking about them today, we shall also need a grasp of the historical and cultural background from which these issues have emerged, how and why they came up. Finally, once we grasp what the issues are and why they are the issues, we shall need to get a handle on the methods with which scholars seek to resolve them, how the issues are being met at present.

Now while this statement of the goal of this book is entirely accurate, it also tells you very little that seems concrete or specific. It still leaves you wondering: what is this going to be about? As a formal statement, it needs to be filled in by the rest of the book. By the end of the book, however, our hope is that you will find that you recognize in that statement, formal though it is, what you have in fact accomplished. Understanding, then, is our goal, understanding the process of inquiry, conversation, and debate that makes up the present stage of thinking about Jesus' religious significance, the present stage of christology.

To start making all this more concrete, we can move into four introductory points. First we shall lay out the specific questions that generate the christology to be found in this book and the general approach to those questions we shall take. At least roughly we can pick up a term used by professionals in the trade to call the approach to christology we are taking a "low, ascending" approach. Second, this approach is a relatively recent development among Roman Catholic scholars. To further clarify it, as well as to explain where a lot of what we have heard from our parents or from the pulpit or in religious education programs is coming from, we can contrast this "low, ascending" approach to the approach that preceded it, namely, of course, a "high, descending" approach. That will involve us in some fairly dry ancient history. Third, the "high, descending" approach was in place for a very long time. Hence it makes sense to ask why it has been felt necessary to replace it, why it has been found inappropriate of late. What criticisms of the "high, descending" approach does one encounter these days? Fourth and finally, given the fact that that approach was in use for such a long time, another question also suggests itself. Why are these criticisms, obvious as they may seem once they are stated, only emerging now?

A "Low, Ascending" Approach to Christology

We can begin to get a sense of what this book will involve by noting that some people (Christians) speak of Jesus as, among other things, the Christ. This simple observation gives us three elements to consider.

First, as we learned in English class long ago, "Jesus" is grammatically a proper noun, and proper nouns designate the names of persons or things. In this case we are dealing with a person, a someone, a who. This someone was a male Jew; he lived in Palestine almost two millenia ago and his life ended violently. Facts like these are a matter of historical record, and they point to the first element we need to take into account, historical knowledge. What do we know about Jesus, the first-century Jew, by the means that historians employ to obtain knowledge about any figure of the past? The methods used by historians give us one lens through which to look at Jesus, a lens that in our time and culture we cannot ignore or disregard.

Now just about anyone will grant that Jesus was a first-century Jew. Talking about him as the Christ is, however, a different matter. Not everyone can, or wants to, say that Jesus is the Christ. What's the difference? Apparently we are dealing with two different kinds of statement. The first, "Jesus was a first-century Jew," is a historical statement. It's the kind of statement that results when you look at Jesus through the lens of history. What about the second? Well, notice who is usually willing to say it—Christians. Christians look at Jesus through another lens besides the historical, and using that lens they end up calling Jesus by titles like Christ. Over and beyond what historians grasp about Jesus, those who use this second lens make statements about Jesus' religious significance. That gives us a second element besides the historical component, namely a religious dimension.

To get hold of our third element we can go on to ask what it means to say that Jesus is the Christ. This, however, may also be slightly, if unnecessarily, embarrassing. It may be slightly embarrassing because as a matter of fact a good number of Christians these days have no clear idea of what the word "Christ" means. As a quick experiment, ask yourself. Occasionally a bright student will suggest that it means Messiah. But that only backs the problem up a step—we have gone from a Greek-based word, Christ, to a Hebrew-based version of the same word. The question remains, what does either of them mean? Did you get to the next step? Christ and Messiah both mean, literally, "anointed," that is, smeared with oil. But it's not clear how calling someone smeared with oil is saying anything about that person's religious significance.

To get beyond this literal sense to the metaphorical sense of Christ or Messiah as someone chosen by God for a special task would require getting into a bit of Israelite history. For the moment, however, the point is that Christ is not a word whose precise meaning is at the fingertips of most contemporary Christians.

This may be true, but it need not be embarrassing. To call Jesus the Christ, as Christians do, is to say something about Jesus' religious significance. Statements of that sort differ from ordinary historical statements, and so we arrived at a second element, the religious significance of Jesus, the first-century male Jew. Yet as our discussion of the meaning of the term "Christ" may indicate, statements of religious significance are themselves historical. Presumably calling Jesus the Christ communicated something very definite and clear to someone at some time. Today, however, it does not. Languages change over time, and words lose their currency. This is nothing to be embarrassed about, but it does give us our third element:

the various ways in which Christians have sought to express Jesus' religious significance in the past, and what those expressions may mean in terms that make sense today.

The three elements we have been gathering up suggest a sequence of questions. What can we know about Jesus historically? In what we know historically, can we discern why some people found him to be religiously significant? At the same time, can we also discern why others wanted him dead? Regarding Jesus' religious significance, how has the Christian community expressed it in the past, in terms that made sense to the first or fourth or thirteenth centuries? How may it be expressed in terms that make sense today?

Taken together these questions amount to what some call a "low, ascending" approach to christology. That is, one starts off "low," down here as it were, with the historical figure of a first-century Jew. Then, by questions of the sort we have just indicated, one moves "up," so to speak, to the religious significance of that figure. In a way, this approach retraces the process by which Christianity began in the encounter between one human being, Jesus, and some of his fellow Jews of the first century. A "low, ascending" approach has become very common among scholars today.

By Way of Contrast: A "High, Descending" Approach

Until fairly recently, however, theological reflection on Jesus followed a different approach. This other approach structured the Latin textbooks used in seminaries. In a watered-down version it was taught in Catholic colleges. It provided the background for materials used in religious education on the primary and secondary levels. Hence, because the influence of this other approach is still operative today, and as a way of further clarifying the "low, ascending" approach we just laid out, we want to get hold of what went into a "high, descending" approach to christology. We can do this by examining (1) its starting point; (2) its central content; (3) a one-word summary; and (4) what a course based on this "high, descending" approach looked like.

First, then, this approach takes its starting point from one particular New Testament text, the prologue found in the first chapter of the Gospel of John. In this text the author of the Fourth Gospel is trying, as do all the gospel writers, or evangelists, as they are called, to express Jesus' religious significance in a way that will make sense to the audience for whom the gospel is composed. This is how the author sets the stage for the story of Jesus:

> In the beginning was the Word,
> and the Word was with [the] God,

and the Word was God. . . .
And the Word became flesh
and lived among us,
and we have seen his glory,
the glory as of a father's only Son,
full of grace and truth (John 1:1, 14).

However puzzling it may sound to late-twentieth-century North Americans—"*What* Word?" we may find ourselves asking—this imagery of Jesus as the enfleshment of the eternal Word of God worked with powerful effect in the early centuries of Christianity.

At the same time, however, questions arose within the framework this imagery offered for thinking about Jesus. Just what is the relationship between the Word and God? If the Word and God are both divine, how is there only one God? Questions like these set off a process of trial and error that lasted several centuries. That process led to the councils of the church, solemn, authoritative assemblies whose teaching comprises the central content of the "high, descending" approach.

The first of these councils met at Nicea, a town in present-day Turkey, in 325. There, in response to what a presbyter, or priest, named Arius from Alexandria in Egypt had been teaching, the Council Fathers doctored a creedal prayer that was already in use at baptismal ceremonies and added some curses to it. This prayer confessed belief in Jesus as God's Son who was, the Council Fathers specified, "true God of true God, begotten, not made, one in being with the Father." Arius apparently had been teaching the opposite. Hence the Council Fathers added curses like this: "If anyone say 'there was a time when he [the Son] was not,' let him be *anathema* (i.e., accursed and excommunicated)." At the Council of Nicea in 325, in response to Arius, the Church defined the dogma of the divinity of Christ.

After this the opposition between two centers of Christianity in the East, one at Alexandria and the other at Antioch in Syria, set things moving toward the Council of Chalcedon in 451. Alexandria focused on the belief that with the coming of Jesus, the divine Word or Son, God was at work saving the human race. Hence they stressed the unity of the divine and the human in Jesus, and they spoke of Jesus, using the language of the prologue to John's gospel, in terms of Word and flesh. With this emphasis, however, they experienced difficulty in maintaining the full humanity of Jesus. Clement of Alexandria, for instance, declared it unthinkable that Jesus, being who he was, would have had to go to the bathroom. Another Alexandrian thinker, Apollinaris, took this tendency to an extreme and declared that in Jesus the divine Word replaced the human soul. This denial of Jesus' full humanity was condemned at the first Council of Constantinople in 381.

Antioch's emphases mirrored and reversed Alexandria's. If with Jesus' coming God was saving the human race, then Antiochene thinkers stressed the full humanity of Jesus. Were there anything about us that Jesus did not share, were he not fully human, then we would not be fully saved. Hence they spoke about Jesus in terms of the Word and a full human being (*anthropos*), while their difficulty lay in expressing how Jesus was one, a single person.

The Council of Chalcedon in 451 sought to bring together the valid insights of both schools. Jesus, it taught, is one and the same, both truly divine, as Nicea had taught, and truly human, as Antioch especially insisted. As one and the same he can be spoken of as one "person," as Alexandria stressed, and if this one person is truly divine and truly human then one can speak, as would Antioch, of the "two natures" that come together in him. Thus the Council of Chalcedon defined what is called the dogma of the "hypostatic union," that is, the union of true divinity and true humanity in the one person (*hypostasis*) of Jesus.

These two dogmas, the divinity of Christ and the hypostatic union, form the central content of the "high, descending" approach to reflection on Jesus' religious significance. From this perspective, what is significant about Jesus is that he is the incarnation, or enfleshment, of the preexistent divine Word or Son. The single term "incarnation" serves as a summary of this "high, descending" approach to christology.

Having reviewed the starting point, central content, and a summary of this approach, we can look briefly at what a course based on it was like. Such a course, taught in Latin to seminarians, was part of a fixed sequence. Before taking the course in christology, commonly entitled *De Verbo Incarnato (On the Incarnate Word)*, students first followed courses on God as one (*De Deo Uno*) and God as triune (*De Deo Trino*), that is, three-personed. Then came the christology course, and it fell into three parts. A first part raised the question of how a divine person could become human and used the discipline of philosophy to answer it. This part of the course worked out what was meant by person and nature in such a way that it became possible for a divine person, possessing the divine nature, to assume or take on a human nature as well. Thus this first section of the course worked out the metaphysics of the hypostatic union.

A next section inquired into the effects of the hypostatic union on Jesus' humanity. How would a humanity be affected by being assumed by a divine person? One effect pertained to Jesus' human will. Morally, in his humanity the Son of God would be incapable of sinning. With regard to Jesus' human intellect, matters got a bit complicated. It was taught that in his humanity Jesus acquired knowledge like everyone else. Like any other Jewish child, for instance, little Jesus had to learn to tie his sandals. In addition to this experiential knowledge, however, he had two further kinds of human knowledge as well. Because his task was to save the human race, he was equipped with what was called infused knowledge, knowledge that was simply poured into him without any learning process, that would help with his task. Thus, for instance, he could read people's thoughts, and he could predict the future.

Beyond this infused knowledge there was something else as well. All human beings were made to be happy with God in heaven by enjoying a face to face knowledge of God. This was called the beatific vision, the vision of God that makes you happy. While everyone else had to wait until the next life for this knowledge of God, it was taught that Jesus, by virtue of who he was, enjoyed the beatific vision from the very beginning of his human life on earth.

A third and final section of the course asked how Jesus, thus fitted out with these moral qualities and various kinds of knowledge, in fact achieved his task. How did he save the human race? In response some version of a theory of satisfaction, originally proposed by St. Anselm of Canterbury at the end of the eleventh century, was usually worked out. By dying on the cross Jesus satisfied, that is, in some sense made up for our sins.

Three Lines of Criticism

The year 1951 brought the fifteen hundredth anniversary of the Council of Chalcedon. Scholars celebrated the occasion, as they are wont to do, by producing learned essays in large tomes. What began coming to light in this flurry of research was an inconsistency. The standard course in christology we just summarized was intended to present and explain the teaching of Chalcedon. As we have seen, the Council of Chalcedon balanced the Council of Nicea by teaching that Jesus was fully human as well as fully divine. In fact, the Council had stated that as human Jesus was "like us in all things except sin." But, scholars began to wonder, is it because of our sinfulness that we cannot predict the future or read people's minds? Similarly, is Jesus really like us if, besides not in fact sinning, he was not able even to experience temptation? With questions like these it began to emerge that the standard course in christology was not fully consistent with Chalcedon's firm teaching of Jesus' full humanity.

In the four decades since that anniversary three lines of criticism of the "high, descending approach" to christology have been voiced. Notice that none of these criticisms is aimed at the content of that christology. None of them is saying that Nicea was a mistake, Arius was right, and we should forget about Chalcedon, too. The criticisms we are about to review in no way deny the Church's dogmas of the divinity of Christ and of the hypostatic union. What they do argue, however, is that as a way of dealing with these questions the "high, descending approach" is inappropriate today. Why is this the case?

First, look where that approach begins. John's gospel begins with the divine Word who is with God in the beginning. The first question the standard course faced was how to get a preexistent divine person, the Second Person of the Trinity, down here as a human being. Notice what that question assumes—that Jesus, a first-century male Jew, is divine, the Second Person of the Trinity. Today, however, the existence of God is not something that can be taken for granted in contemporary culture. Even less so is the divine identity of a first-century Jew self-evident to people today. So, this line of criticism runs, while the "high, descending approach" takes Jesus' divinity for granted, this is inappropriate in today's culture. Rather than taking this belief for granted, a contemporary christology needs to give some account of it. How and why did belief in Jesus' divinity arise in the first place?

A second line of criticism zeroes in on what the course we outlined leaves out. Chalcedon taught that Jesus was both fully divine and fully human, and the standard course followed up on Chalcedon's language by treating Jesus' humanity in philosophical terms. Thus it dealt with Jesus' humanity as "a complete human nature." In taking this philosophical approach, however, the standard course abstracted from the concreteness of Jesus' humanity. It left out the actual course of his life, the fact that he lived one lifestyle rather than another, and that this lifestyle had something to do with why he got killed. It abstracted as well from what follows Jesus' execution in the gospels, namely his resurrection. Hence, besides criticizing the "high, descending" approach for what it takes for granted, namely Jesus' divinity, scholars also criticize that approach for what the standard seminary course managed to leave out, namely Jesus' life, death, and resurrection!

A third line of criticism has to do with what the "high, descending approach" can suggest to people's imaginations in the contemporary cultural context. If you start off by thinking of Jesus first of all as an eternal, divine person who subsequently assumed a human nature, it becomes very easy to imagine Jesus much as Apollinaris thought he was, a divine person walking around in a human body. You are likely to spontaneously follow a reasoning process that goes like this: Jesus, the first-century male Jew, is a divine person. Hence whatever is true of God is true of this first-century male Jew. If God is omnipotent, so is Jesus—so of course he can walk on the surface of a lake, change water into wine, or for that matter, if he wanted to he could fly. So also, if God is omniscient, that is, all-knowing, then so also is Jesus. Of course he can read people's minds and predict the future, nor did anything except modesty prevent him from speaking Chinese or laying out Einstein's theory of special relativity.

The theologian Karl Rahner had a word for this way of imagining Jesus: "cryptomonophysitism." Literally this would mean a "hidden one-natur-ism." The idea is this: when push comes to shove, Jesus is really divine. Period. That means, in classical terms, he has one nature, not two. But while that is how you imagine Jesus, you still repeat what Chalcedon taught, one person in two natures. So your "monophysitism" is hidden, even from yourself. But if you do imagine Jesus along the lines sketched in the preceding paragraph you are far from what Chalcedon affirmed. The Jesus you imagine is hardly "like us in all things except sin." The late bib-lical scholar Bruce Vawter put the matter almost crudely. To imagine Jesus along these lines, he wrote in *This Man Jesus* (Garden City, New York: Doubleday, 1975, p. 15), is to imagine a mythicized figure who never walked the face of this earth.

Thus three lines of criticism of the "high, descending approach" to christology have emerged in the decades since 1951. That approach is found inappropriate because of what it takes for granted (Jesus' divinity), because of what it tends to leave out (Jesus' life, death, and resurrection), and because of what it suggests to people's imaginations (a mythological figure far from one who, in his humanity, is "like us in all things except sin").

Why Now? A Clash of Cultures and a New Task

These criticisms of the "high, descending" approach may seem clear and compelling. Yet that approach in one form or another dominated Christian thinking about Jesus for a very long time, perhaps a millennium and a half or more. Hence the question arises: why are these criticisms only emerging now?

The criticisms, I would suggest, together with the shift from a "high, de-scending" to a "low, ascending" approach in christology, are called forth by a much larger change that Christianity, and particularly Catholicism, is undergoing. To get hold of the character of this larger change let us say that the "high, descending" approach to christology was part of what we can call the traditional self-understanding of Christian faith. That tradi-tional self-understanding, the way Christians thought about God, the uni-verse, and themselves, emerged over a long period of time.

Church historians divide the history of Christianity into a series of pe-riods. The Church begins with the apostolic age, named after the first wit-nesses to Jesus, the apostles. This is the age of the formation of the early

Christian communities and the compilation of the writings that make up the New Testament. There follows, from roughly the middle of the second century to the seventh or eighth century, the patristic age. This age is named after the so-called Fathers of the Church such as Irenaeus, Clement of Alexandria, Augustine, and John Damascene. Many of these writers were also bishops. Next come the Middle Ages with their cathedrals, schools, and eventually universities. This is the period of the Doctors of the Church ("doctor" is the Latin word for teacher), theologians like Thomas Aquinas, Bonaventure, and Duns Scotus. After the Middle Ages historians distinguish the Renaissance, Reformation, and, beginning in the seventeenth century, the modern period.

The point is that the traditional self-understanding of Christian faith of which the "high, descending" approach to christology forms a part was worked out in the periods prior to the seventeenth century, prior to the modern age. Those earlier periods were characterized by what a scholar named Paul Ricoeur has called a "first naiveté." What does this mean? Anthropologists and sociologists tell us that every society and every culture rests on some basic story, some narrative that orders the universe and makes sense out of life. For Christendom prior to the modern period the Bible fulfilled that function of ordering the world. The Bible provided the foundational story upon which European culture was built. In that culture if one wanted to know where we came from, how we ought to live, and what our final destiny was, one naturally turned to the Bible. The Bible, then, was simply taken for granted. This is what Ricoeur means by "the first naiveté:" the unproblematic, taken-for-granted character of the relation to the world of the biblical narrative that characterized the ages of Christian history prior to the modern period.

At least two things make modern culture different from earlier periods. Modern culture rests on the empirical natural sciences and on historical consciousness. These are modern developments, and neither of them was available to the apostolic, patristic, or medieval periods. This is not to say that prior to the modern age, humankind had achieved no scientific knowledge. The opposite is obviously true. But in both the ancient world and the Middle Ages the sciences were considered subdivisions of metaphysics. Metaphysics, as the science of being as such, was regarded as the science of sciences. Other sciences were considered branches of metaphysics. Physics, for example, was the science of being insofar as being is mobile, biology the science of being as animated, and so on. Furthermore these sciences took their terminology and questions from metaphysics, inquiring into the formal, material, efficient, and final causes of the phenomena they studied. All this is what changed when, starting in the seventeenth century, the sciences began breaking out from under the metaphysical umbrella that held them together. The sciences became empirical, a matter of mathematically formalized observation of phenomena and testable hypotheses about their workings.

Historical consciousness was similarly absent from the ages prior to the modern period. Human nature, it was thought, was always and everywhere the same and so differences from place to place and time to time were regarded as merely accidental, while the unchanging permanence of the natural law rendered truth and right and wrong likewise permanent and unchanging.

What happens when the traditional self-understanding of Christian faith encounters modern culture, a culture in possession of the empirical natural sciences and historical consciousness? To continue to borrow Ricoeur's language, the "first naiveté" gives way to a "hermeneutic of suspicion." A hermeneutic is a set of principles of interpretation. Suppose, for instance, you have taken a psychology course and learned about the work of Sigmund Freud. Then, when you are out with friends having dinner in a restaurant, you find yourself giggling knowingly at the man in the smoking section lighting up a cigar. He, of course, thinks he is simply smoking a cigar but you, with your brand new knowledge of Freud, know better. He is really doing something unmentionable! So why are you giggling? You have been applying a Freudian hermeneutic to the man's behavior.

What goes into a hermeneutic of suspicion? Imagine you're a good Christian living in the middle of the nineteenth century. Your religion tells you clearly where we came from. Read the opening chapters of the first book of the Bible, the book of Genesis, about Adam and Eve and the garden. But suppose you have some free time, some money, and a good deal of curiosity. Suppose you fit out a ship named after your favorite kind of dog and you spend some time hanging around some rocks in the Pacific Ocean, and then you come home to England and write a book. Your favorite kind of dog is the beagle, the rocks are the Galapagos Islands, your name is Charles Darwin, and your book is *The Origin of Species*. So what is a good Christian to do? The Bible, it seems, says one thing and modern science another. Thus is generated a hermeneutic of suspicion. As Sportin' Life sings in the show *Porgy and Bess*, "The things that you li'ble to read in de Bible—dey ain't necessarily so."

That unproblematic relationship to the world of the Bible is lost when, as it seems, the Bible and science contradict one another. The "first naiveté" shatters and you begin to read the Bible with a hermeneutic of suspicion. Existentially this can distance you from the religious tradition and alienate you from it. Something like this seems to be the path Western culture took in the modern period, and it is a path many people tread in the process of growing up. For people who go this route, the world of one's religious tradition, the world of the biblical narrative, comes to seem naive and childish, something you outgrow as you come to know more of how the world really is. Auguste Comte, a modern thinker who is regarded as the father of sociology, expressed this attitude when he divided the history of the human race into three phases. The first phase was the age of religion, a primitive phase that gave way when, in ancient Greece, the age of metaphysics dawned. This, however, was only an intermediate phase. Complete enlightenment finally arrived, on Comte's reckoning, when the modern period ushered in the age of science.

The myth of scientific progress that Comte proposed as modern culture's substitute for the biblical narrative has itself encountered a hermeneutic of suspicion of late. Progress that creates a consumer society, that fosters an international market in high-tech instruments of human destruction, and that is not far from destroying the organic systems that make our planet habitable has proven highly ambiguous. With this recognition, some would say, our culture is shifting into a post-modern phase.

In the midst of the cultural shifts we have been outlining one question remains constant: What is it all about? In response to this question we find a variety of available answers. Some are fairly simple. Work hard all week, play hard on weekends and vacations; or follow the right career, marry the right-looking spouse, have the right number of children, drive a mini-van and own a dog. Alternatively, one might bring this question of what it is all about to bear on one's religious tradition. Nothing says you have to turn in this direction. After all, it's a free country. But notice that by its scope, at least, the question itself is religious in nature. What is it *all* about?

The persistence of the religious question makes possible a move beyond the hermeneutic of suspicion. You may turn to the world of the biblical narrative, but not with scientific questions. Science is competent to deal with those. Nor do you look to the Bible for historical information: for that, one turns to the academic discipline of history. But if what Ricoeur called the first naiveté is no longer an option, turning to the biblical tradition with a second, post-critical openness is. Bringing the religious question—what is it all about?—to bear on the biblical tradition sets up what Ricoeur calls a hermeneutic of recovery. Investigating the religious tradition from this perspective you just may, perhaps, find there an answer to the religious question that you judge superior to the many other answers offered by our culture.

We started this section by asking why the criticisms of the "high, descending" approach to christology that we enumerated are only emerging of late. Our response has been that those criticisms, and the shift to a "low, ascending" approach to thinking about Jesus' religious significance, are part of the process set in motion by the encounter between the traditional self-understanding of Christian faith and modern culture. We have suggested that in that encounter what Ricoeur calls a "first naiveté" shatters in the face of empirical science and historical consciousness, while a hermeneutic of suspicion is engendered that leads to alienation from the religious tradition. But because the religious question persists there is possible a further move toward a hermeneutic of recovery and a second, post-critical naiveté. The dynamics of this encounter between the traditional self-understanding of Christian faith and modern culture define the larger context for the project of constructing a christology, that is, of rethinking Jesus' religious significance today.

Part I

The Question
of the Historical Jesus

As we saw when we were introducing the notion of a "low, ascending" approach to christology, one of the questions that generates that approach centers on what we can know about Jesus with the means used by historians. What do we learn of Jesus when we view him through the lens through which historians ordinarily obtain knowledge about the past and about any of the people who inhabited it? Somewhat later we saw that historical consciousness is one of the elements of modern culture that throws the traditional self-understanding of Christian faith into crisis. Together with the empirical natural sciences, the results of historical research often undermine the taken-for-granted character of biblical narrative and thus shatter what Ricoeur calls the first naiveté. Contemporary culture therefore demands that Christian theology deal with the question of the historical Jesus.

We shall begin with what is known as the Old Quest for the historical Jesus, a movement that starts toward the end of the eighteenth century and runs until 1906. Our reasons for delving into the figures and positions that make up this movement are twofold. First, it is through this Old Quest that the encounter between the traditional self-understanding of Christian faith and modern culture gets acted out. The Old Quest exemplifies the process whereby a hermeneutic of suspicion is generated and alienation from traditional Christianity occurs. The Old Quest concretizes the context for contemporary christology that we laid out somewhat abstractly in the final point of our introduction. Second, in the course of the Old Quest certain discoveries were made that are taken for granted by scholars today. It will be helpful to become familiar with these.

Plato held that teachers do not really impart anything new to students; they merely remind them of what they already know. Thus if there was an

Old Quest you already know that there must be a New Quest as well. The beginning of the New Quest occurs in 1953 and its work continues today. After we lay out the Old Quest we shall ask what went on in the interim (1906–1953) as immediate background to the New Quest. Then, having reviewed the launching of the New Quest by a scholar named Ernst Käsemann, and having laid out a statement of its goal and methods, we shall settle down to a consideration of the payoff of the New Quest by constructing an interpretation of the historical Jesus.

Chapter Two

The Old Quest
for the Historical Jesus

Our major source on this topic is a book published in 1906 by Albert Schweitzer. Students of music will recall that Schweitzer was instrumental in the revival of Bach's organ music late in the nineteenth century. He is also widely known for the philosophy of reverence for life that guided a hospital he operated in Gabon in Africa, work for which he was awarded a Nobel Prize. Musician and medical doctor, Schweitzer was also a theologian, and his book entitled *The Quest of the Historical Jesus* (ET New York: Macmillan, 1968) both sums up the Old Quest and brings it to an end.

To keep our bearings as we proceed through the various figures and positions that make up the Old Quest we can begin with an overview of what we need to cover. If we chart the data on the Old Quest, those data fall into three columns.

H. S. Reimarus	Rationalists (H. E. G. Paulus)	Supernaturalists
D. F. Strauss Marcan hypothesis B. Bauer		
W. Wrede J. Weiss, A. Schweitzer	Liberals (A. von Harnack)	

Hermann Samuel Reimarus lived an uneventful life. Having followed a career as a professor of Oriental languages in Hamburg in northern Germany, he died in 1768. After he died a bundle of papers was found squirreled away in his desk, and G. E. Lessing began publishing them in 1774. Four years later, however, the civil authorities ordered Lessing to cease and desist under pain of confinement. Reimarus's papers, apparently, were unfit reading material for decent Christian folk.

What had Reimarus been up to in these *Fragments,* as the English translation is entitled? He sought to ascertain the aims and intentions that had animated Jesus during his lifetime. Reimarus thus wanted to find out just what Jesus had actually been trying to do. As a clue, Reimarus noticed how often in the gospels, especially the synoptics, as Matthew, Mark, and Luke are called, Jesus proclaims "Repent! The kingdom of heaven is at hand!" Reimarus noticed something else as well. Nowhere in the gospels does Jesus offer a clear explanation of what he means by the kingdom. Hence, Reimarus reasons, if Jesus could speak about the kingdom without explaining what he meant by it, this must have been because he could assume that his audience already knew what he was talking about.

For Reimarus, then, the key to understanding Jesus' aims and intentions lay in the meaning of the phrase "the coming of the kingdom of heaven" for a first-century Jew. Jesus and his contemporaries, Reimarus suggests, shared a Davidic-Messianic understanding of the coming of the kingdom. That is, God would raise up a leader, a Messiah, who would rally the Jews to expel foreign domination and restore Israel as a kingdom to the glory it had enjoyed under King David. Jesus would have understood himself in these religious, nationalistic, and political terms, with one further twist. He also calls for repentance. When the Kingdom is restored, it will not be enough just to be Jewish to participate in it. One can't just be a Jew, one must be a just Jew. Beyond race, Reimarus believed that Jesus, as a great ethical teacher, set moral requirements for belonging to the kingdom he sought to restore.

The outcome, of course, was Romans one, Jesus zero. The revolution failed to materialize and Jesus was executed. Where, then, did Christianity come from? Jesus wanted to restore Israel, not found a Church. His disciples, however, having been plucked from obscurity, enjoyed the status they were accorded in Jesus' movement. Hence, Reimarus suggests, in order to keep a good thing going they explained Jesus' failure away. His real kingdom, they said, was not of this world. He had really had a spiritual kingdom in mind. Nor did his death mean that he had failed. No, he died to save us from our sins. Nor for that matter was he still dead. He was risen and they had seen him. Unfortunately, says Reimarus, in fabricating the resurrection stories Jesus' disciples were very clumsy. The various versions of the story that they gave out contradicted each other so often that were they a group of witnesses in a court of law a judge would throw their testimony out.

Reimarus is generally credited with opening the Old Quest. On his account the historical Jesus was a failed religious and nationalistic revolutionary, albeit a great ethical teacher, while Christianity was the result not of Jesus' intention but of a fraud on the part of his disciples.

Because Reimarus's position was extreme and because his writings were suppressed his immediate impact was muted. In the first third of the nineteenth century a debate between groups we can call *rationalists* and *supernaturalists* held center stage. Who were these parties? In the far right column of our chart we find the supernaturalists. Attempting to maintain the traditional self-understanding of Christian faith, they reject anything in modern culture that would contradict it. They emphasize two doctrines about the Bible as the revealed word of God. First, God is the principal author of the Bible and God used its human authors as passive instruments who contributed no more to its content than does your pen or word processor to a paper you are writing. That is, they hold that the Bible is verbally inspired; every word, indeed, every Hebrew vowel point, is directly inspired by God. Second, this doctrine of *verbal inspiration* has a corollary. If God is the principal author of the Bible, since God knows everything and never lies, the Bible contains no error of any sort. In addition to verbal inspiration, the supernaturalists held as well a doctrine of total *biblical inerrancy*. With the supernaturalists the first naiveté is hardening into a biblical fundamentalism.

We place the rationalists in the middle column because they are attempting to be at once Christian and modern. Modern, however, is a relative term. Think of how quaint old movies and TV shows look today. Being modern in the early nineteenth century meant especially being scientific in one's outlook, and the science that set the tone was the classical sort exemplified by Newtonian physics. From this perspective nature was a closed, machine-like system of cause and effect. For this reason while the rationalists were enthusiastic about what they took to be Jesus' teaching, what stuck in their craw were the New Testament miracle stories. As apparent exceptions to the laws of nature these stories went against the grain of a nineteenth-century scientific world view. Hence for the first third of the nineteenth century attention focused on a debate between the supernaturalists and the rationalists regarding the biblical miracle stories.

For the supernaturalists, of course, matters were simple. Each story happened exactly as it was written. The rationalists countered with what they regarded as a more nuanced position, including a general theory and its application. The theory distinguishes two sorts of causality. Think of some event: a leaf falls or a war breaks out. Why did the leaf fall? An answer to that question would involve some knowledge of botany, of what goes on with deciduous leaves, and a smattering of physics, a notion of how gravity operates. Similarly for the war breaking out—understanding its causality would require knowledge supplied by a number of relevant disciplines. Each of these disciplines would offer part of the answer to the question why the event being considered happened. Each of these disciplines would contribute to a grasp of the causality of that event.

In constructing their theory the rationalists locate the explanations offered by botany, physics, political science, economics, and combinations of these disciplines on the level of what they call secondary causality. Now back to Plato. If we know about secondary causality we know there must be primary causality as well. Think again of a leaf falling or a war breaking out. Now if you ask why these events occur, and if you ask from the perspective of primary rather than secondary causality, you get a one-word answer. God! God, if God exists, is the primary cause of everything that is and happens. God is the reason for the existence of a universe in which botanical and physical and political scientific explanations hold.

Besides distinguishing primary causality from secondary causality, the rationalists add one further component to their theory. This component consists in a historical observation. Modern people, they contend, have a scientifically-informed mentality and so they focus on the secondary causes of things and events. The ancient world, however, saw the world more religiously and so they tended spontaneously to describe events from the perspective of primary causality.

With these considerations the rationalists dissolve, as it were, the problem of miracles. If the biblical miracle stories are recounted from the viewpoint of primary causality, the only problem is to figure out what secondary causes were involved. For example, the story is told in Mark 6:35-44 that as Jesus was preaching in a remote place to a large crowd, it got late and people began to get hungry. Jesus told the disciples to begin distributing the five loaves and two fish that they had with them, and by a miracle these proved enough to feed a throng of five thousand people! God, then, saw to it that everyone got fed. But, ask the rationalists, how did God go about it? Through what secondary causes did God work? In this case, they suggest, God used the example of generosity set by Jesus and his disciples. When they saw that it was late and the crowd was hungry Jesus had them begin distributing the food they had brought with them. The idea caught on, others started doing the same, and soon there was enough for everyone. The real miracle, then, was the generosity to which Jesus' example inspired so many people.

One more example: there are three New Testament stories in which Jesus is pictured as raising the dead to life. One involves a synagogue official's daughter (Mark 5:21-24, 35-43), another a widow's son (Luke 7:11-17), and the last Jesus' friend Lazarus (John 11:1-44). What do the rationalists do with these miracle stories? They begin by noting Jewish burial practices at Jesus' time. People were sealed into their tombs quickly, three hours after death. Next the rationalists speculate that such haste must occasionally have had tragic consequences. Every so often in today's world you read a story in the paper about coroners who, just as they are about to perform an autopsy, notice a twitch or some other sign of life. Similarly in the days of Jesus, the rationalists suggest, it must have happened from time to time that someone who fell into a deep coma or otherwise appeared dead was sealed into a tomb, only later to awaken and then, unable to get out, perish miserably. Hence the stories about raisings from the dead were misnamed. Rather in each case Jesus perceived some sign of life and saved the person from being entombed prematurely.

The debate between rationalists and supernaturalists went back and forth until, in 1831–32, *David Friedrich Strauss* came out with a two-volume work entitled *The Life of Jesus Critically Examined*. In this work Strauss goes through the gospel narratives story by story, in each case giving the supernaturalist case for its literal historicity, the rationalist interpretation, and finally his own position. The outcome of his work is twofold. It discredits the rationalist project. This does not, however, give comfort to the supernaturalists, for its second effect is to pull the whole rug out from under their debate with the rationalists.

How does Strauss discredit the rationalist project? He points out that their success comes with a price tag that they overlooked. In order to fashion a Christianity acceptable to modern folk like themselves they needed to get rid of what they saw as a crude and primitive element in the biblical narratives, the miracle stories. These the rationalists explained away, seeking to come up with a plausible explanation for what had really happened in each instance. What they failed to notice, however, was this. On their account, Jesus and the disciples would have known that it was good example, and not a miraculous multiplication, that had gotten everyone fed. Similarly Jesus would have known that the widow's son, the official's daughter, and Lazarus were not really dead. Hence the question arises: since Jesus and the disciples knew what had really happened, why did they let the stories be told the way they were? Does that not make them dishonest charlatans? And in that case, what value is there to the rationalist project of reconciling Christianity with modern culture? Why bother?

Yet Strauss offers no comfort to the supernaturalists either. He picks up a category that had already been applied to parts of the Bible, including certain sections of the Old Testament, the opening chapters of the gospels of Matthew and Luke, and the final chapters of all four gospels. Strauss takes up this category and argues that from beginning to end the gospels are not historical biographies of Jesus. Rather the gospels are myth.

It is important to be precise about what Strauss means. The gospels are myth in the sense of "a creative reminiscence acting under the impulse of the idea [of God-manhood] which the personality of Jesus had called to life among humankind" (Schweitzer, 80). The gospels, Strauss is saying, have a practical intention. They are intended to get people to change their lives. Now one way to do that, perhaps, is through philosophical discourse about happiness and the human good. Such discourse, however, is likely to have very limited appeal. A more effective way is to tell the story of the ideal human life, of God-manhood, as Strauss calls it, in hopes that people will recognize in that story their own aspirations and true selves and will begin changing accordingly. This, he suggests, is what the evangelists were about.

In that case, what is Jesus' relation to the gospels? Negatively the gospels are not about Jesus. They are about God-manhood, and Jesus is not the God-man. For Strauss, as a good Hegelian in philosophy, it is axiomatic that no individual can fully embody the ideal. Hence Jesus cannot be the God-man. Positively, however, it was Jesus whose personality disclosed this ideal; through him it became clear what all human beings ought to aim to be. Furthermore, the evangelists needed materials for their myth and so they drew on their memories of Jesus, but creatively, transforming those memories into the story of the ideal figure, the God-man. Jesus, then, has a twofold relation to the gospels; he inspired the vision of the ideal they hold up, and his life provided raw materials, as it were, for the story they tell.

About the same time as Strauss's book was coming out, Christian Weisse argued that Mark was the first of the gospels to be written, and this *Marcan hypothesis* soon found further confirmation from Christian Wilcke, while Julius Holtzmann pretty much nailed it down for good in 1863. Prior to this development it was assumed that each of the gospels was based on firsthand testimony since Matthew and John were among the twelve apostles, while Mark reported Peter's preaching and Luke had been closely associated with Paul. On this assumption about the authorship of the gospels it was customary to compose a life of Jesus by harmonizing the contents of all four gospels into one account. Furthermore, if there was a conflict of detail among them priority was accorded to John. Look, after all, at where he got to sit at the Last Supper. Would not the testimony of this Beloved Disciple be most trustworthy? Since it was also the Fourth Gospel that provided the framework for the conventional "high, descending" approach to christology and that, among the gospels, portrays Jesus as most obviously divine, this practice of according historical priority to

John sat well with the occupants of our right-hand column. Hence it was something of a blow to them when it was argued that Mark, in some ways the least edifying of the gospels—look at how Jesus dies in Mark, crying out "my God, my God, why have you abandoned me," or how often the Twelve fail in their discipleship—was the earliest and thus, presumably, the most reliable.

Bruno Bauer followed up on the Marcan hypothesis to arrive at a radicalized version of Strauss. Bauer turned to the gospels as the primary data on the origin of Christianity. In John he found eloquent discourses and magnificent imagery. This literary richness indicated, for Bauer, that John was a product of mythopoesis, myth-making, and so of negligible historical value. Moving back to Matthew and Luke, he found in them expanded versions of Mark. For Bauer, then, the question of the origin of Christianity coincided with the question of the origin of the Gospel of Mark.

Bauer suggests that two different cultural backgrounds blend to produce Mark's portrayal of Jesus. Jesus' dying and rising evokes a pattern found among the mystery religions of the Roman empire. According to this pattern a divine hero descends each year into the underworld, the land of the dead, only to arise and renew the cycle of the seasons with the new life of spring. In addition, however, Bauer found in Mark features of Jewish apocalyptic thought. "Apocalyptic" comes from a Greek word for "revealing" or "unveiling" and apocalyptic literature takes the form of visions of heavenly matters that a seer has received. It can be found in the book of Daniel in the Old Testament, in the book of Revelation in the New Testament, and in other Jewish literature current at the time of Jesus and early Christianity. Apocalyptic visions often project a scenario including such motifs as a final conflict opposing God, the angels, and God's friends on earth to Satan, the demons, and powers that oppose God on earth, the tribulations of the just, God's final victory, resurrection of the dead, and judgment.

For Bauer the figure of Jesus in the Gospel of Mark is just what you would expect from the convergence of these two cultural streams, Hellenistic mystery religions and Jewish apocalyptic. Having offered this account of the origin of Mark's gospel and with it of the Christian movement as a whole, Bauer points out a logical consequence. There is no need, beyond that cultural convergence, to postulate the existence of a historical individual, Jesus, at the origin of Christianity. From Bauer's point of view one might say of Jesus what the astronomer Laplace is reported to have said of God: "We no longer need that hypothesis."

In the meanwhile efforts to reconcile Christianity with modernity continued among Protestant liberals, among whom *Adolf von Harnack* was perhaps the leading figure. Renowned for his work on the history of Christian doctrine, Harnack was invited to give a course open to all comers at the University of Berlin in the winter of 1900. As the topic of the course he chose to address the question of the essence of Christianity. The answer he worked out has been published under the title *What Is Christianity?* (ET New York and Evanston: Harper and Row, 1957).

Harnack reviews several approaches one might take to the question. Some people, for instance, regard Christianity as primarily a system of beliefs: what makes you a Christian is that you assent to the proper set of propositions. But on the strength of his multivolume history of doctrine, Harnack rejects this approach. Through the ages Christian belief has displayed rich diversity and change. If others would locate the heart of Christianity in a pattern of behavior or ethics, Harnack again demurs. As with doctrine, history witnesses to variety and flux in the moral precepts by which Christians have structured their living. A final candidate lies in the area of liturgy. Christianity, some might suggest, is a matter of the proper worship of God. But, Harnack might reply, what form of worship is proper? Think of the variety observable on any Sunday morning as Christians gather—some for the solemn ritual of a high Mass, others for the companionableness of folk liturgy, while still others spill out of storefronts with dancing and tambourines. Quakers sit in silence. Christians, it seems, do very different things when they gather for worship.

The essence of Christianity, Harnack concludes, does not lie in doctrine, morality, or worship. It is not a matter of creed, code, or cult. These are only the husk, variable from time to time and place to place. What creed, code, and cult are meant to carry within them, however, the kernel within the husk, is Jesus and his simple message. That is the essence of Christianity. In Jesus and his message, Harnack proposes, are to be found the high point of the religious evolution of humankind, something completely universal and applicable to all times and places. This essence, he contends, can be extracted by historical analysis of the synoptic gospels.

Jesus' message can be summarized under three overlapping headings. Jesus preached the kingdom of God and its coming. He proclaimed the fatherhood of God and the infinite value of the human soul. He taught a higher righteousness and the law of love.

When Harnack reviews Jesus' sayings in the synoptic gospels about the coming of the kingdom he divides the data into two classes. On the one hand, Jesus sometimes speaks of the coming of the kingdom as a future, external event, as what will happen when the world ends. These sayings present an apocalyptic understanding of the coming of the kingdom. On the other hand Jesus also speaks of the coming of the kingdom as a present reality, something interior and wholly spiritual. Having thus divided the data Harnack makes a decision. In understanding Jesus and the essence of Christianity the first class of data can be ignored. If Jesus sometimes spoke of the coming of the kingdom according to the apocalyptic pattern, this was only because he was a first-century Jew reflecting his time and culture. This apocalyptic way of thinking about the coming of the kingdom did not express what was new and unique about Jesus' message.

For Harnack what Jesus brings that is new, and what belongs to the essence of Christianity, is Jesus' message of the coming of the kingdom as a present, interior, wholly spiritual reality. How does the kingdom come? This brings us to Harnack's second heading. When you recognize that God is not a stern judge weighing your every move and ready to get you if you sin, when you recognize instead that God is a loving father, then God's kingdom is established—within your heart. Furthermore, if you recognize that God is father then you know God as father of all. Hence you recognize as well that everyone—the most vicious criminal, the dullest blob—has a soul beloved of God the father and therefore of infinite value. This in turn leads to Harnack's third heading. Recognizing God as father and everyone else as infinitely valuable, you begin to live a higher righteousness. Higher than what? Your righteousness is higher than what you obtain by keeping rules and following laws. The law that now rules you is interior and spiritual, the law of love.

This simple message, for Harnack, is the essence of Christianity. But what of Jesus? By emphasizing the message Harnack creates a problem. When Western Union boys used to deliver telegrams you took the telegram, tipped the boy, and sent him on his way. You did not invite him into your house to live with you. Hence Harnack's problem. Once Jesus has delivered the message, why is he still necessary? Why does Jesus, as well as his message, belong to the essence of Christianity?

Harnack's answer has two aspects. First he emphasizes that Jesus did not proclaim himself. Jesus did not traipse around Galilee and Judea saying "here I am, the second divine person of the Trinity. Fall down and worship me!" Jesus proclaimed the coming of the kingdom. His concern was to direct all to God as loving father. Indeed, Harnack says, it was because Jesus was so aware of God as father that he is called Son of God, and it was to share this awareness with others that he devoted his energies and activity.

At this point Harnack makes a strategic detour. If Jesus pointed away from himself toward God as father, he asks, does not the Church have the cart before the horse? The Church, Harnack asserts, requires you to accept the right beliefs about Jesus—Nicea's dogma of the divinity of Jesus and Chalcedon's dogma of the hypostatic union—before you can accept and live Jesus' simple message. But do not those right beliefs, or doctrines, belong to the husk, not the essence, of Christianity? Perhaps they served well in the fourth and fifth centuries to communicate the essence of Christianity. If today, however, they get in the way, then is not the Church placing an unnecessary obstacle between people and Jesus and his simple message?

Here, by playing the historical Jesus off against traditional Christianity, Harnack is making a move typical of nineteeenth-century liberal Protestants and not uncommon today. The general university audience to which his course was being offered would no doubt include a fair number of students who, at this stage of their lives, had rejected the traditional Christianity of their childhood and joined the ranks of Christianity's cultured despisers. Harnack is suggesting that it is merely the husk of Christianity that they have rejected. In insisting on this husk the Church had kept them from access to the attractive figure of Jesus and his simple, surely unobjectionable message.

But how does Jesus belong to the essence of Christianity? The answer is clearly not, for Harnack, that Jesus is the divine Son of God. That doctrine is part of the husk, not the essence. Rather, he says, Jesus belongs to the essence of Christianity because, with regard to his gospel message, "he was its personal realization and its strength, and this he is still felt to be" (Harnack, 145). What kind of an answer is this? From one angle it rests on what is called a romantic conception of historiography. On this view the key to understanding history lies in identifying the great personalities whose impact accounts for historical movements. Thus Harnack is suggesting that Jesus' simple message caught on and the Christian movement took off because of the power of Jesus' personality. It is that power that keeps the movement alive. Second, Harnack is saying as well that Jesus belongs to the essence of Christianity because Christians feel he does. This basic fact of Christian consciousness helps define the essence of Christianity.

Harnack's portrait of Jesus and his message shows how liberal Protestants tried to reconcile Christianity and modernity. Further developments in the Old Quest, however, knocked out first one leg and then the other from beneath Harnack's proposal. First Harnack claimed to get at Jesus and his message by historical analysis of the synoptic gospels. His assumption was that the synoptics, and especially Mark, since they were written first, were closest to the facts. Therefore if you trimmed out such crudely supernatural material as the miracle stories you were left with a basically reliable account of Jesus' career. This assumption was called into question when *William Wrede* wrote a book entitled *The Messianic Secret in the Gospel of Mark*.

In reading Mark's gospel you may notice a recurring motif. Jesus heals someone, or casts out demons, and when he is hailed as Messiah or by a similar title he enjoins silence. He is indeed the Messiah but it is to be kept secret. The question arises: why does this occur in Mark's narrative? The assumption operative thus far in the Old Quest was that since Mark was written earliest it follows the historical facts most accurately. On this assumption the answer would be that Mark's narrative exhibits this pattern because that is how things happened.

Wrede, however, suggests a different answer. He sees the Messianic secret as Mark's solution to a challenge facing his community. Engaged in conflict and controversy with non-Christian Jews, Mark's community would confront the question why, if Jesus was the Messiah, no one knew about it during his lifetime. Besides, who ever heard of a crucified Messiah? Part of the evangelist's task would be to tell the story of Jesus in such a way as to meet the objection carried by these questions. Mark's community required an apologetic, as it is called. *Apologia* is the Greek word for the reasoned defense one might offer against charges brought in a court of law. Apologetics designates the reasoning one works out to meet objections to one's faith. Wrede is suggesting that the evangelist crafted the motif of the Messianic secret as an apologetic device.

It follows from this analysis that the Gospel of Mark provides excellent historical data on the evangelist's community, its beliefs, and its problems. It also follows that even the earliest gospel to be written, Mark, is not a source of straightforward data on Jesus and his lifetime. Hence Harnack's assumption that with the exception of the miraculous and supernatural elements Mark offered a factually trustworthy account of Jesus' life proves untenable.

Harnack ran into trouble on another front as well when *Johannes Weiss* published a book entitled *Jesus' Proclamation of the Kingdom of God.* Weiss was reacting against the idea espoused by liberal Protestants like Harnack and his own father-in-law, the renowned theologian Albrecht Ritschl, that the kingdom of God was a reality that progressed in history with the advance of culture. For Weiss the idea of evolutionary progress was distinctly modern; it stood in contrast to what a first-century Jew like Jesus would have understood by the coming of the kingdom. From Weiss's perspective Harnack had put his money on the wrong horse when he excluded the apocalyptic understanding of the kingdom from consideration.

Weiss explained that for a first-century Jew the kingdom of God was not a place. Rather it designated God's activity as king of the universe. To Jesus and his contemporaries, however, it seemed that the present age was ruled not by God but by God's enemies. Given the might of the Roman empire there seemed no reasonable hope that Israel could be restored as God's kingdom within history. Hence the coming of the kingdom of God was an event for which God's people could only wait in prayer and hope.

No one but God could act to overcome God's enemies and bring the kind of history they ruled to an end.

As a first-century Jew, Weiss argues, Jesus shared this apocalyptic expectation. Within that context what marked Jesus out as special were two things. First, he thought that the kingdom was about to come. As the rustling of leaves and the blowing of the wind indicate a thunderstorm's approach, so Jesus believed the coming of the kingdom was imminent. Second, he believed that he himself had a role in its coming. The apocalyptic scenario involved the final conflict with Satan and his demons. In Jesus' day, however, illness was attributed to evil spirits. Hence, Weiss proposes, if Jesus healed and cast out demons, this signified for him the onset of the final conflict in which God would prove victorious.

Albert Schweitzer expanded Weiss's apocalyptic interpretation of Jesus' ministry. For Schweitzer, the synoptic story of Jesus sending out the seventy disciples represented Jesus' last-ditch effort to call his fellow Jews to repentance before the end came. To Jesus' surprise, however, the seventy went out, preached, and reported back. The end had not yet come. Then Jesus decided to force the issue. Knowing the place of the suffering of the just in the apocalyptic scenario, he went up to Jerusalem to take on that suffering and thus force God's hand. Schweitzer summarizes his apocalyptic interpretation of Jesus in powerful, graphic terms:

> There is silence all around. The Baptist appears, and cries: "Repent, for the kingdom of heaven is at hand." Soon after that comes Jesus, and in the knowledge that he is the coming Son of Man lays hold of the wheel of the world to set it moving on that last revolution which is to bring all ordinary history to its close. It refuses to turn, and he throws himself upon it. Then it does turn; and crushes him. Instead of bringing in the eschatological conditions, he has destroyed them. The wheel rolls onward, and the mangled body of the one immeasurably great man, who was strong enough to think of himself as the spiritual ruler of mankind and to bend history to his purpose, is hanging upon it still. That is his victory and his reign (Schweitzer, 370–371).

In other words, Schweitzer is saying, Jesus was wrong. The kingdom did not come, the world did not end. Jesus' first-century apocalyptic understanding of the coming of the kingdom—and of himself—was mistaken, and he sacrificed himself in vain.

With Schweitzer the Old Quest comes to a close. Perhaps now the process we laid out at the end of our introduction is clearer. We suggested there that when the traditional self-understanding of Christian faith encounters the empirical scientific and historical consciousness of modernity, what Paul Ricoeur calls the first naiveté goes up for grabs. The truth

of the biblical narrative loses its taken-for-granted character and a hermeneutic of suspicion comes into play. That process is clearly operative in the
movement, from Reimarus to Schweitzer, that we have sketched.

Several observations suggest themselves. First notice that most of the
movement in the Old Quest takes place in the left hand column of our
chart. Among the figures in that column Reimarus, Strauss, and Bauer
were motivated by a sincere and profound hatred of the Christian Church.
To their mind the Church stood for the opposite of what they valued most,
human freedom and rationality. Be that as it may, it was only because of
the questions they asked that Christianity has been able to discover alter-
natives to the fundamentalism of the supernaturalists as it seeks to communicate its message to the modern world. Perhaps there is a lesson here.
Perhaps even in matters of religion the appropriate response to questions,
no matter how shocking or impious they may appear, is to pursue and answer them rather than squelching them. Only in this manner can a religious tradition avoid becoming fossilized at some past stage of its growth.

Second, in the course of the Old Quest certain advances were made that
find a place in contemporary scholarship. To cite the most obvious, most
New Testament scholars take the Marcan hypothesis, that Mark was the
first of the gospels to be composed, as a given. In addition Reimarus,
Weiss, and Schweitzer were correct to recall that Jesus was a first-century
Jew and thus to be understood historically in terms of that cultural context.
Again in their own way Reimarus, Strauss, Bauer, and Wrede point to the
creativity of the early Christian movement as it sought to express the religious significance of Jesus, while Strauss's category, myth, has found
widespread acceptance, though a somewhat different definition, of late.
The Old Quest made it clear that the gospels are something other than
what a modern historical biography would encompass.

Last, we can ask what options were available at the close of the Old
Quest. This is simply a matter of scanning the bottom line of our chart.
Four options emerge. To begin at the right, the *supernaturalists* represent
the first naiveté hardening into a fundamentalism. Wishing to preserve
Christian faith in its traditional self-understanding, they resolutely reject
those developments in modernity that would challenge that understanding.
This, of course, places them in a position similar to that of an ostrich who
responds to danger by sticking his head firmly into the sand. This is a vulnerable posture.

In the middle column are the *liberals* like Harnack. Rather than oppose
their faith to modern culture, the liberals try to reconcile them. To this end
they seek release from what they experience as the shackles of the traditional self-understanding of Christian faith by playing that understanding
off against what they take to be the historical Jesus and his simple message.

They identify Jesus and his message with the essence of Christianity while doctrine, moral precepts, and forms of worship are merely the historically variable husk. By this maneuver liberals are freed to base their living on a message modern culture can find attractive.

There is, however, a problem with the liberal maneuver. The English Jesuit George Tyrell, himself eventually excommunicated for his efforts to reconcile Christian faith with modernity, likened the liberal quest for the historical Jesus to a person looking down a deep, dark well. What would someone see at the bottom of the well? Tyrell suggested that these people would see a blurry image of themselves. That is, the historical figure of Jesus constructed by liberals like Harnack looks suspiciously like the figure of a nineteenth-century liberal German professor of theology who has studied philosophers like Immanuel Kant and Georg Friedrich Hegel. Hence the question must arise: Is Harnack replacing the traditional self-understanding of Christianity with an understanding really based on Jesus and Jesus' message, or is he replacing traditional Christianity with a religion based on Harnack's own self-image?

The left-hand column yields two options. For *William Wrede* the quest for the historical Jesus halts at the communities for whom the New Testament documents were composed. As we saw, Wrede regards the Gospel of Mark as excellent historical data on the beliefs and problems of the evangelist's community, while the figure of the historical Jesus remains an unknown, hidden from historical scrutiny by the faith and needs of the early Christian movement. *Weiss* and *Schweitzer*, on the other hand, quite confidently constructed an ample image of the historical Jesus but their first-century apocalyptic preacher and healer remains firmly stuck in his times; to the modern world he can only appear grotesque in his fatal error.

Chapter Three

An Interim Period and the Launching of the New Quest

Albert Schweitzer's review of the Old Quest marked its close in 1906. In this chapter we want to ask how, in the ensuing period, Schweitzer himself and two major theologians of the generation after him handled the outcome of this first round in the encounter between historical consciousness and Christian faith. If that outcome seemed to be a contradiction between historians' images of Jesus and the gospel stories, how did Schweitzer nonetheless not only remain a Christian but muster heroic commitment as a missionary doctor in Africa? Similarly, in the generation after Schweitzer, how did the theologians Karl Barth and Rudolf Bultmann, both of them scholars of enormous stature and worldwide influence, handle that same apparent contradiction?

With Bultmann we come to the immediate background to the launching of a New Quest for the historical Jesus in 1953. As we shall see, one of Bultmann's own students was able to seize upon a method of analyzing the Bible that Bultmann himself had been instrumental in developing and turn it in a direction that Bultmann had claimed was barred. A grasp of how Bultmann urged that claim and why his student, Ernst Käsemann, rejected it will lead us into an overview of the methods of analysis upon which the New Quest depends. Then, beginning in our next chapter, we can begin to assemble some results.

In the Interim (1906–1953): Making a Virtue of Necessity

If the New Quest for the historical Jesus was launched in 1953, what went on in the interim? The Old Quest represents the first round in the encounter between Christian faith and modernity, and none of the results available to Christians at its close seems satisfactory. Supernaturalists rejected modernity. Liberals accommodated themselves to it all too well. Wrede concluded to historical scepticism—Jesus is simply unavailable to historical inquiry. Weiss and Schweitzer came up with a historical Jesus of little relevance to contemporary Christians.

All four options share a common assumption. Each of them accepts the existence of a dichotomy, the two poles of which received their names when, toward the close of the Old Quest, Martin Kähler wrote a book which he entitled *The So-Called Historical Jesus and the Historic Christ of Faith*. What emerged from the Old Quest was the recognition that when the New Testament is submitted to historical scrutiny, the resulting historical image of Jesus differs from the gospel portraits of Jesus as the Christ. That difference, in turn, appeared to be a dichotomy. From Reimarus's failed Davidic Messiah to Schweitzer's mistaken apocalyptic preacher, from Bauer's denial of Jesus' existence to Wrede's claim that Jesus is unknowable by historical methods, the contrast between what is thought to be known of Jesus historically and how he is regarded by traditional Christian faith seemed no less than a contradiction. Harnack, as we saw, thought he could forge a Christianity suitable for modern culture by playing the historical Jesus off against traditional Christian belief. The Old Quest, it seemed, left Christians stuck with Kähler's dichotomy between the historical Jesus and the Christ of faith.

What all parties had in common was an understanding of the relationship between the results of historical inquiry and the Christ in whom Christians believed as a dichotomy. Given that situation, how did people maintain their Christian faith? Albert Schweitzer wrote learned tomes of theology stressing what he took to be the apocalyptic character of Jesus' career. He also, however, moved to Africa and set up a hospital in a remote section of the Congo, where he spent the rest of his life as a missionary doctor. The outcome of Schweitzer's research on the historical Jesus, it seems, in no way lessened the fervor of his Christian commitment.

A common response to the intellectual situation was to make a virtue of necessity. If historical research either came up dry, as with Wrede, or arrived at results that seemed inimical to Christian belief, that did not matter. Kähler, for example, had no problem with the unsatisfactory results of historical inquiry. As he saw it, it was not the so-called historical Jesus but rather the real, historic Christ of faith who counted. We can look at how this effort to immunize Christian faith from any possible results of critical historical research panned out for Schweitzer, and then for two of the most significant thinkers in the generation after him, Karl Barth and Rudolf Bultmann. With Bultmann, in turn, we find ourselves in possession of the immediate background from which the New Quest emerged.

Schweitzer casts the results of the Old Quest, including his own research, in dramatic terms. As he saw it, the Old Quest meant that he and his contemporaries "were coming closer to the historical Jesus than men [sic] had ever come before." Indeed, he says, "[we] were already stretching out hands to draw him into our own time." People like Harnack were hoping to reach back behind traditional Christianity in order to base their religion on the historical Jesus. Instead, Schweitzer writes, "we have been obliged to give up the attempt and acknowledge our failure. And further we must be prepared to find that the historical knowledge of the personality and life of Jesus will not be a help, but perhaps even an offense to religion."

Schweitzer was well aware that historical research seemed to fuel the hermeneutic of suspicion. How would he avoid this? What was his own solution that enabled him not only to remain a Christian but to live a life of intense commitment? He makes a distinction. "But the truth is, it is not Jesus as historically known, but Jesus as spiritually arisen within men [sic] who is significant for our time and can help it. Not the historical Jesus, but the spirit which goes forth from him and in the spirits of men strives for new influence and rule, is that which overcomes the world" (Schweitzer, 401). Unfortunately, the relationship between the historical Jesus and the spirit that goes forth from him remains vague.

In the generation after Schweitzer, Karl Barth and Rudolf Bultmann both participated in a movement centering around what is called the "theology of the word." According to this theology the Bible by itself is a dusty old text from an ancient and long-vanished world. When, however, the text is taken into a pulpit and proclaimed, then in that situation, by the power of God's Spirit, the dusty text of the Bible becomes for those who hear it God's saving word. Responding in faith, they are saved, but if they reject God's word they thereby undergo judgment and are lost. The theology of the word contends that proclaiming the Bible as God's word plunges those addressed into a crisis situation in which nothing less than their standing before God, their eternal destiny, is at stake.

Given the dramatically decisive character of the preaching situation, what difference do the results of historical critical scholarship make? Barth's answer is: none. He expresses this with an image. Suppose you are in an office building and you hear a commotion on the street below. Looking out, you see a group of people looking up. From your vantage point you can describe in great detail how many they are, what each looks like, and what each is wearing. You cannot see, however, what it is that has them all looking up. That lies outside your field of vision. Similarly, Barth suggests, the historical critic is free to examine and analyze the biblical documents in great detail, but none of that analysis enables the critic to grasp—or better, be grasped by—the object to which those documents bear witness, what they are looking up to, as it were, namely God's

powerful and saving word. Historical criticism misses what is most important about the biblical text; it is therefore in an important sense irrelevant.

Again, Barth reflects, the proclaimed word places a demand for response upon its hearers. You can answer yes and be saved, or no and be
judged. What you cannot do in the situation of crisis into which the proclaimed word places you is to call time out in order to check that word out
historically. To do so would be to act like Adam and Eve who, after they
had eaten of the forbidden fruit, tried to hide from God among the trees of
the garden because they knew that they were naked. God's word does not
allow such evasive tactics.

In a similar vein Rudolf Bultmann argues that the quest for the historical Jesus is as a matter of fact practically impossible, and as a matter of
principle illegitimate. As we shall see when we consider the methods the
New Quest will use, Bultmann bases his first point on the nature of the
biblical documents. They are, he contends, so impregnated with the faith
of the early Church that it is practically impossible to get behind them to
the historical Jesus. This is a point we have already seen made by Wrede.

With his second point Bultmann ups the ante. Not only is the quest for
the historical Jesus practically impossible; it is also illegitimate. One
should not even attempt it. In arguing this point Bultmann draws upon his
Protestant heritage. Against the corrupt practices of the medieval Church
Martin Luther had insisted that human beings are made right before God
by God's grace received in faith, and not by their own efforts apart from
grace. "Faith, not works" became one of the rallying cries of the
Reformation in the sixteenth century. On this basis Bultmann rejects the
quest of the historical Jesus as an effort to save oneself by one's own
works, in this case intellectual works, rather than relying in faith on God's
grace.

At the close of the Old Quest, Martin Kähler conceived the relation between the results of historical inquiry into Jesus and the gospel portraits of
Jesus as the Christ in terms of a dichotomy between the historical Jesus
and the Christ of faith. Accepting that dichotomy Albert Schweitzer, Karl
Barth, and Rudolf Bultmann tried to make a virtue of necessity, immuniz-
ing Christian faith from any possible results of critical historical research.
This position largely prevailed until 1953.

The New Quest: Goal and Methods

Bultmann trained a generation of students who, once they had completed their degrees and found positions as professors, formed the habit of
returning each year for a reunion in Marburg, where they had studied
under the master. At these gatherings of the Old Marburgers, as they were

called, their idea of a good time was to read learned papers to one another in the presence of their revered mentor. At the 1953 meeting one paper roused Bultmann from the grandfatherly benevolence with which he presided over his academic progeny, making him sit up and take notice.

Bultmann's former student Ernst Käsemann delivered a paper entitled "The Problem of the Historical Jesus." In it he argued that a New Quest for the historical Jesus was legitimate, necessary, and possible. First, it was legitimate. When you read the gospels, it is clear that their authors intend to tell their audience about Jesus. Today, with the invention of critical historical method, we have an additional way of learning about Jesus. Using that method of access to Jesus, Käsemann argues, coheres with the evangelists' basic intention and is therefore legitimate from the viewpoint of Christian faith. It is not an attempt to save oneself by human works.

Second, a New Quest is necessary. Acceptance of Kähler's dichotomy leaves Christians in an untenable position. Someone might object that a Christianity centered wholly on the Christ of faith is just one more of the myths that human beings have created for themselves, with no demonstrable relation to the historical figure of Jesus of Nazareth. From the perspective that we saw operative in Schweitzer, Barth, and Bultmann during the period after the Old Quest one has no answer to that objection. Hence, Käsemann urges, it is necessary to take up anew the question of continuity between the historical Jesus and the Christ of faith.

Finally, Käsemann points out, a New Quest is possible because scholars have at their disposal research methods that were not available to the Old Quest. In fact, he can argue, Bultmann himself is largely responsible for the introduction and success of one of these methods. What methods does Käsemann have in mind? It will help to become familiar with three methods of modern biblical scholarship. These methods are known as source criticism, form criticism, and redaction criticism; they develop in the order in which we have named them, and each builds on the one before it.

Source criticism is interested in the literary sources of the biblical documents. Given one of the biblical documents, it asks, is it possible to discern a prior document on which the document under consideration depends literarily? That is, is it possible to discern a literary source of the present document?

One outstanding result of source criticism is known as the two-source synoptic theory. The gospels of Mark, Matthew, and Luke are called the synoptic gospels. The reason for this is that if you publish them in columns next to each other, much of the material in one parallels that in the others. Hence they can be published in what is called a synopsis, from the Greek σύν, with, and ὄψις, having to do with sight. In other words, you can look at them with one another. The Fourth Gospel, however, follows a quite different order and does not fit well into a synopsis.

During the Old Quest it was established with high probability that among the synoptics Mark was the first to be composed. This revised the traditional order in which the gospels are still published, according to which Matthew comes first. This traditional order goes back to a second-century writer named Papias. The idea of the priority of Mark revised a very longstanding tradition.

Besides the fact that Mark was written before Matthew and Luke, scholars also notice that when Matthew and Luke follow the same order, it is Mark's order they are following. This suggests that whoever composed Matthew and whoever composed Luke used Mark as a source. Thus far, then, we have a one-source synoptic theory. Mark is a literary source for both Matthew and Luke.

Matthew and Luke also have in common many sayings placed on Jesus' lips that are not found in Mark. This indicates that, besides Mark, Matthew and Luke have a second source in common as well. This source, a collection of sayings of Jesus, is called the Q source after the first letter of the German word for source, *Quelle*. The Q source is a hypothetical construct, a collection of sayings of Jesus whose existence scholars deduce from the presence of those sayings in both Matthew and Luke. According to the two-source synoptic theory, then, Matthew and Luke have in common two sources on which they depend literarily, namely Mark and Q.

Around 1920 three books appeared independently of one another; their effect was to revolutionize New Testament studies. The books were *From Tradition to Gospel*, by Martin Dibelius; *The Framework of the History of Jesus*, by Karl-Ludwig Schmidt; and *The History of the Synoptic Tradition*, by Rudolf Bultmann. In each book the author had begun applying a new method, form criticism, to the New Testament.

Like source criticism, form criticism is interested in what we can call the prehistory of the New Testament documents. Form critics notice that in the period between Jesus' execution and the Easter experience of his disciples that followed it, on the one hand, and the writing of the first New Testament documents, namely Paul's letters, on the other, the only Bible Christians possessed was what they came to call the Old Testament. In that period the memories of Jesus' deeds and sayings were passed on orally in ways that met the needs of the various Christian communities who drew on them. Out of that dynamic oral tradition process the various documents that went to make up the New Testament first emerged, and from that process the evangelists drew their material. Form criticism seeks to move back from the text of the New Testament documents to ascertain the origin of the units of oral tradition those documents incorporate. Thus, like source criticism, form criticism inquires into the prehistory of the New Testament, though with a different focus.

To reach its goal form criticism moves through a set of three questions. When form critics analyze a particular section of a New Testament document, or a pericope as it is called, they first try to ascertain how much of the section represents the original unit of oral tradition and how much is the framework supplied by the evangelist. Imagine a gospel as a brick wall. The point of this first question is to ascertain, within a given pericope, what is brick, drawn from the oral tradition, and what is mortar, supplied by the evangelist to integrate the unit into the document.

Second, bricks are of various sorts. Once one has ascertained how much of a pericope represents the original unit, the next question focuses on the literary genre of the unit. What kind of a brick is it? To get hold of the idea of literary genre, think of today's newspaper. If you can read the paper, then without thinking about it you know how to distinguish a whole set of literary genres. You know the difference among news stories, editorials, and ads, for instance, and you do not get them mixed up. If you did, you would misread the paper. Similarly, scholars of the ancient world learn to distinguish among the many different genres found in the literature of that world, and this in turn allows form critics to ask about the literary genre of the units of the oral tradition that the evangelists have incorporated into their gospels.

Third, once you have determined what kind of brick the original unit is, what it is made of, you can ask where they make bricks like that. You can ask about what the Germans call the *Sitz im Leben*, literally the "situation in life" of the original unit. The idea is that different literary genres can correspond to different cultural contexts. In the first stages of the Christian movement scholars distinguish between Palestinian Jewish Christians whose language was Aramaic and Greek-speaking Hellenistic Jewish Christians. Cultural differences involve different thought patterns, and so the literary genre of an original unit can provide the clue to its *Sitz im Leben*, where it came from.

With the question of the *Sitz im Leben* form criticism arrives at its goal. Focusing on the prehistory of the New Testament documents, form criticism seeks to trace the material in those documents to its origins in the oral tradition of the early Christian movement. Thus Dibelius could reconstruct the movement *From Tradition to Gospel* and Bultmann could trace *The History of the Synoptic Tradition*.

The final stage of its investigation, with the question of the *Sitz im Leben*, is where form criticism pays off for the New Quest. The payoff comes with the use of a negative criterion or yardstick called the principle of dissimilarity. If a unit of oral tradition does not correspond to what you would expect from an early Christian community, if it does not fit one of the cultural contexts of the early Christian movement, then, by the principle of dissimilarity, one concludes with some probability that that original unit goes back to Jesus himself. When he was delivering his paper to the Old Marburgers, Käsemann was able to point out how often such judgments recur even in Bultmann's own work. Bultmann's actual practice of form criticism, Käsemann could argue, belied his claim that a quest for the historical Jesus was as a matter of fact next to impossible because of the nature of the sources.

Form criticism sets up the principle of dissimilarity with which a start can be made on compiling probable historical data on Jesus. By itself, however, the principle of dissimilarity has a weakness. By ruling out any material from the oral tradition corresponding to the cultural contexts of the early Christian movement it rules out material from Jesus' own cultural context. Jesus was, after all, an Aramaic-speaking Palestinian Jew. By itself the principle of dissimilarity is likely to exclude data that may in fact originate with Jesus himself. To compensate for this possibility scholars employ a second criterion, the principle of coherence. On this criterion, material from the oral tradition can be judged historically probable even if it fails the first test, the principle of dissimilarity, as long as such material nonetheless fits in with, that is, coheres with, material that passes the first test. Once form critics have begun to amass a certain amount of data on Jesus through the principle of dissimilarity, then further material betraying a Palestinian Jewish background, which of itself might go back either to Jesus or to an early community, can be ascribed to Jesus if it coheres with the material already compiled.

A similar criterion used to determine authentic Jesus material is called the principle of embarrassment. If Jesus is reported as saying or doing something that would seem an embarrassment to the early Church, something that the early Christian movement would have no good reason to invent, then chances are that it is found in the New Testament because it is something that Christians were stuck with as a historical fact. Examples that come readily to mind are Jesus' undergoing John's baptism of repentance, a situation the structure of which assigns John the superior place and Jesus the inferior, or Jesus' execution by the Romans as a criminal.

Beyond source and form criticism, redaction criticism came on the scene in the years after World War II. Redaction criticism builds on form criticism and corrects it in one important aspect. Form critics so focused on the prehistory of the gospel material that they downplayed the role of the evangelist or, as the person who had a final hand on the documents is otherwise known, the redactor. Form critics tended to regard the redactors as mere compilers who gathered units of oral tradition and strung them together like beads on a necklace. Yet once form criticism determines what the original units of tradition are, if one focuses on the text itself rather than on its prehistory it is possible to notice that the redactors integrate those units differently in their respective compositions. If the original units are like bricks of various sorts, then once the bricks have been identified you can notice that the redactors build them into walls with very distinctive patterns. Mark's gospel has a pattern all its own, and this holds for Matthew, Luke, and John as well. Each redactor incorporates the elements of tradition into a document held together by a particular slant on Jesus and his significance. Each gospel is governed by a distinctive theology.

The redactors, it turns out, are by no means mere compilers. They are imaginative, creative theologians who integrate their materials in a way that expresses an individual and distinctive slant on Jesus and his meaning. For example, both Matthew and Luke assemble sayings of Jesus into a major sermon. Thus Matthew gives us the famous Sermon on the Mount, while Luke combines much of the same material to produce a sermon that Jesus preaches not on a mount but on a plain. Why the difference? It is not a matter of one redactor having better geographical information than the other. Matthew, it seems, is trying to make sense of Jesus to an audience to whom God's dealings with Israel are familiar and alive. Who was the most important Israelite of all, the one through whom God had acted to establish Israel as God's own people? Moses, of course, who had given God's law to Israel from the mountain. To Matthew's audience Jesus' significance becomes clear when Matthew presents him as God's new Moses, giving the new law on the mount. Hence Matthew composes a Sermon on the Mount. Luke, addressing a different audience, can locate his great sermon elsewhere.

This example indicates how redaction criticism builds on the identification of the original units of oral tradition provided by form criticism, how it corrects the form critics' neglect of the creative role of the redactor, and how it brings attention back from the prehistory to focus anew on the New Testament text itself.

Käsemann had argued that a New Quest was legitimate, necessary, and possible. The task of the New Quest was to ascertain whether any continuity might be discerned between what could be learned about Jesus by critical historical method and the figure of Jesus as the Christ presented by the New Testament and Christian tradition. With this task the New Quest takes on a far more positive goal than that animating the Old Quest. While participants in the Old Quest sought to play Jesus as historically construed off against the Christian tradition, the New Quest refuses to accept the dichotomy that obtained at the close of the Old Quest. This is not, of course, a matter of proving Christian faith. Faith remains a prerequisite for grasping the correctness of the Christian interpretation of Jesus as the Christ. While the New Quest does not aim to prove Christian faith it does seek to determine whether Christian faith and its interpretation of Jesus can be seen as a possible, if not necessary, response to Jesus as he appears through a historian's lens. Unlike the Old Quest, the New Quest has a very positive goal.

In method, however, the New Quest is far more rigorously critical than the Old Quest. Just because the New Testament presents Jesus as saying or doing something does not of itself provide sufficient grounds for judging historically that he in fact said or did it. The New Testament provides data on Jesus, but in each instance those data must undergo a process of scrutiny involving criteria like the principles of dissimilarity, coherence, and embarrassment discussed above. Only at the end of such a process can those data be counted as enjoying some degree or other of historical probability, or lacking it. From the historian's viewpoint the New Testament provides data and no more. As in any other field judgments about those data can only emerge on the basis of a process of disciplined inquiry. Thus whereas someone like Harnack could accept the synoptics as basically reliable historically with the exception of their supernatural elements, methods like form criticism render the New Quest more critical in evaluating the data than was the Old Quest.

In 1953 Ernst Käsemann reacted against Rudolf Bultmann's position by arguing that a New Quest for the historical Jesus was legitimate, necessary, and possible. Three years later the first response to Käsemann's call appeared with Günther Bornkamm's slender but enormously influential *Jesus of Nazareth*. Within two decades Roman Catholic scholars had joined the movement; in 1974 the Flemish theologian Edward Schillebeeckx published a massive and encyclopedic synthesis of biblical scholarship entitled *Jesus. An Experiment in Christology*. The movement reached a watershed of sorts when, in 1985, in his book *Jesus and Judaism*, E. P. Sanders offered a critical review of the New Quest to that point in some ways similar to Albert Schweitzer's critique of his predecessors in the Old Quest.

In its present phase the quest is characterized by a debate among three positions. For Sanders, in the book just mentioned, Jesus' hopes for God's kingdom were fixed wholly on the future. Against this position a group of scholars known as the Jesus Seminar, most notably John Dominic Crossan, argues that the kingdom with which Jesus was concerned was an ever-present reality. Thirdly, in *A Marginal Jew*, a multivolume project that is likely to set the standard on the topic for at least a generation, John P. Meier argues that Jesus considered the kingdom of God to be a future reality that had already begun with his own activity.

Having examined the background to the New Quest, the circumstances under which it began, its goal and methods, we can turn next to its payoff. What does Jesus look like through the lens of contemporary historical scholarship? Does that scholarship offer a glimpse of why some people would have found him religiously significant while others would have sought his death?

Chapter Four

Jesus and the Nearness of the Kingdom

Contemporary biblical scholars do not believe that historical methods like form criticism allow them to produce a full-scale biography of Jesus. To that extent, at least, Wrede and Bultmann were right. The sources do not provide adequate data for writing Jesus' biography.

One reason for this has to do with the order of the events recounted in the gospels. We can plant a few flags to mark the parameters of Jesus' career. Jesus' baptism by John marks the outset of his public life. It ends with a final journey to Jerusalem, a last meal, and execution.

The order of the events between these basic markers, however, is a different matter. The order provided by the gospel narratives, beginning with the earliest gospel, Mark, comes by and large from the redactor. It forms part of the mortar, as it were, with which the redactor holds together the pieces drawn from the oral tradition. Mark's order and those of the gospels after Mark are devices whereby the redactor structures the disparate elements of the oral tradition into a story and plots that story to express a particular theology. Beginning with the gospel of Mark the order of events is part of the framework supplied by the evangelist to give form to the gospel narrative. This means that we do not possess the actual chronological order a biography would demand.

Besides chronological order in general, biographers have an interest in the interior development of their subject, in the process whereby character is formed and identity achieved. In Jesus' case, however, this interest cannot be met, and for the same reason. The gospels just do not furnish data on the process of Jesus' interior development. The gospels do not allow us to glimpse the route by which Jesus' self-understanding took shape nor what its major stages were. Hence, in the absence of adequate data on chronological order and on personal development, there can be no question of the New Quest yielding a full-blown biography of Jesus.

What the New Quest does claim to make accessible is Jesus' typical fashion of speaking and acting. If we cannot put together the biography that would allow us to make a movie of Jesus' life, we can at least get hold of a series of revealing snapshots. This means that we can hope to answer some questions. In this chapter we shall first ask about the central theme of Jesus' public ministry, the focus of his career. Next, the background to Jesus' theme will allow us to digress very briefly on the figure of his mentor, John the Baptist. Then, getting back to Jesus' central theme, our next move will be to explore how Jesus expressed that theme both in word and deed. This chapter will investigate what Jesus had to say for himself by focusing on his parables. Moving in the next chapter to Jesus' activity, we shall consider first the question of his miracles and then the people with whom Jesus associated, the significance of the company Jesus chose to keep.

After having probed in these two chapters what Jesus had to say and what he did during his public career, we shall be able to ask in a further chapter what positive response Jesus was looking for, what he was trying to make happen. This will allow us to step back to ask the "why" question: what motivated Jesus? Finally, of course, we need to consider as well the negative response he received. Hence we shall also devote a chapter to asking why Jesus was killed.

By working through the sequence of questions we just outlined, we can get a sense of the payoff of the New Quest. What does Jesus look like through the historical lens of contemporary scholarship?

Central Theme: The Kingdom of God and Its Coming

A broad consensus among contemporary scholars identifies the coming of the kingdom of God as the theme that defines and sums up Jesus' mission and activity. Jesus proclaimed the nearness of the coming of the kingdom of God. This fact leaves open a crucial further question. What did Jesus mean by these words? When he proclaimed this central theme, what was Jesus talking about?

We shall introduce this topic by recalling three interpretations of the theme that we saw proffered in the course of the Old Quest. Next we shall pause to ask a question to which the Old Quest did not advert. What kind of language are we dealing with when we pursue the meaning of Jesus' central theme? What is the logical status of the language in which he announced his theme? This will lead us next into a brief review of the historical background to the theme, and then we can wrap up this introductory section by suggesting what we shall call a functional definition of the theme. These moves will put us into a position where, bringing in further data on Jesus' public activity, we can settle down to solving for *x*, as it were, with *x* standing for what Jesus was talking about when he talked about the coming of the kingdom of God.

Three interpretations

From the Old Quest we have already gleaned three quite different interpretations of Jesus' theme. Reimarus, Harnack, Weiss, and Schweitzer all agreed that Jesus' central concern was the coming of the kingdom of God. They differed widely, however, on what they thought that meant. For Reimarus the coming of the kingdom meant a this-worldly restoration of Israel to the splendor it had once enjoyed. As the Messiah, Jesus hoped to rally his fellow Jews to throw out the Romans and establish Israel as a kingdom of justice. Unfortunately, Reimarus notes, Jesus failed. Harnack, we saw, thought Jesus was really concerned with establishing God's kingdom in people's hearts. He would do this by pointing them to God as father and leading them into a life of love. Thus the kingdom was a spiritual reality that progressed in time as more and more people came to accept and follow Jesus' simple message. If, for Harnack, Jesus had also spoken of the coming of the kingdom as an apocalyptic event yet to come, this was only because he was a first-century Jew conditioned by his culture. This aspect of his message, Harnack suggested, did not really count. Weiss and Schweitzer, however, insisted that Jesus was indeed a first-century Jew and therefore ought to be understood precisely in those apocalyptic terms. Jesus thought the end was near, the final conflict was already breaking out, and he himself was instrumental in bringing about the coming of the kingdom. And in all of this he was mistaken. The wheel of history rolls on, and despite Jesus' effort to force the issue the end did not arrive.

Logical status

Are these interpretations the only ones available? A path beyond them may open up if we ask a question Reimarus, Harnack, Weiss, and Schweitzer did not pursue. None of them paid particular attention to what we may call the logical status of Jesus' language about the coming of the kingdom. But if we reflect upon it, we can notice that the language in which Jesus expressed his central theme is peculiar. A monarch is someone we can readily imagine, drawing on newspaper photos or television footage. As queen of England, Elizabeth II occasionally wears a crown, carries a scepter, issues edicts, and reads speeches written by her prime minister. Hussein of Jordan is another contemporary monarch. Monarchy is one political arrangement among the many that human beings have created; within this arrangement the monarch carries out certain duties, enjoys certain privileges, and on occasion wears certain insignia.

Of course none of this applies literally to God. The reality to which the word "God" points is, literally, unimaginable. Thomas Aquinas taught that while we can come to know *that* God is, *what* God is, the divine essence, exceeds the grasp of human intellect. The reality of God, the divine mystery, is not bounded by space and time. Every image, on the other hand, is intrinsically spatial. For this reason when we refer language about a spatial and temporal reality like monarchy to God we are not using that language literally. Language about the kingdom of God is not literal language. It is metaphorical, symbolic language.

Furthermore, it may not be too gross a generalization to say that symbolic language falls into two classes. On the one hand, thus far all of us have come into this world from a woman's womb and for the first part of our lives we live in utter dependence on a nurturer. All of us have experienced the hormonal stirrings that signaled the onset of puberty. All of us face the certainty of death. Mother, sex, and mortality are constants in the structure of human existence and every culture devises symbolic systems to enable people to negotiate them, to deal with these constants in a humanly meaningful manner. In this sense one can speak of some symbolisms as archetypal or universal.

Other symbolic language is more tied to a particular historical experience. In Washington, D.C., Americans flock to the Mall for picnics, concerts, and fireworks on the Fourth of July. In Paris it is just another day. Parisians are waiting to dance in the streets on July 14. Each of these dates has become symbolic. The Fourth of July sums up for Americans the story of their nation's founding, the story of the Boston Tea Party, Bunker Hill, the Declaration of Independence, Valley Forge, and so forth. On July 14 the French recall the storming of the Bastille and their founding story of prisoners released, tyranny overturned, and liberty won. In each case, both date and event have come to sum up a nation's story and thus symbolize that nation's identity.

Historical background

Jesus' language about the coming of the kingdom belongs to this latter sort of symbolism. Kingdom of God is a symbol that finds its home in the particular historical experience of Israel and appeals first of all to those who shared that experience. Jesus was a first-century Jew addressing himself to his fellow Jews in language drawn from their common heritage. To appreciate that language we need a crash review of Bible history. We shall briefly recall four moments in Israel's story: Israel's first experience as a monarchy, the subsequent role of the classical prophets, the emergence of apocalyptic writers, and finally the role of John the Baptist.

Israel's first experience of monarchy was also the high point. Organized as a loose confederation of tribes, they had followed the life of wandering herdsfolk. About a thousand years before Jesus' time the Hebrews came into possession of territory of their own and settled down to farming while they enjoyed as well the benefits of the trade routes on which their territory lay. Under these changed circumstances the more centralized system of monarchy became necessary.

When Israel became a monarchy, however, they differed from their neighbors. They did not divinize their kings, nor were the kings absolute. Even Israel's kings always remained subject to Yahweh, the God of Israel, who had entrusted the kingdom to them, and to whom the kingdom belonged.

Under their first kings, David and Solomon, Israel prospered, but the honeymoon with monarchy did not last. The kingdom split in two and first one half, then the other was overrun by enemies and the people carried off into exile. Ordinarily this would have meant the end of the worship of Yahweh. Ordinarily it would have meant that other gods were more powerful than Israel's and were to be worshiped in Yahweh's stead.

What interrupted this ancient religious logic was the message of Israel's prophets. Israel's prophets took an unheard-of step. They smashed the assumption that Israel's national interests and the will of God were one and the same. Yahweh was not simply a national cheerleader. Yahweh had a plan for all of history. If even Israel, the people chosen to be God's own, scorned and neglected the values God had revealed to be what God willed and desired, then God would marshal the forces of history to chastise them.

Amos, for example, proclaimed the doom impending as Israel's mighty neighbors armed themselves as Yahweh's punishment about to fall upon the "fat cows of Bashan," women of wealthy families who lounged in the back yard eating grapes while the widows and orphans among them starved. Thus the prophets announced a message of woe and destruction. Yahweh, Lord of history, was preparing to flail a people who, though God's own, were neglecting the demands of justice and solidarity that went with being a chosen people.

Disaster struck, the kingdom was overrun, the people were carted off to exile. Then the prophetic message became one of hope and consolation. If God had chastised them it was only for a little while. God's faithfulness endured forever and God would lead them back. From woe the prophetic message became a promise of restoration. God's punishment would not last forever and God's people could look forward to something better than what they were experiencing, to a new creation and a new covenant.

Restoration did finally occur under Cyrus the Great of Persia but its reality fell far short of the prophetic imagery. Life was hard. Nor did the restoration last. Alexander the Great's progeny, the Ptolemies out of Egypt and then Seleucids from Syria, swept the region and after a brief interlude of liberty under the Maccabees mighty Rome marched in.

Through all of this the prophets fell silent, and as we saw, Israel's hopes found new expression in apocalyptic. Restoration of the kingdom within history seemed implausible; yet God remained God, and God would demonstrate God's kingship by bringing this kind of history to a close. In literature from the book of Daniel, written a century and a half before Jesus, through the book of Revelation in the New Testament, apocalyptic writers wove visions of the final tribulations of God's just ones and the appearance of an Antichrist. They wrote of a final conflict, both cosmic and earthly, that would pit God's angels above and Israel below against Satan, the other demons, and the beastly kingdoms who tormented God's people on earth. With God's victory the dead would be raised and a world of oppression, injustice and suffering would yield to God's rule. The kingdom of God would come.

John the Baptist, the key figure in launching Jesus' public career, revivifies the old negative prophetic proclamation. The Day of the Lord is about to come, doom is impending, judgment is about to fall upon God's people. With urgency John calls Israel to the repentance symbolized by undergoing his baptism in the waters of the Jordan. Only thus can they hope to escape the judgment God is about to execute when God sends one greater than John to winnow God's people and burn off the chaff among them.

Functional definition

Such is the background to Jesus' message from which his central theme of the nearness of the coming of the kingdom of God draws its evocative power. Does this historical background tell us what Jesus meant by the coming of the kingdom? Does this history lead us to a choice, for example, among the three options afforded by the Old Quest? It does not.

What the historical background does allow us to venture is what we might call a functional definition of Jesus' central theme. We can get at what this means this way. Perhaps you have had the experience of coming across someone in a public place, standing on a street corner, say, or on a subway platform, who was speaking loudly to all comers about Jesus' second coming or the near approach of the end of the world or a similar topic.

How do most people react? How would you react? I do not think you have to be cynical to doubt that people will come rushing out of the subway to hear this good news. Most of us are probably inclined to hurry by, avoiding even eye contact with the preacher. Enthusiastically proclaimed religious language feels out of place in a public setting. Such language belongs in church, if anywhere at all, where those with a taste for it can indulge themselves without offending their fellow citizens.

In his day, however, Jesus found an audience. At that time public speaking about his theme did not strike people as weird or out of place. In Jesus' day, speaking publicly about the coming of the kingdom of God had an appeal that it does not have today.

Hence we can ask what that appeal was. To what interest did this language of Jesus appeal? What were people hoping for when they hoped for the coming of the kingdom? Functionally, what were people expecting the coming of the kingdom would do for them? That is, what function would the coming of the kingdom perform?

The answer we want to suggest has two aspects. In most general terms, the coming of the kingdom meant to Jesus' contemporaries that which would make everything all right. It was a way of talking about what Jesus' contemporaries believed would bring them fulfillment, both as a people and as individuals. Such fulfillment involves a second aspect as well. Hope for fulfillment is at the same time hope for a solution to the problem of evil. We are suggesting that Jesus' language about the coming of the kingdom appealed in his day to people's aspirations for fulfillment and for a solution to the problem of evil. Functionally, then, the coming of the kingdom is what brings fulfillment and solves the problem of evil.

The definition we are working with is functional. It tries to pin down the job that the coming of the kingdom is supposed to do. As functional it leaves open the further question of what the coming of the kingdom is, specifically, of just what would meet that definition and do the job. Perhaps some of Jesus' contemporaries hoped for the revolution that Reimarus thought Jesus had in mind when he spoke of the coming of the kingdom. Perhaps others expected the apocalyptic scenario to unfold.

And what of Jesus himself? We still need to discover what Jesus had in mind when he proclaimed the nearness of the coming of God's kingdom. Given our functional definition, we can let x equal what Jesus meant by his central theme. To solve for x, we can review the data the New Quest offers on what Jesus had to say and what he chose to do. By bringing together our functional definition and what the New Quest tells us about Jesus' words and deeds, we can hope to arrive at the aims and intentions of Jesus' public ministry.

John the Baptist

First, however, at the outset of our treatment of the historical Jesus we want to pay just a bit more attention to the figure of John the Baptist. In our previous section we mentioned John when we were reviewing the historical background to Jesus' central theme, and before that we noted that while the actual order of events of Jesus' public life is largely inaccessible, Jesus' baptism by John does serve to mark its beginning.

Starting with Mark, all four gospels locate Jesus' encounter with John at the beginning of his public life, and when they do this, they cast John as Jesus' forerunner or precursor. In Mark this happens in the very first few verses of the gospel:

> The beginning of the good news of Jesus Christ [the Son of God]. As it is written in the prophet Isaiah, "See, I am sending my messenger ahead of you, who will prepare your way; the voice of one crying out in the wilderness: 'Prepare the way of the Lord, make his paths straight'" (Mark 1:1-3).

Matthew, Luke, and John make the same appeal to the Hebrew Scriptures to set up John's role as the messenger sent by God to get things ready for Jesus.

These data give rise to a question: why? If all four gospels present John as Jesus' precursor, why is this the case? Why do they do this? Following up on this question will serve two purposes for us. On the one hand it will fill in a bit more of Jesus' historical background. On the other it will illustrate what happens when contemporary biblical scholars bring a historical critical perspective to bear on the gospel narrative.

In considering our why-question scholars pull in two further pieces of evidence. First, the Acts of the Apostles relates that while Paul was at Ephesus he encountered and baptized a group of followers of John the Baptist (Acts 19:1-7). John's movement, this indicates, apparently continued and even spread in the years following his death, and data found in the gospels point in the same direction.

Second, when we were laying out the background to Jesus' central theme, we suggested that John represented a revival of the old negative prophetic message that appealed for conversion in face of impending doom. In Matthew (drawing on Q material), for instance, John addresses his audience harshly:

> "You brood of vipers! Who warned you to flee from the wrath to come? Bear fruit worthy of repentance. Do not presume to say to yourselves, 'We have Abraham as our ancestor'; for I tell you, God is able from these stones to raise up children to Abraham. Even now the ax is lying at the root of the

trees; every tree therefore that does not bear good fruit is cut down and thrown into the fire" (Matt 3:7-10).

John expects this judgment to be carried out by one who will come after him:

"I baptize you with water for repentance, but one who is more powerful than I is coming after me; I am not worthy to carry his sandals. He will baptize you with the Holy Spirit and fire. His winnowing fork is in his hand, and he will clear his threshing floor and will gather his wheat into the granary; but the chaff he will burn with unquenchable fire" (Matt 3:11-12).

These data are puzzling. If John was Jesus' forerunner, why did his followers continue as a distinct and independent group, perhaps even in rivalry with Jesus' followers, throughout Jesus' ministry and afterwards when Jesus as well as John had died? Again, how does John's message of impending doom and the coming of a judge who will bring unquenchable fire work as preparation for the gospels' story of Jesus' coming as glad tidings? John's message of itself would lead one to expect something rather different.

There are tensions in the New Testament portrait of John the Baptist as Jesus' precursor. To resolve these tensions, consider that Christians who encountered a rival group for whom God's chosen one was not Jesus but John could not reply by simply putting John down. The fact that Jesus had undergone John's baptism and had regarded John highly would block this avenue of response. Instead, Jesus' followers could reason as follows. Jesus was clearly God's main man, the Messiah, Son of David, and so forth. But John also had a positive significance. John also was from God. And God knows what God is doing. Hence if God sent Jesus, and if God also sent John the Baptist just before Jesus, then John's function was to get things ready for Jesus. This was true whether John knew it or not. John was Jesus' forerunner.

On this position, casting John in the role of Jesus' precursor expresses John's religious significance from a Christian point of view. The New Testament picture of John is not a historical statement about how John understood himself. Rather it expresses how John fit into God's plan as Christians find that plan revealed and worked out in Jesus.

Notice how one other New Testament passage makes this same point about John's status vis-à-vis Jesus. Luke 1–3 tells tales of the infancy of both John and Jesus according to the pattern we have just suggested. On the one hand John is clearly from God. Look how John comes on the scene. God's hand is patently at work when John's parents, Zechariah and Elizabeth, conceive a child despite their great age. Yet on the other hand

Jesus is clearly superior to John and this becomes evident from the manner of Jesus' conception. The way Jesus is conceived tops John's. In Jesus' case power from on high overshadows a young girl named Mary, and her child will be Son of the Most High, ruler of the house of David. Jesus' conception, with no man involved, is even more marvelous than John's.

The gospels' portrait of John the Baptist as Jesus' precursor expresses his significance from a Christian point of view. That viewpoint rests, in part, on the fact that before Jesus began his own ministry he found John's call for the renewal of Israel compelling and urgent. Jesus joined those who went out into the desert to listen to John and he underwent John's baptism in the Jordan. Even when Jesus' message took on accents different from John's, Jesus continued throughout his career to honor John as his mentor.

The Kingdom Expressed in Words: Jesus' Parables

Among the sayings of Jesus recognized as historically authentic we shall focus on the parables. Many of these parables, like the Prodigal Son or the Good Samaritan, the Lost Coin or the Mustard Seed, have become woven into the fabric of Western culture. They are familiar even to people with little contact with organized religion.

The question, of course, is how to read them. At this point the issue of genre becomes important. If you mistake an editorial for a news story when you read the newspaper, you will find yourself misinformed and confused. In order to avoid this sort of confusion, because of the familiarity of the parables through their constant use in the Church and through their diffusion in Western culture, a quick scan of the history of their interpretation, the ways in which they have been read down through the centuries, will be helpful. A review of the history of parable interpretation, helpfully set out by Norman Perrin in *Jesus and the Language of the Kingdom* (Philadephia: Fortress Press, 1976), will allow us to focus clearly on what contemporary scholars are saying about parable as a genre. This in turn will set up the tie-in between Jesus' parables and his central theme.

We can use the parable of the Good Samaritan, found in Luke 10:29-37, to illustrate the history as we go. As the parable appears in the Gospel of Luke it is introduced by the inquiry of a scholar of the Jewish law who asks Jesus what he needs to do to inherit eternal life. Jesus gets him to answer his own question with the double great commandment that enjoins love of God with all one is and love of neighbor as oneself. Still trying to get one up on Jesus, the scholar then asks who counts as his neighbor. Jesus replies with the parable:

"A man was going down from Jerusalem to Jericho and fell into the hands of robbers, who stripped him, beat him, and went away, leaving him half dead. Now by chance a priest was going down that road; and when he saw him, he passed by on the other side. So likewise a Levite, when he came to the place and saw him, passed by on the other side. But a Samaritan while traveling came near him; and when he saw him, he was moved with pity. He went to him and bandaged his wounds, having poured oil and wine on them. Then he put him on his own animal, brought him to an inn, and took care of him. The next day he took out two denarii, gave them to the innkeeper, and said, 'Take care of him; and when I come back, I will repay you whatever more you spend'" (Luke 10:29-35).

Luke then has Jesus ask which of the three was really neighbor to the mugging victim, and when the scholar answers correctly, Jesus further enjoins him to "Go and do likewise."

As the parable stands in the Gospel of Luke, that final line is also the punch line. It is the message that the reader is supposed to carry away. Be like the Samaritan traveler, not like the priest or the Levite. Let your compassion extend to all. Boundaries like those that separate Samaritans and Jews ought not count. Within the framework of the Gospel of Luke, the parable functions as a moral example story. It holds up an example of conduct to be imitated.

If the redactor of Luke transforms the parable of the Good Samaritan into a moral example story, other parables, as they pass through the oral tradition and get taken up by the evangelists, become allegories. An allegory is a way of saying indirectly something that for some reason or other you do not want to express directly. Imagine, for example, that you are a French playwright in Paris in 1943. Your capital is overrun with jackbooted, goose-stepping Nazis. You may end up writing a play about Caligula, the corrupt Roman emperor, and the various thugs who make up his court. Your play is, of course, really about Hitler, Goebbels, Ribbentrop, and the whole evil crew. In interpreting allegory, detail is significant. The appropriate question to ask is what this detail stands for, and what that.

Perhaps the most obvious example of a parable that has become an allegory in the gospels is the parable of the Sower and the Seed in Mark 4:1-9, for which the evangelist provides an interpretation in the eleven following verses that leaves nothing vague or to chance. The evangelist informs us that the seed stands for the word of God and that the various places where it lands stand for different ways in which people respond to the word. This style of interpretation, already operative in the formation of the gospels, became a favorite for centuries afterwards. The influence of Hellenistic culture led people to distinguish the literal sense of a text from its spiritual sense.

St. Augustine, living in north Africa in the fifth century, interprets the parable of the Good Samaritan in this allegorical vein. The man journeying from Jerusalem to Jericho represents every man (or every woman), the soul on its journey through life. Who attacks the soul, stripping it, beating it, and leaving it half dead? Satan and her demons, of course. For Augustine the priest and Levite represent the Old Law, God's covenant with Israel, which Augustine believes was powerless to heal and restore the wounded soul. Who then is the Samaritan traveler whose heart is filled with compassion? It can be none other than Jesus Christ our Lord. Oil and wine represent the sacraments, the inn Holy Mother the Church, and there the wounded soul receives care until the Lord's second coming. For Augustine the parable of the Good Samaritan is a parable about salvation history: sin, the Old Testament, Christ, sacraments, church, and final coming.

This kind of allegorical interpretation prevailed for centuries. In the nineteenth century, however, a liberal Protestant named Adolf Jülicher called a halt. Edifying and ingenious though these allegorical readings were, they also seemed arbitrary and uncontrolled. The only limit on allegory appeared to be the interpreter's ingenuity and imagination. Allegory left people free to find whatever they wanted in the parables.

Jülicher suggested a different approach. Instead of approaching the parables as a bundle of details to be deciphered, he argued that literarily each parable was an organic unity. All the parts of the parable conspired to deliver a single point. The appropriate question to ask of a parable was not what this detail, and this, and this, really stood for. Rather, the question to ask was: what is the point?

As a liberal Protestant Jülicher had definite ideas about what kind of point the parables must be delivering. Jülicher accepted the suggestion made by Immanuel Kant in a book entitled *Religion Within the Limits of Reason Alone*. Kant had argued that religion is really dressed-up morality and liberal Protestants tended to regard Jesus as primarily a great moral teacher. Hence Jülicher took it for granted that each parable delivered a single point of universally applicable moral teaching. In that case the message of the Good Samaritan would be that one's charity should be universal. Why? It is only rational to recognize that our common human nature makes such differences as nationality unimportant. That is why, in the parable, Jesus has a Samaritan overcome the hostility that separated his people from the Jews and offer assistance to the wounded Jew. Notice that on Jülicher's interpretation the basis for the course of action the parable commends is a philosophical one. Religion, he believes, is really morality.

We can divide parable interpretation in the twentieth century into two phases. C. H. Dodd and Joachim Jeremias represent the first phase. Jeremias is significant for the form-critical work he did on the parables, reversing the transformation they had undergone through the oral tradition and at the hands of the gospel redactors. Jeremias thus reconstructed the parables in a form as close to the original as we are likely achieve. Regarding the interpretation of the parables, both Dodd and Jeremias agreed with Jülicher that the parables functioned as organic literary units to deliver a single point. Allegory was out.

They differed from Jülicher, however, on the kind of point Jesus was making in the parables. They did not believe that religion was merely dressed-up morality, nor that Jesus was simply a great moral teacher. Hence they did not find in the parables points of universally applicable moral teaching. Instead they believed that Jesus' teaching was what they called eschatological. The word comes from the Greek for what is final, last, or ultimate. Dodd and Jeremias are both reacting to Weiss and Schweitzer's construction of Jesus' message as apocalyptic. Weiss and Schweitzer, we saw, believed that Jesus thought of the coming of the kingdom as a wholly future event and, furthermore, that Jesus mistakenly thought it was breaking in through his own ministry. Against this thoroughgoing eschatology, as it is called, Dodd stressed those sayings of Jesus that indicate that the kingdom has already arrived with his own activity; this position is called realized eschatology. Jeremias in turn modified Dodd's position. Recognizing that in some of Jesus' sayings the kingdom is a future reality, in others a present reality, he proposes that Jesus thought of the kingdom as in process, already present but not totally.

This discussion of eschatology pinpoints how Dodd and Jeremias differ from Jülicher on the interpretation of parables. For them Jesus' teaching is not merely ethical but eschatological, that is, about the kingdom of God that has at least begun its entry into history with Jesus' ministry. From this perspective the point of the parable of the Good Samaritan would still be universal compassion but the reason behind the point would be different. Jesus would be commending universal compassion, not on the basis of our common human nature, but on the basis of the reign of God that has begun to take hold in his activity. St. Paul would make a similar point when he wrote that in Christ "there is no longer Jew or Greek, there is no longer slave or free, there is no longer male and female; for all of you are one in Christ Jesus" (Gal 3:28).

In the second, contemporary phase of parable interpretation, the action moves to this side of the Atlantic and takes a decidedly literary turn. Authors like Robert Funk, Dan O. Via, and John Dominic Crossan continue to regard the parables as organic units. On their account, however, the parables are not mere didactic devices aimed at communicating some point of Jesus' teaching, even eschatological teaching. Rather, they argue, the parables are intended to make something happen. Parables have an event-like character, and this dimension is lost when they are reduced to pedagogical tools. Parables are not simply means of delivering a lesson; their telling is itself an event, a happening. When they are viewed this way, these parable-happenings help us solve for *x*. They bring about what we shall call anticipatory experiences of the reality symbolized as the coming of the kingdom of God.

Robert Funk sets up the theory for this approach to parables in conversation with the definition of parable that C. H. Dodd had offered. According to Dodd, four elements go into a parable. A parable is, first, a simile or metaphor. Second, it is drawn from everyday life or from nature. Third, it holds your attention by its intensity or strangeness. Fourth, its meaning is open-ended, to be grasped by each hearer in his or her own situation.

Beginning from the last point, Funk argues that Dodd was inconsistent with his own definition when interpreting the parables. Dodd asked what point of teaching about the kingdom as a present reality each parable communicated. But this ignores his own stipulation that the meaning of a parable is open-ended, not to be pinned down in some timeless formulation. Dodd's practice of interpreting the parables in terms of eschatological teaching transgresses his definition of what a parable is.

Second, Funk points out that if the parables are metaphors, they must be seen as real metaphors, which have an event-like character. The material for the parable may be drawn from nature or everyday life but it becomes clear in the course of the parable that the particular aspect of nature or everyday life is not what the parable is about. The literal sense is one thing, but what the parable is about, the referent, is another. How does this become clear? This is where the elements of intensification and distortion come in. The parable draws its hearer in by beginning with a plausible, familiar situation. Soon, however, the details become both so vivid and so extravagant or exaggerated that through this intensification the effect becomes surreal.

This occurs in the parable of the Good Samaritan. The parable begins with an event common enough both then and now, a mugging. The mugging is made very vivid. We are not simply told that the traveler is robbed; he is robbed, beaten, stripped, and left half dead. At this point the parable starts becoming strange as well. As the traveler lies there, a priest comes along. Help is on the way. But the priest walks on by on the other side of the road. What? That is odd. It must have been a fluke. Right behind the priest comes a Levite, a Jew of the tribe of Levi, the tribe to which the Temple service was entrusted. This Levite looks at the wounded traveler. And he walks on by on the other side.

What John Dominic Crossan analyzes as a reversal of expectations is setting in. Twice help has been anticipated, and twice that anticipation has been denied. Now, as the story continues, a Samaritan comes upon the scene. Who are the Samaritans? In the first century they played the role of modern Catholics to northern Irish Protestants. They played the role of the PLO to Israelis. They played the role of abortionists to Operation Rescue. Samaritans worshiped the same God as the Jews, but in a different place and according to their own customs, and they claimed that their way and not the Jews' was how God should be worshipped. Rival claims to a common heritage led Jews and Samaritans to hate each other intensely.

The wounded traveler lies there, half dead. Priest and Levite have passed him by. Enter the Samaritan. To Jesus' Jewish audience the very word evokes loathing and disgust. Yet that audience has to entertain the unthinkable as they hear that it is the Samaritan whose heart is filled with compassion. And by again heaping up details the parable insists on this and rubs it in the audience's face. Jesus' hearers have to watch with their mind's eye as the Samaritan tends the victim's wounds, pouring oil and wine on them. The Samaritan hoists the victim onto his own animal and, having given up his seat, walks beside him until they come to an inn. There the Samaritan devotes himself further to caring for the victim and then, as if this were not enough, in effect writes a blank check to the innkeeper to continue this care until his return.

Contemporary interpreters would have us regard the parables as metaphors. Metaphors, when they are alive, when they have not become familiar and routine, generate new meaning. This new meaning is not imparted like a lesson. It happens, dramatically. The Good Samaritan becomes a metaphor through the intensification and extravagance of its details and especially through the reversal of expectations it brings about. The audience settles in for a story about a familiar event, a mugging. But if the parable draws them in by appealing to their familiar world, its effect is to undermine and shatter that world. In the familiar world of Jesus' hearers it is perfectly clear who Jews are and who Samaritans are. The parable pulls the rug out from under that world.

How is this parable-event related to Jesus' central theme? In the apocalyptic scenario the coming of the kingdom of God meant the end of the world. Jesus' parables can evoke an anticipatory experience of this. The planet does not collapse physically into a black hole, of course, or flare up into a ball of fire. Each of Jesus' hearers, however, has a life-world of his or her own. That world has its structure determining who is in and who is out, who deserves respect and care and who deserves scorn and contempt. Jesus' parables would subvert that world as too narrow, too confining, as a world in which one constricts one's own humanity in denying that of others. That subversiveness, of course, begins to explain the hostility Jesus evoked. People protect the worlds that render them secure.

The meaning of the parable is open-ended. Beyond shock and possibly outrage, the parable evokes questions. The first question for Jesus' audience is: will I allow this to happen? Will I allow my world to go up for grabs like this? If I do, how do I find the new source of identity that letting go of my old security requires? This open-endedness extends beyond Jesus' original audience. People today can also ask: who are my Samaritans? Who are my priests and Levites? Can I let go of this neat and comfortable structure and open to what it cuts me off from?

Jesus' parables indicate that as it draws near, the coming of the kingdom is something that subverts, undermines, and shatters the worlds we construct. Parables evoke an anticipatory experience of the coming of the kingdom as end of the world.

Jesus symbolized what he believed would genuinely fulfill human beings and resolve the problem of evil for them as the coming of the kingdom of God. His parables, we are suggesting, evoke anticipatory experiences of the coming of the kingdom. The coming of the kingdom, as it draws near, radically calls into question the worlds people construct for themselves. Those worlds block genuine fulfillment and feed, rather than solve, the problem of evil. The coming of the kingdom means an end to such worlds.

Chapter Five

The Kingdom Expressed
in Deeds

In our effort to solve for x, to determine what Jesus meant by the coming of the kingdom of God, we are examining Jesus' characteristic ways of speaking and acting. What was it that Jesus thought would provide both authentic human fulfillment and a solution to the problem of evil? Moving from his speech in parables to his actions we want to inquire first into his miracles, then into the significance of the company Jesus kept, the people with whom Jesus chose to associate.

Jesus' Miracles

Like many of his parables, the stories of Jesus' miracles have become familiar through the art and literature of Western culture. Perhaps best known are the raising of Lazarus from the dead and the changing of water into wine at the wedding feast at Cana, both recounted in the Fourth Gospel. Other stories, such as those in which Jesus calms a storm with a word of command, or walks on water, or heals various people, have also entered the Western imagination. As we saw when we were reviewing the Old Quest, these stories have become problematic in the encounter of traditional Christian belief with modernity. They meet resistance from a modern sense of reality informed by scientific and historical consciousness. If previous ages readily found them plausible, the stories of Jesus' miracles no longer enjoy that taken-for-granted status.

In approaching the topic of Jesus' miracles we shall first ask just what we mean by the term miracle. Having clarified the meaning of the term, we shall next pose the unavoidable modern question, that of the historicity of the New Testament miracle stories. Modern scientific and historical consciousness cannot help raising the question: did it happen? Then, having established what we mean by a miracle and having suggested a position on what actually happened, we can ask about the significance of this aspect of Jesus' behavior. We shall suggest that like the parables, Jesus' miracles advance our understanding of his central theme. They help us grasp what Jesus believed was involved in the coming of the kingdom.

Two definitions

What is meant by a miracle? Many people, when they hear the word, think of something unexplainable. Pushed for a bit more precision, they speak of something that violates the laws of nature. On this common understanding of the term miracle, the world of our experience contains many happenings. It starts raining, a baby is born, politicians sign an arms reduction treaty, a family drives off on vacation. Each of these happenings has an explanation. If we ask why something occurred, an answer is usually available. We can turn to some discipline, or combination of disciplines, for an explanation. Occasionally, however, there is a ringer. Something occurs that cannot be explained. It violates the laws of nature. God did it. Occasionally an event occurs that is caused directly by God. God has intervened, interrupting the normal course of things, setting aside the laws of nature, and this direct divine intervention produces a miracle.

The key to this common understanding of miracle lies in the question of causality. Either there is some natural explanation or God did it. If the event can be explained, it is not a miracle. "Either/or" characterizes the approach this understanding of miracles takes to the question of their causality.

Common though it is, this understanding faces a number of objections. One objection is this. On this understanding something is a miracle if it cannot be explained. "Cannot," however, is a tall order. There is a large difference between saying that we do not, in fact, understand something and saying that we cannot, in principle, ever come to understand it. The history of science suggests that we should exercise a good deal of modesty in making the second kind of statement. What we do not understand at present may well find an explanation sooner or later.

A next observation notes that to move from the statement that something is inexplicable to the further statement that God caused it involves a leap. The inexplicable is just that, something that we cannot explain. Of itself it does not necessarily imply divine intervention. Bringing in God as the explanation for what we cannot explain is a further step that does not follow necessarily or automatically.

Third, defining the miraculous as the inexplicable ties into a dynamic that Dietrich Bonhoeffer, a German pastor who was hanged for participating in a plot against Hitler, described as "the God of the gaps." In Bonhoeffer's eyes the encounter with modern science sent the Church on an inglorious path of retreat. If science seemed to be pushing God out of the world, the Church responded by staking out the gaps in scientific knowledge, the lacunae in scientific explanation, to claim room for God. As science progressed and these gaps were filled, however, the Church retreated farther. This defensive strategy of the "God of the gaps," Bonhoeffer finds, is unworthy of the reality of God. God exists at the center of all reality, not on the fringes of scientific explanation.

For the past several decades some Catholic biblical scholars have been suggesting an alternative understanding of the term miracle. They claim this alternative understanding accords better with the New Testament witness. On this understanding a miracle is some extraordinary event that bears religious significance. The event must be extraordinary; not everything is a miracle if the word is to serve any purpose; and what makes the extraordinary event a miracle is the meaning, the religious significance, it bears.

This second understanding of the term miracle shifts the focus of attention from causality to meaning. As far as causality goes, this understanding allows a "both/and" approach. On one level or from one perspective the extraordinary event may have a "natural" explanation, but that explanation is not exhaustive. The event also bears religious significance. As the rationalists correctly perceived, God can work through secondary causes.

There are, however, conditions that must be present for religious significance to be grasped. It is not self-evident to all. On the first understanding of the term miracles were hard facts that could be used as clubs against nonbelievers. On the second understanding that arsenal is emptied. Believers and unbelievers may agree up to a point on the causality of the extraordinary event but where unbelievers find the "natural" explanation exhaustive believers discern a further level of meaning in the event. The point at issue between believers and unbelievers becomes not a difference over a particular empirical fact as on the first understanding, but a difference on the deeper level of worldview. If one's worldview is secular, miracles never happen, although some extraordinary events may be quite puzzling. From the secular perspective, however, claims about religious significance are merely subjective oddities.

Historicity

The term miracle can be understood in two quite different ways, and some biblical scholars recommend the second. Having clarified the term, let us move our attention to the stories told about Jesus in the gospels.

Jesus heals and casts out demons; he raises the dead, calms winds, walks on water, and changes water to wine. The gospels picture Jesus performing these signs and deeds of power, as the New Testament calls them, and others as well. What are we to make of such stories? Does Christian faith commit one to accepting them all as actual events in Jesus' life?

Two decades ago the late Bruce Vawter, a noted Roman Catholic biblical scholar, sought to make the discoveries of his discipline available to a broad audience in a book we have already cited, *This Man Jesus.* On pages 139–144 of that book he addressed the question that concerns us. The answer he suggested then can serve to orient our thinking on the matter.

Vawter begins his discussion by noting that one cannot raise the question seriously if one starts with dogmatic assumptions. There is no sense raising the question of the historicity of Jesus' miracles if you have already decided that that kind of thing is simply impossible and there is no room for miracles in the real world. Similarly, you also exclude yourself from the conversation if you have already decided that whatever the Bible says must have happened, and just the way the Bible says it happened. Questions, if they are genuine, require openness.

Vawter makes a second preliminary comment. Strictly speaking, he points out, you would have to go case by case through each of the New Testament miracle stories to arrive at a judgment of historicity. If you were to do this you might well discover that what looks like a miracle story to a twentieth-century reader of the Bible might not have struck the story's original audience that way. If, for example, the story of the timely catch of a fish with something in its mouth was a commonplace in the world of Jesus' day the reaction would not be astonishment at the miracle. Rather the audience would recognize the story as familiar and wonder what novel twist the storyteller was going to give it.

With these two preliminary cautions Vawter goes on to suggest that the miracle stories fall into two classes. Some depict healings and exorcisms, others what he calls nature miracles. The former, he argues, enjoy high historical probability. Vawter is not saying that each story occurred just as it is recounted; the creative contributions of the oral tradition and the redactor rule that out. He is arguing, however, that behind the stories about healings and exorcisms lies a highly probable tradition that Jesus in fact did that sort of thing.

One reason for judging this tradition probable is the witness of those who would have an interest in denying it. In the gospels Jesus is accused by his enemies of healing by the power of the ruler of the demons, Beelzebul, as he is called (Mark 3:22), or Satan. The accusation shows that even his opponents are granting that he did this sort of thing although they offer an unfriendly explanation for it. Their charge is echoed later in the

Jewish tradition when the Talmud refers to a Nazorean who was hanged for sorcery. Jesus' enemies did not deny that he healed and cast out demons; acknowledging this activity, they attribute it to black magic. Vawter also offers a second reason for accepting this tradition; as we shall see, this healing and exorcising activity coheres with what else we know about Jesus' ministry.

The nature miracles receive low historical grades from Vawter for two reasons. First, the point of some of them at least seems to be to extol Jesus' power, but this contradicts the constancy with which Jesus rejected requests to validate his ministry by showy signs. Second, similar stories are told of other figures in the ancient world, suggesting that these are legends, of themselves unhistorical, whose purpose is to keep alive the memory of important people.

For Vawter the stories of Jesus healing and casting out demons have a reliable historical tradition behind them. The question to be put to the stories of nature miracles is how the story is used to express something about Jesus' religious significance, not when or how it might have really happened. This position, which Vawter drew in large part from Rudolf Bultmann, has evoked criticism. Most seriously, the distinction between healings and exorcisms on the one hand and nature miracles on the other has been judged arbitrary. One might venture to guess that the reason for making it is philosophical rather than something based on the biblical text. Healings and exorcisms are perhaps more plausible to the modern sense of reality than walking on water or raising the dead.

Perhaps, however, this modern sense of reality needs to be expanded beyond the limited experience of Western culture that informs it. Phenomena that lie outside the boundaries of that experience have been amply documented; think, for example, of Indian fire walkers who can stride over a bed of glowing coals without injury. Phenomena such as these, while seemingly inexplicable, do not necessarily entail the dualistic worldview that would invoke direct divine intervention as their explanation. They do, however, indicate that our culturally conditioned sense of what is possible may need to become less rigid.

Where does this leave us? Certainly Vawter's preliminary caution still holds good. To genuinely pursue the question of the historicity of the miracles attributed to Jesus in the New Testament requires openness to the question; dogmatic presuppositions, one way or the other, disqualify one from the discussion. In addition, the positive side of Vawter's position still stands. There exist very good reasons for holding that in all probability Jesus healed people and cast out demons. The so-called nature miracles, however, ought not be ruled out of court *a priori*. A grasp of the narrowness of the sense of reality typical of contemporary Westerners cautions against this. Hence Vawter's second point regarding the necessity of dealing with the miracle stories case by case becomes all the more urgent.

As it happens a contemporary biblical scholar has done precisely that. John P. Meier is in the process of researching a multivolume work, *A Marginal Jew*, that will serve as the standard for research on the historical Jesus for at least a generation. In the second volume of this work, subtitled *Mentor, Message, and Miracles* (Garden City, New York: Doubleday, 1994), Meier both confirms Vawter's position on Jesus' healings and exorcisms, challenges the usefulness of the category "nature miracle," and works one by one through every miracle ascribed to Jesus in the gospels. While he finds some grounds that would incline him to regard one story of a raising from the dead as possibly historical, the rest of the so-called nature miracles remain where Vawter left them.

Miracles and the Nearness of the Kingdom

Having clarified the meaning of the term miracle and having explored the question of the historicity of the miracles attributed to Jesus in the gospels, we can now turn to the payoff for our inquiry. Historically it is highly probable that Jesus at least healed people and performed exorcisms. What is the significance of this behavior in the context of his ministry?

Negatively, Jesus was not seeking to demonstrate his divinity by exercising superhuman power. On this Harnack was correct: Jesus' concern in his earthly ministry centered on the coming of the kingdom, not on his own identity as second person of the Trinity. Whether Jesus thought of himself explicitly as divine is a question we have yet to examine. Again negatively, Jesus was not out to prove that he was the Messiah by acting out a script that he found written for him in Israel's Bible. As we shall see, titles like Messiah were probably chosen by Jesus' followers after Easter to express and communicate his religious significance. Finally on the negative side, Jesus did not heal people simply because he was kind. He was indeed kind, but the hierarchy of values that places being nice at the peak as the ultimate good was foreign to him and his world. Rather, Jesus' concern was the nearness of the coming of the kingdom.

His parables, we saw, evoked anticipatory experiences of that reality. Kingdom of God in the apocalyptic scenario meant the end of the world; when God's reign draws near, it subverts the worlds we construct. Undermining, threatening, and even shattering our worlds, that nearness anticipates the end of every world in which God does not reign. Jesus' parables, by evoking an experience of the nearness of the coming of the kingdom of God, exercised that negative, world-shattering function.

His healings and exorcisms are more positive. Again in the apocalyptic scenario the coming of the kingdom meant liberation from oppressors and victory over Satan. In our functional definition the coming of the kingdom provides a solution to the problem of evil. Healing people from illness, Jesus offers an anticipatory experience of that reality. In the ancient world all illness, and especially mental illness, was attributed to evil spirits. If you had a migraine, there was an evil spirit in your head. Museums of ancient history document the remedy; you can see skulls into which holes had been drilled to allow the evil spirit to depart. The operation was, no doubt, a success; the headache was cured, even if the patient also died.

In healing people and performing exorcisms Jesus evokes anticipatory experiences of the coming of the kingdom. If that coming meant the definitive conflict with and victory over Satan and the demons, then from that perspective Jesus' ministry launched an assault on all that renders people unfree. Evoked in Jesus' parables, the coming of the kingdom shatters worlds. Jesus' cures and exorcisms suggest that beyond those shattered worlds lies a reality that heals and liberates all that needs to be freed and made whole. The nearness of God's kingdom brings wholeness and freedom.

The Company Jesus Kept

The gospels portray Jesus journeying to Jerusalem to worship at the Temple. He reads and preaches in the synagogues. He dines with Pharisees and engages the scribes in debate. He is also found at table with tax collectors, conversing with women, and in the company of the poor.

This behavior is significant. The world of Jesus' day was highly structured and a clear line ran through it to separate those with whom it was acceptable to associate from those whose company rendered one unclean. To appreciate the significance of this aspect of Jesus' behavior, of the company he kept, we need to know a bit about the various groups who made up the world of his day.

At Jerusalem the center of Israel was the Temple, the only place where the sacrifices prescribed in the Law could be offered. Over the Temple liturgy presided the high priest and his associates, part of a wealthy, aristocratic group known as *Sadducees*. Religiously this group was very conservative. If something was not found in the Torah, the first five books of the Hebrew Scriptures, which they believed had been composed by Moses himself, the Sadducees would not hear of it. Resurrection of the dead, for instance, was an idea they dismissed as a novelty. Politically the Sadducees were in bed with the Roman occupation. So long as Rome allowed them to maintain their privileged status they would go along to get along. In the eyes of the Jewish populace the high priestly party was regarded as corrupt. According to the Law priests were to be drawn from the tribe of Levi. The incumbents of the high priesthood in Jesus' day, however, came from a line that had bought the office under a previous occupation.

If the Sadducees' response to the Roman occupation was compromise, *Realpolitik*, the *Essenes* represented the extreme opposite. Regarding Jerusalem and the Temple as hopelessly corrupt, they withdrew back out into the desert where, prior to the rise of monarchy, Israel had enjoyed its honeymoon with God. Here they established communities much like monasteries, with goods pooled for common support, a daily round of pious observances, and for some members at least, a life of celibacy. From their settlement at Qumran have been recovered the Dead Sea Scrolls, documents that provide a wealth of information on this form of Judaism at the time of Jesus. Apocalyptic-minded, the Essenes of Qumran expected two messiahs, one priestly and one royal, and they looked forward to the final conflict that would purge the world of God's enemies.

The New Testament depicts the *Pharisees*, another Jewish group at the time of Jesus and one with common roots with the Essenes, as hypocritical legalists. This picture is a historical distortion. It reflects not so much the situation in Jesus' day as later developments. The Gospel of Matthew, for example, is likely to have been written for a Christian community whose members have recently been excluded from the synagogues by the Pharisees' successors, the rabbis. The latter had the task of redefining what it meant to be a Jew once Jerusalem, and with it the Temple, had been destroyed in the aftermath of a failed revolt against the Romans. In the eyes of some scholars the destruction of Jerusalem gave birth to two new religions, Judaism as it has existed for the past two millennia and Christianity. It was from this newly emerging Judaism that Matthew's community had been excluded, and Matthew's portrait of the Pharisees projects back into Jesus' day the conflict and hostility that characterized his own situation.

In reality the Pharisees represented something like a lay holiness movement. In order to remain faithful Jews under the abomination of Roman rule they would live in daily life the numerous prescriptions found in the Law governing the behavior of the priests in the Temple. Extending these regulations to daily life, the Pharisees would thus be a people set apart, a holy and priestly people. In some ways they seem similar to the "Holy Club" behind the emergence of the Methodist church under the leadership of John Wesley, or like the Third Orders whose Roman Catholic members adapted the rules of groups like the Franciscans or the Dominicans to the life of laity in the world.

Whether the *Zealots* were an organized group during Jesus' time is unclear. What is certain, however, is that a constant thread among the Jewish responses to foreign occupation favored violence. A good Roman, on this account, was a dead Roman. This dynamic would in fact lead to revolts against Rome that brought disastrous results upon Israel in 70 C.E. and again in 135 C.E. These revolts brought the Sadducees, centered on the Temple liturgy, and the Essenes, warlike in their apocalyptic hopes, to an end. Israel as it had existed since the time of King David was also wiped out, and for almost two millennia the Jews would live dispersed in exile without a state of their own until after World War II. Under those circumstances the future lay with the Pharisees and their successors, the rabbis.

In Jesus' day, however, a variety of groups flourished in Israel, including Essenes, Sadducees, and different schools of Pharisees. This society included others as well. Tax collectors, for example, appear in the story of Jesus. While the Internal Revenue Service is not the most beloved of American institutions, things were different in Jesus' day. Jewish tax collectors can be described as quislings, a word taken from the name of a Norwegian prime minister who sold out to the Nazis during World War II. They worked for the foreign occupation. The tax system was somewhat different, too. These publicans, as they are called, made their living by gouging as much as they could out of their fellow Jews in order to make a profit for themselves over and beyond what they had to pass on to the Romans. Collaborators with the enemy, enriching themselves at their countrymen's expense, they were regarded as beyond the pale, renegades, no longer to be considered Jews.

Besides the tax collectors among Jesus' friends, there were women. As the ad goes, "You've come a long way. . . ." In Jesus' day women's place generally was in the home and their purpose was to care for husband and children. Period. If they had to go out they were to veil themselves, and they were not to be greeted on the street. Contact with blood was taboo among Jews, and since one never knew whether a woman might be menstruating, they were better avoided. Besides, proximity to a woman might lead a man to a loss of self-control, to lust.

Women, it seems fair to say, and the Scriptures could indeed be read as saying this, existed for men. They also depended on men. Widows, for example, could not inherit, leaving them at the mercy of their sons' or in-laws' good will for their very subsistence, while wives, of which a man was allowed as many as he could afford and cared to have, were easily divorced. Divorce, of course, was primarily, if not exclusively, a male prerogative.

Religiously also, women's role was circumscribed. They were excluded from the priesthood and their access to the Temple at Jerusalem was restricted to the Court of Women. It is not clear that they were allowed any function in the synagogue, the local house of prayer and study. A text from a period later than Jesus' day forbids in strongest terms teaching one's daughter to read, while another preserves a prayer with which Jewish males thanked God for not creating them female.

Besides women and tax collectors around Jesus, there were the poor. Roman occupation placed a crushing burden of taxes on the peasant farmers who eked out their subsistence in the countryside. Over and above the Temple tax that supported the wealth of the high priestly party in Jerusalem, the financial demands of the Romans had to be met. A life of grinding poverty was the result, and this system of oppression wielded the power of religious sanction; inability to pay the tithe required for the Temple rendered one a sinner. These conditions spawned the banditry that made travel through the countryside a dangerous proposition, a situation we have seen reflected in Jesus' parable of the Good Samaritan.

Among all these people, Sadducees, Pharisees, tax collectors, women, and the poor, Jesus comes proclaiming the nearness of the kingdom of God and healing and exorcising. Sadducees and high priests were unlikely to find Jesus' message interesting. They were doing just fine as things were. Pharisees were much closer to Jesus' own thinking but the key strategy for maintaining their identity as God's holy people was one of separateness, and this Jesus transgressed. By the company he kept Jesus attacked the line that defined the world of his day. Within that world it was self-evident that those above the line should enjoy wealth and status, and equally self-evident that those below the line deserved scorn and contempt. Jesus, however, proclaiming the nearness of God's kingdom and acting that nearness out in the company he kept, attacked that assumption and pulled the rug out from under the world it structured. Like the parables, then, Jesus' associations evoked anticipatory experiences of the end of the world, the end of the humanly constructed world, a world structured on oppression and injustice in such a taken-for-granted way that its sinfulness becomes invisible.

This aspect of Jesus' activity has a positive side as well. What message did the world of the day send to tax collectors and the poor? It defined them as human trash, contemptible, unfit for the company of good, godfearing folk. Tax collectors were no longer counted as Jews. Women, in particular, were regarded as sources of uncleanness and temptation. From Jesus, however, these people receive a different message. From him they experience simple human acceptance. He seeks out their company, he dines with them. He speaks to women publicly, extends a healing touch, teaches them and sends them out as his disciples. He does all this, not out of some generic niceness, but as an exercise of his ministry. In Jesus' simple human acceptance he makes available a fragmentary glimpse, a foretaste, of the reality symbolized as the coming of the kingdom of God.

That coming is, in the apocalyptic scenario, the coming of God as God of the universe. The nearness of that God, Jesus demonstrates, brings acceptance to those who are contemned, care to those who are cast aside, freedom from society's demeaning definitions. Like his miracles, the company Jesus chooses to keep anticipates the coming of the kingdom as the nearness of healing from whatever needs to be healed, of liberation from whatever enslaves and oppresses.

Chapter Six

Responding to the Nearness of the Kingdom

Having identified Jesus' central theme and having explored how he expressed that theme in the happenings of his parables, in his deeds of healing and exorcisms, and in the company he chose to keep, we are ready to ask a further question: In all of this activity, what was Jesus after? What was he trying to make happen? What response was he looking for? This will allow us to ask further what Jesus' own standpoint was throughout the activity we have been reviewing. While on the topic, we can also digress only a bit in order to ask another question prompted by the later Christian tradition, namely whether Jesus knew he was God. Finally, we need to account for the negative response Jesus evoked. Hence in our next chapter we shall investigate why Jesus ended up getting killed.

The Positive Response: *Metanoia*

Reimarus, we may recall, had identified Jesus' central theme at the very beginning of the Old Quest. "Repent, for the kingdom of God is at hand." Contemporary scholars focus on repentance, *metanoia* in Greek, as the response Jesus was seeking. But insofar as the English word "repentance" may suggest that you should feel bad about yourself and grovel it translates the New Testament Greek term poorly. *Metanoia* derives from the root word *nous*, which designates how you operate from the neck up, your mind. Literally, then, *metanoia* would mean a change of mind, a change in the way you think. A more Jewish way of expressing it would be to speak of a change of heart. The prophet Ezekiel, for instance, looked forward to a time when God would give God's people a new heart and a new spirit, removing their heart of stone and bestowing instead a heart of flesh.

Nowadays instead of repentance *metanoia* is more commonly translated as "conversion." To understand this, however, we need to exclude one common meaning of the term. You sometimes hear Catholics divided into two classes. There are, on the one hand, "cradle Catholics" who were baptized as infants and have been Catholic all their lives. On the other hand there are converts. On this understanding conversion is the process whereby, having been a member of one denomination, after a good deal of prayer and soul-searching one switches to another. Having been born Presbyterian, for example, one undergoes a conversion, comes to a better understanding of the one true church, and becomes a Lutheran. Conversion in this sense, understood as denomination switching, is not the response Jesus was looking for.

Rather, to put the matter somewhat technically, the *metanoia* Jesus was seeking to elicit can be understood as the transformation of persons on the level of what we shall call spontaneous felt meaning. Given that technical phrase, however, we are no doubt guilty at this point of trying to clarify the obscure by the even more obscure. To escape that charge we need to answer two questions. First of all, what do we mean by "the level of spontaneous felt meaning?" Then, how is what we have seen of Jesus' words and activity geared to transform it?

First we need to clarify what we mean by a level of spontaneous felt meaning. Suppose you were assigned to write an essay: "My Philosophy of Life." You would be trying to articulate in that essay the pattern of meanings and values that guides your living. Having written it, you might share the essay with a good friend. Based on your friend's close knowledge of you, she might congratulate you on how well you know yourself. Or she might point out how idealized your essay is—you may think this is the way you live, but come on, you're kidding yourself.

Perhaps you've never been assigned to write that essay. Perhaps you've never even given the matter much thought. Nonetheless, we would suggest, you do have an operative philosophy of life, a more or less coherent set of meanings and values out of which you live. Furthermore, that pattern of meanings and values shows up spontaneously in how you react to everything that happens to you. It shows up in how you feel about what comes your way.

For example, imagine this situation. It is the first day of class. The professor walks in and points to one student, another, and another, telling each of them to leave the room. Out in the hall, the professor explains: she has decided that learning requires community, and to get that started each student is to go back in and spend five minutes introducing himself or herself to the class. Now what are the possible reactions to this bizarre situation? One student may develop a sly grin. She hasn't announced it yet, but she intends to run for student government president, and here's a chance to begin selling herself to her constituency. Another student reacts differently. Where's the bathroom? Getting up in front of other people is torture, very nervous-making. The third? Well, this is pretty silly. On the other hand, it's equally silly to sit in a room for fifteen weeks and never meet anyone, so all right, let's get on with it.

Notice that the same thing has happened to each of the three students, yet each of them experiences the event very differently. Each of them feels very differently about what has happened to them. Their feeling, moreover, is not simply irrational. It indicates a whole set of meanings and values. Take our first student, rubbing her hands in anticipation of getting back in the room to start her campaign. Life is a series of opportunities to get ahead and the trick is to grab them and exploit them as they arise. The second student, on the other hand, finds little value in himself, perceives other people as threatening, and would rather hide, making his way through life attracting as little attention as possible. For the third student we are all in this together and even if the exercise is foolish, the company and support of other people is a good thing.

Each of us, we are suggesting, carries around a coherent set of meanings and values, a philosophy of life, if you will, and it shows up spontaneously in how we feel about whatever happens to us. That pattern of spontaneous felt meaning determines how we experience whatever we experience.

Now how might what we have seen Jesus saying and doing work to transform people on this gut level out of which we live? To at least illustrate the connection we can borrow some ideas from developmental psychology. From our perspective, developmental psychologists investigate how one's level of spontaneous felt meaning takes shape. According to the late Erik Erikson this development occurs as we proceed through a distinct set of stages in the life cycle. The shape of our pattern of spontaneous felt meaning is determined incrementally by how we negotiate each of these stages.

For our purposes we can focus on Erikson's very first stage. It begins when, after we have wriggled and pushed our way down the birth canal, our entrance into the world is celebrated with a slap on the rear. We've begun our career as an infant. What that career was like is very hard for us to imagine. On the one hand there was not a thought in our heads. On the thinking score, the lights had not yet been turned on. Otherwise, however, lots was going on. As infants we were bundles of sensations, needs, and affect. And while we did not yet know where we left off and other things began, one other figure was crucial in our experience as an infant—the nurturer, most often our birth mother but not always.

Even though we were not yet thinking, during our first few months our earliest experience of being in the universe was being imprinted on us. To the extent that our nurturer was on deck, alert and attentive to our needs, this was a positive experience. The universe, we "learned," was a good place to be. It supported us and met our needs as they arose. If we were hungry, something warm and soft supplied us with warm, sweet milk. If we were wet or worse, we were wiped and powdered. Often we were held and rocked in a comforting embrace.

Or perhaps things did not go so well. Perhaps we found that if we were hungry or messy we could cry our little lungs out to no avail. Perhaps the occasions on which we were held and rocked were few and far between. In that case a very different message was being imprinted on us about what kind of universe it is.

On Erikson's analysis the first few months are critical in developing a sense of basic trust that the universe is a benevolent, supportive place to be, that we can confidently expect our needs to be met and can thus move openly and confidently into new experiences and new situations. But no nurturer is perfect, and some do a very poor job. To that extent the message we absorb is a different one. We learn that the universe is a cold and indifferent place, that we are fundamentally alone, that we can trust only what we can control. Besides basic trust there is basic mistrust. And all of this occurs before we have thought a single thought.

As we move through life, basic mistrust inclines us to overload the roles we play and status we obtain. It is fine to knock down good grades, but every so often you meet people who seem to feel that unless they receive an "A" they are total failures. Or one can be proud of running a successful business, but every so often you read about the suicide of someone who goes bankrupt. Basic mistrust enslaves people to the sources of their security, makes them rigid in the roles they play, and has much to do with the lines we draw to demarcate who in our world is OK and who is not.

All of us, one might venture to assert, come out of those first few months with some mix of basic trust and basic mistrust. The latter saddles us with a very dehumanizing dynamic, an insecurity that drives us to seek to control our roles, status, relationships, and possessions. Basic mistrust tells us that without them we are nothing. As we grow up, it also fits us well into those aspects of our society and culture that embody previous generations of mistrust. Thus we learn the superiority of our nation, race, class, or religion, and the inferiority of those who do not belong, of those who are different from us.

We are proposing that what Jesus was seeking in response to his ministry was *metanoia*, conversion, a transformation on the level of spontaneous felt meaning. To glean a sense of how that might happen we have been taking a brief detour into developmental psychology and, by way of illustration, noting Erik Erikson's analysis of the first stage through which we pass as newborn infants. We come out of that stage with some mix of basic trust and mistrust, and the latter skews both our own development and the dynamics of the worlds we construct.

As anticipatory experiences of the apocalyptic scenario's end of the world, Jesus' parables subvert worlds based on mistrust. In such worlds it becomes self-evident that some people and groups should enjoy wealth and status while other people and groups deserve to be excluded. But those assumptions are challenged when Jesus comes on the scene, proclaims the nearness of God's kingdom, and acts that nearness out in his parables. From a God's-eye point of view, a world divided into Jews and Samaritans is inhuman and unreal; such worlds must pass.

On the other hand, mistrust is a real affliction and security a real human need. If Jesus' parables would strip away false security, his healings and exorcisms betoken the nearness and availability of an unfailing source of care and compassion; they act out the nearness of a reality that makes whole and liberates, as does his availability to all, to Sadducees and Pharisees but also and especially to those like the tax collectors, women, and the poor whom the Sadducees and Pharisees would exclude.

We are suggesting, then, that by shaking up worlds ruled by basic mistrust and by making available a source of acceptance, healing, and liberation Jesus might evoke a transformation of people on the level of spontaneous felt meaning. Conversion, in the sense of this fundamental transformation effected by the nearness of the kingdom is the response Jesus was seeking.

Ethics?

At this point a further question arises. Suppose a tax collector encounters Jesus, thrills to his message, and accepts the infinite care betokened by Jesus' companionship. Does this mean that, healed and liberated from the message of contempt his society sends, our tax collector can continue as before, contentedly and peacefully gouging his fellow Jews for his own enrichment? Having encountered Jesus and accepted the nearness of the kingdom, can he continue to serve the Roman occupation, now feeling good about himself as he does so? This is the question of ethics. Does *metanoia* have an impact on one's behavior or is it entirely an interior, spiritual, private affair?

We shall approach this question from two angles. First of all, in the premodern world religion, morality, politics, and economics came as a package. The neat distinctions—and separations—that our twentieth-century culture makes among these spheres of reality are a peculiarly modern development. Hence, to ask about ethics in the context of Jesus' culture is to raise first of all the question of where Jesus stood in relation to the Torah, to Israel's Law. Next, to get a further perspective on our issue we shall turn to one classic New Testament passage, Luke's Sermon on the Plain (Luke 6:20-49).

Jesus and the Law

Christians have at times characterized their religion as a religion of love and contrasted it to Judaism as a religion of law. On this view Jesus sought to liberate his people from the oppressive legal burden that comprised the essence of their religion.

Such a caricature misunderstands both Judaism and Jesus. In Judaism there is in principle no contradiction between love and law. In fact the opposite is the case. The Hebrew scriptures express Israel's conviction that it exists as a people by God's free choice. Having led the Jews out of slavery in Egypt, God made a covenant, that is, a treaty with them in the desert. According to this covenant God would be their God, they would be God's people, and they would show themselves to be God's people by living out the laws God had given them.

In this context law—from the ten commandments that Moses brought down from Mount Sinai to the total of seven hundred thirteen regulations that one can find in the Pentateuch—expresses Israel's specialness to God. Living according to God's law allows them to express their gratitude to God, and possessing God's law makes Israel a light to all the nations.

Within this general framework that bound Jewish identity to God's holy law there was room for a variety of styles of living that identity. As Israel's history unfolded, traditions of interpretation evolved that kept the law a living reality so that by Jesus' day the same kind of diversity existed within Judaism that can be observed within Christianity today. Sadducees, for example, focused as exclusively as possible on what was written in the Pentateuch while various schools of Pharisees developed a lively, ongoing oral tradition.

Besides diversity of interpretation, of course, Israel also developed a history of failure to live out the law, a history of infidelity to God's gift. This was the context in which, as we have seen, Israel's prophets rose up to denounce the evils that festered in the community and to warn of the doom those evils would bring upon them. The rhetoric of such denunciation was extreme. God could, for instance, be said to hate Israel's religious practices because they were carried out without justice and compassion binding the community together. In none of this were the prophets claiming to abrogate Israel's law, including its cultic provisions; rather they sought to recall Israel to an authentic observance of that law as the means of living out their love and gratitude to God.

In calling his people to conversion, Jesus too can be said to be radicalizing the law, bringing people back to its center in the double great commandment—love of God with all one's heart and all one's strength, and love of neighbor as oneself. No more than the prophets before him, however, was Jesus' aim to abolish the law that embodied his people's identity as a people chosen by God.

The Sermon on the Plain (Luke 6:20-49)

We are asking what difference *metanoia* makes, whether it is a purely interior, spiritual, and private affair or whether it has an impact on behavior as well. Moving for the moment beyond the framework of historical Jesus research we can gain light on this question by consulting one particular New Testament text. As we noted when we were discussing redaction criticism, Matthew's gospel presents Jesus' famous Sermon on the Mount while Luke, following a different theological symbolism, gives us the Sermon on the Plain.

In Luke's narrative Jesus, having spent the night in prayer on a mountaintop, chooses the Twelve from among his disciples. He then comes back down from the mountain and, with his eyes on his disciples, addresses the large crowd that has come out to hear him and be healed. He begins with a series of blessings:

> Blessed are you who are poor,
> for yours is the kingdom of God.
> Blessed are you, who are hungry now,
> for you will be filled.
> Blessed are you who weep now,
> for you will laugh.
> Blessed are you when people hate you,
> and when they exclude you, revile you,
> and defame you
> on account of the Son of Man.
> Rejoice in that day and leap for joy, for surely your
> reward is great in heaven; for that is what their
> ancestors did to the prophets.

Jesus next utters a series of curses:

> But woe to you who are rich,
> for you have received your consolation.

> Woe to you who are full now,
> for you will be hungry.
> Woe to you who are laughing now,
> for you will mourn and weep.
> Woe to you when all speak well of you,
> for that is what their ancestors did to the false prophets.

The sermon continues with sayings about how to deal with enemies and how to handle one's possessions:

> But I say to you that listen, Love your enemies, do good to those who hate you, bless those who curse you, pray for those who abuse you.
> If anyone strikes you on the cheek, offer the other one also; and from anyone who takes away your coat do not withhold even your shirt.

Jesus further develops these ideas:

> Give to everyone who begs from you; and if anyone takes away your goods, do not ask for them again. Do to others as you would have them do to you. If you love those who love you, what credit is that to you? For even sinners love those who love them. . . . If you lend to those from whom you hope to receive, what credit is that to you? Even sinners lend to sinners, to receive as much again. But love your enemies, do good, and lend, expecting nothing in return. Your reward will be great, and you will be children of the Most High; for he is kind to the ungrateful and the wicked. Be merciful, just as your Father is merciful.

Jesus' focus shifts to forgiveness:

> Do not judge, and you will not be judged; do not condemn, and you will not be condemned. Forgive, and you will be forgiven; give, and it will be given to you. A good measure, pressed down, shaken together, and running over, will be put into your lap; for the measure you give will be the measure you get back.

The sermon concludes with further sayings about self-knowledge, the correspondence between one's deeds and the kind of person one is, and the need not only to hear but also to act on Jesus' words.

To begin our inquiry into this section of Luke's gospel we should note that the evangelist prepares for it carefully in two ways. First, he begins his account of Jesus' ministry in chapter three when Jesus is baptized by John. Then, having withstood Satan's temptations in the desert and having nearly incited a riot in his home town, Jesus settles down to preaching, healing, and gathering disciples.

From the outset he evokes very strong reactions. At Nazareth they "were amazed at the gracious words that came from his mouth" (Luke

4:22). At Capernaum "they were astounded at his teaching, because he spoke with authority" (Luke 4:32). His fame spread; "many crowds would gather to hear him and to be cured of their diseases" (Luke 5:15). Not everyone, however, was wildly enthusiastic. The scribes and Pharisees "were filled with fury and discussed with one another what they might do to Jesus" (Luke 6:11).

From the outset of Jesus' ministry, then, Luke portrays him as healing and preaching and thereby evoking very strong reactions, some enthusiastic, others enraged. But only well into chapter 6 does the author give a full account of just what Jesus has been saying to evoke so strong a reaction. In that sense he sets up Jesus' Sermon on the Plain as a mini-climax to the action of the story thus far.

Luke prepares for the sermon in a second way as well. In chapter 3 Luke, like Matthew, draws on the Q source to present the preaching of John the Baptist. Addressing the crowds who come out to be baptized, John takes a hard line:

> You brood of vipers! Who warned you to flee from the wrath to come? Bear fruits worthy of repentance. Do not begin to say to yourselves, "We have Abraham as our ancestor"; for I tell you, God is able from these stones to raise up children to Abraham. Even now the ax is lying at the root of the trees; every tree therefore that does not bear good fruit is cut down and thrown into the fire (Luke 3:7-9).

At this point in John's sermon Luke interrupts the Q material that he shares with Matthew. He inserts a passage in which John gives advice to those before him:

> And the crowds asked him, "What then should we do?" In reply he said to them, "Whoever has two coats must share with anyone who has none; and whoever has food must do likewise." Even tax collectors came to be baptized, and they asked him, "Teacher, what should we do?" He said to them, "Collect no more than the amount prescribed for you." Soldiers also asked him, "And we, what should we do?" He said to them, "Do not extort money from anyone by threats or false accusation, and be satisfied with your wages" (Luke 3:10-14).

After this interruption Luke rejoins Matthew, and Mark as well, by having John predict the coming of one mightier than himself who would baptize not with water but with the holy Spirit and fire.

Now, how does the material placed on Jesus' lips in the Great Sermon in chapter 6 relate to the material placed on John's in chapter 3? At first glance, perhaps, Jesus and John may seem to be saying more or less the same thing—be kind, be generous, the usual religious sort of thing. On a closer reading, however, the differences between them may seem sharper. Recall, for example, John's advice to the soldiers; basically he recommended that they be honest, content with their wages. Does this have the same implications as what Jesus enjoins? What would happen to a soldier whose response to the enemy was to love them, pray for them, do good to them and, if they struck the soldier on one cheek, to offer the other as well? Or again John tells the crowd that if they have extra food or clothing they should share it. Is this really the same as telling people, as Jesus does in the sermon, to give to whoever asks, and to lend without expectation of receiving anything back?

We are suggesting that on closer examination the difference between what Luke has John tell people to do and what he has Jesus enjoining is fairly sharp. Furthermore, among the gospels only Luke presents the material in verses 10 to 14 of John's sermon in chapter 3. This expansion of John's preaching, it seems, is deliberate on Luke's part, and it serves as preparation for the Sermon on the Plain. By setting up a contrast between the two Luke insists on the radical nature of the material attributed to Jesus.

We can confirm this point somewhat by recalling what we said earlier about the treatment of John the Baptist in the New Testament, where his positive but subordinate religious significance is expressed by making him Jesus' forerunner. That pattern, common to all the gospels, emerges also in Luke's infancy narrative, where the manner of John's conception is certainly marvelous—look at how old his parents were at the time—but also certainly not so marvelous as that of Jesus, who is conceived when power from on high overshadows a young girl. Now in comparing the sermons Luke attributes to John and to Jesus the same pattern appears once more. John's advice is just fine—be generous people and honest in your professional life—but Jesus' advice exceeds it. (Parenthetically, comparing the material in the two sermons to what one most often hears from the pulpit one might wonder whether Christians are not more often "Baptists" in the sense of followers of John the Baptist, after all. Think, for example, of Thanksgiving Day; whose sermon, John's or Jesus', is represented by the usual advice to drop off some canned goods for the poor before proceeding to one's own turkey feast?)

At any rate we are suggesting that Luke carefully prepares for the Sermon on the Plain in chapter 6, and that his insertion of verses 10 to 14 into John's preaching in chapter 3 is part of that preparation. At this point, in order to make that somewhat lengthy sermon manageable, we can offer a summary. In the Sermon on the Plain in Luke 6:20-49, Jesus makes four points:

(1) Love everyone, especially those you would ordinarily consider your enemies.

(2) Claim nothing as your own, but use all you are and have to meet the needs of others.
(3) Forgive everyone everything.
(4) Judge no one but yourself.

Now if Luke deliberately contrasts Jesus' message to that of John, one question that suggests itself is whether Jesus' message is practical. Given the way the world goes round, how far up the corporate ladder would loving everyone get you? Where would you end up if you claimed nothing as your own? For that matter, where did all this get Jesus? Except for an occasional Mother Teresa, it seems that in the real world in which we all live what Jesus calls for in the Sermon on the Plain is not very practical.

Just as an experiment, however, try to imagine this. Imagine that tomorrow morning, as the sun rose in time zone after time zone around the world, everyone as they got up began living what the Sermon proposes. Will this happen? Of course not. But if it did, what would be different from the previous day? What would be missing from the daily news? Violent crime? Poverty? Wars and revolutions? Sex scandals? But, someone might say, with all this goodness life would become pretty boring. Would it? What are the things you really enjoy? What are the things that really make you happy? Would they disappear or would they be enhanced? At any rate we can conclude our thought-experiment with a final question. If the impossible were to happen, if all at once everyone everywhere were to begin practicing what Jesus preaches in Luke's Sermon on the Plain, would we have solved the problem of evil insofar, at least, as evil is a human product? Granted that earthquakes and microbes would remain, still, insofar as evil is something that human beings do to themselves and to each other, would we not have stopped doing that?

Thus far in our consideration of the Sermon on the Plain we have noted on the one hand that in the real world it seems quite impractical. On the other hand, if by some miracle everyone were to begin following it, it would solve the problem of evil insofar as evil is a human product. This suggests a further question: what does one do with this material?

The question arises on two levels. On a more general level the Bible belongs among the classics of Western civilization. Among the things that make a classic a classic is the power to suggest alternative worlds to the actual one, to free us from the tyranny of the way things are at any given time, to draw us to a vision of our fuller humanity. Classics thus possess a liberating and transforming potential, and one is not living at the level of one's culture if one has not encountered that culture's classics. In that sense, as a classic text of Western civilization Luke's Sermon on the Plain claims our attention.

Some of us also use the Bible religiously, as sacred Scripture. In that context the Bible is read and proclaimed as God's word. Christians read the gospels precisely as such, as what the word "gospel" means, good news. For those who thus read Luke's Sermon on the Plain as the good news of the Lord Jesus Christ, the question seems even more urgently imposed: what do you do with this material, on the one hand so impractical, on the other a solution to the problem of evil?

A common sense response deals with Jesus' radical ethical sayings by regarding them as an ideal. Ideals are important because they orient our action. On the other hand, because we have to live in the real world we can only expect to get so far with them. After all, one has to be practical. Honoring Jesus' teaching as an ideal, this common sense response at the same time makes practicality its first concern.

A second response arose within Catholic culture, if not official Catholic doctrine. Again recognizing the impractical nature of Jesus' radical gospel sayings, this response divided the population into two groups. The aim for all people was salvation, understood as getting to heaven. The condition for achieving this aim was keeping the commandments, with the sacrament of penance as a safety valve. If one committed a mortal sin, a sin that of itself would block one's access to heaven and land one instead in hell, one could go to confession to have that sin removed. Out of the general population a smaller group were called to a higher way of living. They "had a vocation." This vocation was to a religious life structured by what were called the evangelical counsels—literally, gospel advice. Following these counsels, this advice, these chosen ones entered religious life and took vows of poverty, chastity, and obedience. In this way the radical, impractical side of Jesus' teaching was taken care of by an elite, leaving the general population to live an ordinary life focused on keeping the commandments.

A third, scholarly response was formulated toward the end of the Old Quest by Johannes Weiss and Albert Schweitzer. They sought to relate the radical gospel sayings to the context of Jesus' ministry. Recall how, for them, Jesus understood his ministry in thoroughly apocalyptic terms. The last days were at hand, the kingdom was beginning to break through in his own activity. In that case Jesus' radical ethical teaching was an "interim ethic." It spelled out how people were to act in the very short period of time left before the end-time arrived. Notice that precisely because the time left was so short, Jesus' demands on people's behavior could be radical. There is no need to think about tomorrow if there isn't going to be a tomorrow. Ultimately, of course, the world did not end, and so Jesus' teaching becomes impractical in a world that has settled in for the long haul. In that context, back to position one.

Fourth and finally, we can make the same moves that Weiss and Schweitzer made, but because the understanding of Jesus' ministry that we have been working out is different from theirs so will be our results. On this position the radical material in Luke's Sermon on the Plain is not simply a set of lovely and worthwhile ideals, nor is it addressed to an elite minority, nor is it an interim ethic.

Jesus, we have seen, came proclaiming the nearness of the kingdom of God and acting that nearness out in his parables, his miracles of healing and exorcisms, and his associations. Seeking to recall his fellow Jews to their proper covenant relationship with God and thus renew them as God's people, his preaching and deeds looked for a response of conversion, that transformation on the fundamental level of spontaneous felt meaning evoked by the nearness of God's kingdom. In that case, we would suggest, Luke's sermon spells out the direction one will find one's experience taking on the basis of *metanoia,* and to the extent that one is undergoing it. Apart from that basis, the radical gospel sayings become at best ideals, certainly impractical, and from the viewpoint of the way the world ordinarily goes round, irrelevant and foolish.

Our answer to the question of what to do with the radical material in Luke's Sermon on the Plain pivots on *metanoia*, conversion. Thus, to recall the points with which we summarized the sermon: (1) To the extent that one experiences oneself as infinitely accepted, cared for, and loved, one is freed to love all others. On that basis, and to that extent, one has no need to play the usual enemies-game of meeting hostility with hostility, violence with violence, all in defense of a threatened self. (2) Similarly, to the extent that one experiences all one is and has as gift freely and lovingly bestowed, one has no need to find one's security in piling up and clinging to possessions. One is freed to pass the gift along, using all one is and has to meet the needs of others. (3) So also with forgiveness; knowing oneself to be infinitely and totally accepted and loved, accepted not just for one's strengths and goodness but in one's weakness, failings, and dark collusion in evil, one is freed to forgive others everything, (4) judging no one but oneself. Judgment, after all, belongs to God.

We began this section by asking what difference the conversion that Jesus was seeking to evoke might make on the level of one's behavior. This is the question of ethics. Examining this question within the context of the religion and culture of Jesus' day, we discovered that contrary to a popular Christian caricature Jesus did not aim to abolish Torah, the God-given Law that founded his people's identity as Jews. Instead of wanting to abolish the Law, Jesus radicalized it. Like the prophets before him, he recalled his people to an authentic life according to the Law, a life centered on the double great commandment of love of God and neighbor.

We turned next to one New Testament author's perspective on our question, moving into a consideration of Luke's Sermon on the Plain. Noting especially the contrast Luke is at pains to establish between the preaching of John the Baptist and Jesus, we suggested that Jesus' radical sayings about love of enemies, freedom from possessions, and forgiveness spell out the direction in which *metanoia* heads. Given the way the world is, those sayings seemed enormously impractical. Yet if everyone were to embrace them, they would offer a solution to the problem of evil. Hence we can now add that with conversion a force counter to that of evil enters history. With the occurrence of conversion history becomes, among other things, a history of salvation.

What About Jesus Himself? (Didn't He Know?)

At this point we can turn our attention back to Jesus himself. Proclaiming the kingdom of God and acting its nearness out in speech and deed, seeking his people's renewal through conversion—in all of this, what was he thinking?

Like any first-century Jew, Jesus would have appropriated the religion of his people simply by growing up. Keeping Sabbath with the family at home, studying Torah and praying in the synagogue, perhaps journeying to Jerusalem for Passover or other feasts, he would have learned the stories of his people's God and approached that God in prayer and ritual. Their God was of course YHWH, the God of the Hebrew scriptures, creator of the universe and ruler of history, a God fierce in demanding justice for the downtrodden and oppressed and yet a God whose heart was filled with mercy and lovingkindness for the people of Israel. So holy was this God that should the divine name, YHWH, occur when the Scriptures were being read aloud, mere human lips were unworthy to pronounce it; one read instead Adonai, the Lord.

Precisely through his religious experience as a Jew, it seems, Jesus was wholly seized by the reality of this God. He arrived at a point where, some scholars suggest, he came to address this God as "Abba." The word is Aramaic, the vernacular of Jesus' day, and not Hebrew, the formal language of the Scriptures and liturgy. It means "father," but not father in the sense of a Victorian household in the last century, where it designated a distant parental figure who occasionally visited the nursery to inspect his offspring, not father in the titular sense with which Catholic priests are addressed, but father in an intimate sense. Even today, in some Jewish communities in this country, the men can be found sporting T-shirts, sweatshirts and baseball caps bearing the inscription, "World's best Abba."

Jesus arrived at a point at which it made sense to him to address as "Abba" the transcendent mystery to which the word "God" points. That overwhelming sense of the character of ultimate reality as near and full of care led Jesus into the activity we have seen. His parables and associations sought to subvert worlds constructed as though ultimate reality were other than Abba; such worlds were in fact unreal, founded on a lie. Through his healings, exorcisms, and associations Jesus sought to communicate a taste of the nearness of the divine mystery of infinite lovingkindness, a nearness that made whole and liberated, a nearness that provided a basis upon which to construct new worlds, worlds transformed by compassion and justice.

We are speculating that the secret of Jesus' activity lay in the sense of God that grasped him though his religious experience as a Jew and that was, perhaps, focalized in his addressing God as Abba. At this point, however, a question arises to distract us from our historical consideration of Jesus. The question arises from the viewpoint of the subsequent Christian tradition. The Gospel of John has Jesus averring that "the Father and I are one" (John 10:30). In the same gospel the apostle Thomas, confronted with Jesus after the resurrection, exclaims "My Lord and my God" (John 20:28). In 325 C.E. the Council of Nicea pronounced Jesus "true God of true God," in 431 the Council of Ephesus affirmed that his mother was rightly called "mother of God," and in 451 Chalcedon confessed the dogma of the hypostatic union of two natures, the divine and the human, in Jesus' one person.

Given the traditional Christian doctrine of the divinity of Christ, one may well ask how we can talk about Jesus learning about God through his religious experience as a Jew. After all, didn't he know who he was, namely God, the Second Person of the Trinity?

Traditional dogma teaches both the full divinity and the full humanity of Jesus Christ. To be human is, among other things, to be historically situated, and in his humanity Jesus Christ was a Jew of the first century. Reflect, for a moment, on the meaning of the word "God" in that context. We have just sketched, at least in part, its content. "God" referred to YHWH, creator of the universe, covenant-maker with Israel, the one whom Jesus addressed as Abba. It refers to the one whom the later Christian tradition would identify as God the Father, the First Person of the Blessed Trinity. Hence to imagine someone asking Jesus, during his lifetime, whether he knew he was God is to imagine an almost silly situation. The question would be asking whether Jesus thought he was praying to himself when he prayed in the synagogue, whether he thought he was celebrating his own feasts when he journeyed to Jerusalem.

The question whether during his lifetime Jesus knew he was God overlooks the historicity of language. During Jesus' lifetime the only available meaning of the word "God" was one that could not apply to Jesus. Given that fact, the question turns out not to make sense. It rests on an oversight.

If, however, one holds as true the dogmas of Nicea and Chalcedon and so believes Jesus to be both human and divine, then it becomes possible to reformulate the question in a manner that does make sense. To do so, however, requires us to make a technical distinction between two terms that we ordinarily use interchangeably. As reformulated, the question would go as follows: Granted that because of the meaning of the word in his lifetime Jesus could not have made the explicit judgment, "I am God," are there nonetheless indications that he was at least aware of his divine identity, even if he could not explicitly express it?

This reformulation requires us to distinguish knowing from being aware. Ordinarily, to say that you know something is equivalent to saying that you are aware of something. In the technical sense that we are trying to grasp now, however, there is a difference. In this technical sense we are aware of far more than we know. Awareness is like a large container; only some of its contents attract our attention so that we ask about, understand, and thus know them fully and explicitly. At this moment, for example, you may be focused on trying to understand just what the difference we are trying to get at may be. At the same time, however, unless your senses are impaired, much else that is going on in the room is registering in your awareness—sounds, sights, and so on. But only if I ask you what that humming sound is, for example, will you advert to it and explain that the fluorescent light bulbs tend to make a bit of noise. Until then the sound has been registering but you haven't focused on it. It has been in the container, as it were, of your awareness, but you haven't known it. That is, you haven't paid attention to it, wondered about it, tried out one or two possibilities of what it might be, and then arrived at your judgment—it is the lights making that noise.

Knowing, in this technically precise sense, is a compound of all the activities we just listed. If we are awake, then our senses are functioning, things are pouring into the pot of our awareness—our experience is providing us with data on what is going on. But experience or awareness is not yet full knowledge. To illustrate the difference one more time, suppose you have a friend who has a bizarre problem. This friend goes out for sports and inevitably he gets kicked off the team. Every time a coach tries to give him direction your friend gets very angry and blows up. His work experience isn't much better. Job after job, he ends up clashing with the boss. Now something is driving this behavior; something in the container of your friend's awareness is making him act this way. But it might take a lot of money and many hours sitting with someone who says very little beyond, "I see," and "Uh huh," for your friend to come to understand what's going on and name it: "I have a huge hangup with my father." Or whatever.

On this technical distinction awareness is much broader than knowing. Awareness provides data, but only those data that get our attention, that we wonder about and strive to understand, become known in the full sense of the term. In that case, getting back to the point at hand, we have argued that because of the historicity of language, even though he was what Nicea and Chalcedon affirmed, Jesus could not during his lifetime have made the judgment "I am God." Therefore to ask, as we did, whether Jesus knew he was God is to ask a poor question. The question overlooks the historicity of language.

Now, however, we might want to reformulate the question. Even if Jesus could not have known, in that full sense, that he was God, are there any indications that his identity as divine Son entered his human consciousness? Are there any indications that he was aware of this identity even if he could not fully articulate it?

From the viewpoint of this question one might wish to review the notion of Jesus' Abba-experience. In light of the later doctrines of the divinity of Jesus and the hypostatic union, that Abba-experience may appear as how Jesus' divine sonship registered in his human awareness. Note that the Abba-experience does not prove the doctrine of Jesus' divinity but rather, in light of that belief, the historical datum of the Abba-experience gains a deeper significance.

Chapter Seven

Jesus' Execution

Besides *metanoia*, the positive response he sought, Jesus evoked a negative response as well. He did not die in bed, full of years and honored for the wisdom of his teaching. His public ministry was cut short. After only a year, or three, depending on whether you find John or the Synoptic tradition more probable, he was killed. The Roman colonial administration imposed on Jesus a violent, painful, and humiliating death, publicly executing him as a criminal. Roman soldiers nailed him to a cross on a hillside outside Jerusalem and there, a naked spectacle for all to behold, after some hours of agony he died.

Jesus' execution concludes our examination of Jesus' earthly life through a historian's lens; with it our pursuit of the question of the historical Jesus comes to a close. We shall begin with a brief consideration of the Christian response to Jesus' death, moving from the passion narratives in the gospels to three earlier interpretations with a word on their subsequent development. Turning then to the question of what historical phenomenon this material is interpreting religiously, we shall note two standard positions on why Jesus was executed and work our way to a third, more adequate answer. As a final step we shall delve briefly into the further question of how Jesus reacted to the imminent prospect of his death.

Christian Responses to Jesus' Execution

Gospel Narratives

Each of the gospels contains a lengthy narrative of Jesus' last days and death. In the formation of the gospel tradition the account of Jesus' passion seems to have been the first part of the overall story of Jesus to have been woven into a continuous narrative. So prominently does it figure within the gospels that Mark, the earliest gospel to be composed, has been characterized as a passion narrative with a prologue.

Each evangelist's passion narrative is, of course, gospel, written to communicate the religious significance of Jesus' final days from a Christian point of view. This means that, like the gospels in general, the passion narratives are guided by other interests than the concern for factual accuracy that we would expect from a modern historical account. Their overriding concern seems to be to show that Jesus' earthly fate occurred "in accordance with the Scriptures." The evangelists' Scriptures were, of course, the Hebrew Bible, what Christians call the Old Testament. In order to communicate the religious significance of the closing events of Jesus' life the gospel writers discovered in their Scriptures models on which to construct their narrative. In doing so the redactors of the gospels continued a process of interpretation that began at the outset of the Christian movement.

Three Early Interpretations

Moving back from the text of the gospels into the oral tradition from which they emerged, we can identify three different very early patterns of insight into Jesus' death.

The first of these interpretations took shape in a polemical context, under the pressure of external attack on the Christian movement. "Anyone hung on a tree is under God's curse" reads a line from Deuteronomy (Deut 21:23), and this verse offered their opponents a stone to throw at Christians. Jesus' fate would prove that he was a false prophet, cursed by God, and that his followers were rightly cut off from the true Israel.

A Christian riposte to this charge turned it back on those who made it. It was a commonplace among first-century Jews, Christian and non-Christian alike, that it was the fate of the prophets to suffer rejection and even death. Jesus' execution, it could then be argued, proved exactly the opposite of what the opponents of Jesus' followers were averring. Far from demonstrating God's displeasure with Jesus it followed the regular pattern whereby, when God raised up a prophet, God's people rejected and persecuted that prophet. Jesus' death, then, is the death of the final or eschatological prophet-martyr who, when God raised him, became a light to all the nations.

A second interpretation arose within the Christian movement in a context of prayerful reflection. Drawing again on the fund of Jewish religious insight, Christians found special relevance in the traditional recognition that for some mysterious reason it is God's will that, given the kind of world we live in, the upright suffer in this life. Though mysterious, however,

God's plan is not arbitrary, and so this pattern contains a second element as well. Those whose righteousness involves them in suffering can also hope that God will in some manner vindicate them. Evil does not have the last word. All of this clearly applied to Jesus' death. Thus it was seen as a death in accordance with God's will, the death of a righteous suffering one who can look to God for vindication.

Third, Christians also very soon came to regard Jesus' death as somehow linked to their own experience of wholeness and liberation. In some sense, they affirmed, he died for our sins. This confession of faith was formulated very early. It was available when Paul, writing in the mid-fifties, cited it in a letter to the Christian community at Corinth (1 Cor 15:3).

Scriptural metaphors

These three originally independent views of Jesus death began circulating, interacting, and developing further. If Jesus' death was according to God's will, and if God's will was to be found in the sacred Scriptures, then Christians could find in those Scriptures rich sources of further insight into Jesus' death, metaphors with which to spin out its significance.

To take one example, in Israel special obligations fell upon the eldest son of a family. Should a younger brother die childless, for instance, leaving no one to keep his memory alive, it was up to the eldest brother to join with the deceased sibling's wife in order to bring forth a child to honor him. Again, if an Israelite had to sell himself into slavery in order to meet his debts the eldest brother was obliged to come up with the funds to buy him back, literally, to redeem him.

This role of redeemer had provided Israel with a metaphor with which to express its faith that its escape from slavery in Egypt had been through God's action: God had acted as Israel's *go'el*, redeemer. Note, however, that redemption, buying back, has now become a metaphor. No one thought to ask literally how much God had had to come up with to in order to pay off the Egyptians.

Christians were quick to seize upon this Israelite metaphor to express the meaning Jesus' death had for them. If as followers of Jesus they experienced a new wholeness and freedom in their life of conversion they attributed this to Jesus, his ministry, and his faithfulness even unto death. By that death, they could say, he had redeemed them. He had offered his life as a ransom.

To give another example, the religion of Israel included the practice of offering various kinds of sacrifice. God was honored as the God of life, and the symbol of life par excellence was blood. To sin was to cut oneself off from God, and hence from life. The ritual of sacrifice, however, was

God's gift, the God-given means of overcoming sin and getting back in touch with God. Blood served to enact this restoration; blood drawn from an animal and sprinkled on the people restored them to God's life, blood smeared on objects sanctified them.

From the perspective of their conversion Christians could regard Jesus as the God-given means by which their relationship to the God of life had been restored. Metaphorically, then, his death was the sacrifice that took away their sins; his blood was the price of their redemption.

It is important to remember that we are dealing with metaphors. Jesus' death was not literally a commercial exchange or a ritual act. Failure to keep this in mind can lead to bizarre images of God as a bloodthirsty tyrant who requires the death of an innocent son to appease his wrath, images of Jesus' death as a supreme case of divine child abuse. Distortions along these lines have at times been present in the Christian tradition.

Why, Historically?

Jesus' followers learned to understand his death as the death of a prophet-martyr, as the suffering of a righteous one who can hope for vindication from God, as a death for their sins. From their Scriptures, the Old Testament, they drew metaphors that expanded upon these understandings. Jesus' death was the ransom paid by their redeemer. The blood of his sacrifice washed away their sins. But, we can ask, why did he die in the first place? What historical forces came together to bring Jesus to the cross? Why, from a historical point of view, did he end up crucified?

That Jesus was crucified is among the most certain facts we possess about him. It is amply validated by the principles of embarrassment and multiple attestation. There is no reasonable doubt that he was executed at the hand of the Romans along with one or more *lestai*. The latter term means bandit, outlaw, violent troublemaker.

One classic explanation of this fact argues that this occurred because Jesus was himself a *lestes*. We encountered this position at the outset of the Old Quest when Reimarus limned Jesus as a Davidic-Messianic revolutionary whose aim was to evict the Romans and restore the kingdom of Israel to its former glory. More recently this position was represented by S. G. F. Brandon, who tried to locate Jesus within the Zealot movement of his day. His arguments have been somewhat undercut of late, however, with the recognition that the existence of the Zealots as an organized group cannot be documented until a later period. Still, on the current scholarly scene efforts have been made to understand Jesus within the dynamics of the opposition between rural peasants and an urban elite supported by the taxes that weighed on the former as an overwhelming burden.

Against the Jesus-as-*lestes* view Christians have generally espoused what we might call a "bad mistake" theory of Jesus' death. According to this line of thought, which a literal interpretation of the gospels can suggest, the Romans made a bad mistake when they crucified Jesus, taking him for something that he was not. Had they really understood him they would have recognized him as a religious, not a political figure. They would have realized that the kingdom of which he spoke was not of this world. Hence from the Roman perspective Jesus was really harmless. But, this theory often continues, Jesus was set up and the blame for this lies with the Jews who deceived the Romans into thinking Jesus was a threat to their interests.

We want to suggest that neither the Jesus-as-*lestes* theory nor the bad mistake theory is adequate. In order to move beyond them both to a better understanding of the circumstances of Jesus' death, we want to consider in turn the role of the Romans, then that of the Jerusalem Jewish leadership, and finally that of Jesus himself.

The Romans

One way to get hold of the role of the Romans is to review some of the arguments people like Brandon offer. While we shall deny that these arguments make the case that Jesus was something like a Zealot, they can serve to give us some idea of what Jesus would have looked like to the Romans, should he come to their attention.

First, then, look at the inner circle of the Twelve whom Jesus chose to accompany him. Among them is listed Simon the Zealot. Two others, the brothers James and John, have a violent nickname even if the slang is not our own; they were known, we are told, as the "Sons of Thunder." Then there is the ultimate villain of the piece, Judas Iscariot. Was he known as "Iscariot" because he was a *sicarius*, a Latin word that can be translated as "dagger man"? Finally, recall Simon Peter's reaction the night Jesus is arrested: he slices off the ear of the high priest's servant. This implies, of course, that Peter was packing a weapon. In short, then, one might argue that Jesus' inner circle, the Twelve, looks like a violent group of armed thugs.

Add to this the idea that Jesus shared the typically Jewish disdain for non-Jews. Recall the story of his encounter with the Syrophoenician woman (Mark 7:24-30; Matt 15:21-28), whom he meets while he is in Gentile territory outside of Israel proper. When this woman, a non-Jew, asks him to cure her daughter he at first refuses, "for it is not fair to take the children's food and throw it to the dogs." Only after she accepts her place as one of the dogs (Mark softens this to "puppies") who get the scraps that fall under the table does he grant her request.

Similarly, Jesus appears to have shared his fellow Jews' contempt for the Roman occupation and its puppets. Luke's gospel recounts that on an occasion when some Pharisees (!) warned Jesus that Herod was looking to kill him, Jesus instructed them to "Go and tell that fox . . ." (Luke 13:32). "That fox" is hardly a term of respect for duly constituted authority.

Do these considerations, together with the fact that he was talking about a kingdom, clinch the case that Jesus was in fact some sort of violent revolutionary? No. For one thing, the lists of the Twelve also include one and sometimes two tax collectors. In a group of Zealots, however, even if such groups could be documented in Jesus' day, a tax collector's life expectancy would be very brief. More generally, the understanding of what Jesus meant by the nearness of the kingdom that we have been working out is not the sort of thing that could be brought about at the point of a knife or by force of arms.

Even if these arguments do not make the case, however, they can illumine what Jesus might have looked like to the Romans, and the Roman occupation was not known for scruples about due process when dealing with a subjugated people. Their response to the dynastic unrest that followed the death of Herod the Great in 4 B.C.E., shortly after Jesus' birth, had been to crucify thousands of Jews. Even the appearance of opposition won a swift and massively violent response. Hence even if the sorts of argument we have reviewed do not make the case that Jesus was in fact a Zealot or something like one they serve to explain how the Romans would have been likely to react to Jesus, should he come to their attention. That in turn raises a question: why did they pick on Jesus? Israel in his day was swarming with all sorts of groups and movements. How did Jesus come to the Romans' attention?

The Jerusalem Jewish Leadership

At this point we turn from the Romans to the Jerusalem Jewish leadership. To understand their role in Jesus' execution we need to consider first, as background, the hostility Jesus was likely to have evoked, and then the circumstances of his last days in Jerusalem.

As background to the role of the Jewish leadership in Jesus' death we can recall the subversive dimension to Jesus' ministry. We saw that in his parables and in the company he kept Jesus called into question the world of his day. If that world drew a line between those who self-evidently deserved the status and wealth they enjoyed and those who self-evidently deserved the poverty and contempt that were their lot, Jesus proclaimed such a world unreal and intolerable from a God's-eye view. Proclaiming the nearness of God as God, he acted that nearness out in ways that contradicted the assumptions and expectations of those whom the world of the day favored. Sadducees and the high priestly party were making out very well under Roman occupation while Pharisees pursued a strategy of separateness, using ritual purity to mark them off from the unclean. Jesus, however, transgressed those boundaries and denied their ability to define who was acceptable to God. His was a ministry likely to evoke at least the same hostility that greeted the prophets before him.

That hostility turned deadly on Jesus' final visit to Jerusalem. We find a clue to the circumstances that led to Jesus' execution in the Fourth Gospel, which has the high priest Caiaphas tell the Sanhedrin that "it is better for you to have one man die for the people than to have the whole nation destroyed" (John 11:50). This statement of the high priest gains significance if we recall the place and the time of year.

The place is Jerusalem, capital of ancient Judea and seat of the Temple. Occupied by the Romans, at the period in question the area was administered by a Roman prefect, Pontius Pilate. Because it was the site of the Temple, Jerusalem was the only place where Jews could offer the sacrifices stipulated in the Torah, and so it was a center of pilgrimage. Several times a year on the occasion of the major Jewish festivals the population of the city swelled several times over.

The time of year is Passover, a very nervous-making time for the Romans. At Passover Jews from all over swarmed into Jerusalem in order to celebrate —what? They were celebrating their deliverance from slavery in Egypt in the days of Moses. Passover was the Jewish feast of national liberation.

Precisely at this volatile time of year Jesus brings his ministry to Jerusalem and, when he enters the city, makes a stir. Even though we have argued that he was not a Davidic-Messianic revolutionary figure, it is not unlikely that there were some who hoped he was. Besides making a stir, it is during this visit to Jerusalem (according to the synoptics) or earlier (according to John) that Jesus strikes a symbolic blow at the political and economic as well as religious center of Israel under Roman domination, the Temple. Whether the incident known as "the cleansing of the Temple" was in fact a demand for reform or a symbolic acting out of the destruction of the Temple is currently debated, but in either case Jesus' action posed a direct challenge to the power structure of the time.

Under Roman occupation the Sanhedrin, composed of the chief priests, scribes, and elders of the city, was responsible for good order. Although the Sanhedrin was dominated by Sadduccees, it is possible that some of the scribes among its membership were Pharisees. The head priest of the day was Caiaphas, whose long term of office indicates that over the years he and the prefect, Pontius Pilate, had established a working relationship.

The words ascribed to Caiaphas in the Fourth Gospel become plausible under these circumstances. Angered by Jesus' symbolic attack on the system that supported the wealth and status of the priestly aristocracy, and concerned lest the stir Jesus was making among the people bring Roman troops down hard on the entire pilgrim-swollen population, the Sanhedrin decides to neutralize the situation by removing Jesus. Taking him into custody with the assistance of Judas, a member of his inner circle, they hand him over to the Romans as a troublemaker. The Romans then make short work of him.

What was Jesus' own role in all this? Negatively, he was not looking to get himself killed. At times in the history of religions one encounters a pathology that inclines people to seek suffering and death as the ultimate religious high. None of this applies to Jesus. Nor are we to think that he used the Old Testament as a sort of manual for the Messiah, following its instructions step by step on the way to Calvary.

On the other hand, Jesus was not utterly naive. Jesus would have been aware of the hostility he was evoking. He also knew of the fate of John the Baptist, executed under Herod. And he knew that Passover was a particularly volatile, dangerous time at Jerusalem. Nonetheless he felt impelled to bring his ministry to the center of his people precisely at this holy time of year, when they celebrated the saving act of God that had made them a people. It follows that while Jesus was by no means seeking to get himself killed he accepted the possibility of death out of faithfulness to his mission as he understood it.

Taking our cue from Caiaphas' line in John we have arrived at a position that takes into account the respective roles of the Romans, the Jerusalem Jewish leadership, and Jesus himself. On this account Jesus was not a *lestes*, a Zealot, or a Davidic-Messianic revolutionary. To that extent the bad mistake theory is correct. On the other hand, however, Jesus was not simply harmless. His ministry of the nearness of the coming of the kingdom undermined the world of the day and struck directly at the center of that world, the alliance of foreign oppression and domestic collusion centered on the Temple. Hence, as opposed to the bad mistake theory, one might rather say that from their own viewpoint the Romans did the right thing, albeit for the wrong reason. The reason was wrong if they took Jesus for a violent revolutionary. He was not. Nonetheless their action was the right thing because it defended their system against a real challenge. In light of the nearness of the reality of Jesus' God a colonial system based on coercion, a system that legitimated itself religiously by paying divine honors to the emperor, had to pass away.

In the Face of Death

Jesus, we have suggested, accepted the possibility of death out of faith-fulness to his mission as he understood it. Knowing the risks, he nonethe-less took his ministry to Jerusalem. At this point we can ask a further question. How did Jesus react once matters had progressed beyond the risk stage, once it was clear that his death was in fact imminent? How did Jesus handle the certitude of impending execution?

The starting point for scholarly discussion of this question is set by Rudolf Bultmann's position. On this question Bultmann was perfectly consistent with his overall position on the quest for the historical Jesus. For Bultmann, we should recall, that quest was in principle illegitimate and as a matter of fact next to impossible. That being the case, it comes as no surprise that his answer to our present question is that we do not and cannot know how Jesus reacted to his impending fate. The gospels do not provide adequate data to answer it. In setting forth this position Bultmann added a rhetorical flourish. We do not know how Jesus died, he says. For all we know, Jesus died in despair. Notice that Bultmann is not saying that Jesus despaired. He is simply underlining his main point. We do not know, and if we do not know, then we should recognize that anything is possible.

Bultmann's skepticism about our chances of arriving at historical knowledge about Jesus has not prevailed. As we have seen at great length, the New Quest for the historical Jesus started among Bultmann's own stu-dents and has recently entered a whole new phase. On the question that we are presently addressing, two very different views have emerged. We shall examine first Jürgen Moltmann's position, and then that of Edward Schillebeeckx.

Moltmann reviews the diverse ways in which the gospels portray Jesus' final moments. In John, Jesus is in complete control. Having earlier de-clared that he has the power to lay down his life and take it up again (John 10:17-18), on the cross Jesus declares, "'It is finished.' Then he bowed his head and gave up his spirit" (John 19:30). Fully in charge throughout his entire passion, he remains so at the end. If we back up to Luke we find that the Third Gospel pictures Jesus as a man of prayer throughout his min-istry. Now, at the very end, he prays one last time: "'Father, into your hands I commend my spirit.' Having said this, he breathed his last" (Luke 23:46). Matthew in turn follows his source, Mark, quite closely. In Mark Jesus cries out in Hebrew, "'Eloi, Eloi, lema sabachthani?' which means, 'My God, my God, why have you forsaken me?'" and after this "Jesus gave a loud cry and breathed his last" (Mark 15:34, 37).

In Moltmann's view Mark's scenario is likely to enjoy historical accu-racy. John and Luke are clearly toning down Mark's account of Jesus' death and making it more edifying. For that very reason, by the principle of embarrassment, Mark's view becomes more likely. Granted, the words placed on Jesus' lips are a citation from Psalm 22, and yet, Moltmann contends, they express very well the significance of Jesus' final death shriek.

How so? Moltmann sees Jesus dying in triple isolation. Rejected as a blasphemer by his fellow Jews and as a rebel by the Romans, Jesus also experiences abandonment at the hands of the Father whose nearness he had proclaimed. It is this godforsakenness that wrings a final, horrified cry from Jesus at the moment of his death.

If, for Bultmann, our ignorance of how Jesus died means that for all we know he died in despair, Moltmann proceeds to argue that Jesus died with a shriek of horror at being abandoned by the God whose kingdom he had proclaimed. It is interesting to note that Moltmann's answer to the historical question about Jesus dovetails neatly with his own Protestant tradition. If you were to ask the sixteenth-century Reformers Martin Luther or John Calvin how Jesus' death saved us, the answer they would come back with is penal substitution. On the cross Jesus suffered the penalty that we have incurred for our sins. He substituted for us and suffered in our place. What is the penalty for sin? Hell. And what is hell? It is the experience of separation from God, the absence of the God with whom we were made to be united. On the cross, then, for Luther and Calvin, Jesus saved us by suffering in our place the pain of hell, separation from God. Moltmann arrives at this same position on historical grounds when he seeks to determine how Jesus underwent death.

Edward Schillebeeckx arrives at a different position. Scanning the gospel stories of the Last Supper for clues to Jesus' view of his impending death, Schillebeeckx notes first of all what Jesus is doing. As he had throughout his ministry, Jesus celebrates a fellowship meal. These meals, like Jesus' parables and healings, signified the nearness of the kingdom of God. Celebrating such a meal in the face of impending death, Jesus apparently did not think that his coming death called his previous activity into question. He persisted in that activity right up until the end.

Schillebeeckx finds a further clue in Mark 14:25, which has Jesus saying "truly I tell you, I will never again drink of the fruit of the vine until the day when I drink it new in the kingdom of God." The first part of this saying shows Jesus' awareness of his coming death. He will drink wine no more in this lifetime. Yet, as the second part of the saying indicates, Jesus is also aware that the fellowship he shares with his followers is stronger than death. Like his living, his dying also somehow enters into the offer of God's saving nearness. Thus, in Schillebeeckx's view, Jesus goes into the darkness of death trusting that God will somehow use his dying as God had used Jesus' living to communicate the nearness of the kingdom. How

God will do this remains unclear. No more than Bultmann or Moltmann does Schillebeeckx imagine that Jesus breezed into death secure in the knowledge that he would be back in three days. If the gospel writers place detailed prophecies of his fate on Jesus' lips, at least the details have been gleaned by hindsight, supplied after the fact. On this Schillebeeckx and the others agree. But for Schillebeeckx, unlike Moltmann, Jesus' death does not call into question the value of his whole previous activity. Jesus dies as he had lived, his last meal one more act of service to others on behalf of God.

Part II

The Origin and Meaning of Belief in Jesus' Resurrection

Death, of course, does not end of the story of Jesus. At every Sunday liturgy, Christians profess the Nicene Creed. It states that the same Jesus who suffered, died, and was buried also was raised on the third day. Every year, after observing the forty days of Lent, the Christian Churches celebrate Easter. Each of the gospels carries the story of Jesus beyond his execution with tales of an empty tomb and of the disciples' encounters with Jesus as risen Lord. Well before the gospels were written, St. Paul could remind a quarrelsome community of Christians at Corinth that if Christ were not raised, the faith they shared was in vain (1 Cor 15:17).

Belief in Jesus' resurrection is plainly a central feature of the Christian tradition. Somewhat less plain is just what that belief actually affirms. For example, when we were discussing the nineteenth-century rationalists we recalled that the gospels contain several stories in which Jesus raises people from the dead. Lazarus, John's gospel tells us, already stank when, four days after he had died, Jesus called him to come hopping forth from his tomb still wrapped in his burial shroud. Luke narrates how Jesus interrupted the funeral procession of a young man and restored him to his widowed mother, and Mark tells the story of an official's daughter and how, having awakened her from death, Jesus told her family to give her something to eat.

These gospel stories suggest a question. Does belief in Jesus' resurrection mean that what these stories say Jesus did to these three other people happened to him as well? Did he, like they, come back to life? What, precisely, does it mean to say that Jesus was raised from the dead? And where did this belief come from? How did it get started?

From the question of the historical Jesus we turn now to the question of the origin and meaning of Christian belief in the resurrection of Jesus. Our investigation of this belief will take us through four steps. First, if we are not going to weave our answers out of thin air we need something to go on. To get started, then, it will be wise to ask: what are the data? That is, what do we have to go on? A second step will then quickly force itself upon us. Once we become familiar with the data, a close and thorough examination of them will leave us asking a second question. Why are the data the way they are? Only when we have met that issue will we be in a position to ask a third question, the pesky modern question. Why are there any data at all? That is, what happened to kick off this whole business of belief in Jesus' resurrection? How did it get started? This is the modern historical question, so oblique to the gospel writers' concerns but unavoidable in our cultural situation. Finally we shall be able to raise a fourth question, the one of most interest to the New Testament writers and really the most important of all. So what? What difference does it make if Jesus was raised from the dead? Is this just another odd fact to add to the list that Christians carry around? Or is there more, far more, to it than that?

Our questions about the origin and meaning of Christian belief in the resurrection of Jesus are four. What are the data? Why are the data the way they are? Why are there any data at all? And so what?

Chapter Eight

What Are the Data?

If we are after both the origin and the meaning of belief in Jesus' resurrection, we want to begin at the beginning. What we want first of all are the oldest data on this belief. Furthermore, the data we need to carry our inquiry forward have a double job to do. Obviously they have to document belief in Jesus' resurrection. But Jesus' resurrection is something that happened to him, and in the texts that offer themselves as relevant no one claims to have observed Jesus actually being raised from the dead. Whether Jesus' resurrection is even the sort of thing that anyone could observe is a further question. For the moment, though, the point is that no relevant text speaks of a witness to the event of Jesus being raised as such. That fact gives the data we want a second assignment. Besides documenting belief in Jesus' resurrection the data also need to indicate how, if no one saw it happening, anyone came to know about it.

So where do we start? As was true when we were trying to reconstruct Jesus' career from a historical perspective, non-Christian authors from the ancient world give us little or no help. No reports from the Roman garrison at Jerusalem, no archival records from the Jewish Temple are available. Once again the New Testament provides our primary data bank. Within the New Testament we certainly find Easter stories in all four gospels. These, however, are not our earliest data. Remember, Paul was writing his letters well before even the first of the gospels, Mark, was composed. And while Paul does not give us narratives of either Jesus' life or the Easter events, neither does he consider them unimportant or ignore them.

1 Corinthians 15:3-8

As it happens, one particular text in Paul's letters fits our job description very neatly. The text appears in the first letter Paul wrote around the year 56 C.E. to the Christian community he had founded at Corinth, in

Greece, some five years earlier. In 1 Cor 15:3-8 Paul reminds the Corinthians of the message he had proclaimed to them:

> For I handed on to you as of first importance what I in turn had received: that Christ died for our sins in accordance with the scriptures, and that he was buried, and that he was raised on the third day in accordance with the scriptures, and that he appeared to Cephas, then to the twelve. Then he appeared to more than five hundred brothers and sisters at one time, most of whom are still alive, though some have died. Then he appeared to James, then to all the apostles. Last of all, as to one untimely born, he appeared also to me.

This text gives us what we need to get started. It documents belief in Jesus' resurrection when it states that "he was raised on the third day in accordance with the scriptures." It also indicates how anyone would have known about Jesus' resurrection: "he appeared"—to Cephas, to the Twelve, to more than five hundred, to James, to all the apostles, and to Paul himself.

A few features of this text may be puzzling. For instance, Cephas may be a less familiar name than Simon or Peter; they all refer to the same disciple of Jesus, the eventual leader among the original Twelve whom Jesus had called. The passage also indicates that in the early Church the Twelve were one group, while the term "apostle" referred to another, larger group. Only since the writing of the Gospel of Luke have we become accustomed to thinking of an original band of twelve apostles. In our present text, however, the apostles are associated with James, whom Paul elsewhere calls "the brother of the Lord" (Gal 1:19) and who emerged as a leader of the Church at Jerusalem although he had not been a follower of Jesus during Jesus' lifetime.

Having identified our earliest relevant data, we should also point out just how early they are. Paul wrote his letter in 56 C.E., but notice how the passage begins: "I handed on to you . . . what I in turn had received." This indicates that what follows is not simply Paul's own composition. He is quoting. The material he quotes is a very old statement of belief, a creedal statement. Certainly Paul added to it the observation that of the five hundred some are still alive, as well as the claim that last of all in the series Jesus had appeared to Paul himself. If we subtract these additions what we have is an ancient creedal formula, ending perhaps at "Cephas," onto which Paul has stitched traditions about other appearances of the Lord as well. In that case our earliest data are earlier than the letter in which Paul quotes the creedal formula.

Perhaps he received the main formula at Damascus when he went there upon being converted to Christianity about 36 C.E. That would place our data very early indeed, only three years after Jesus' execution. Other possibilities for where Paul got some or all of this material would be

Jerusalem, where he first visited the Christian community in 39 C.E., or Antioch a year or so later. In any case, our earliest data on belief in the resurrection and how that belief arose come from a very early date indeed, certainly no more than a decade and perhaps only three years after the events recounted.

The formula Paul quotes contains two key phrases for our inquiry: "he was raised," and "he appeared." Given the importance of these phrases for the question we are pursuing, we should try to bring each of them into sharper focus.

"He was Raised"

First, then, can we determine more precisely just what Paul is saying when he takes up and hands on an ancient formula that says of Jesus that "he was raised"? Does he mean, for example, that like the official's daughter, the widow's son, and Lazarus in the gospel stories Jesus was brought back to life, that his corpse was resuscitated?

Notice first of all what grammarians call the voice of the verb. In English we have two voices, the active and the passive. Greek adds a third, the middle voice. "He was raised" is, grammatically, the passive voice. Throw that fact into the context of the Judaism of Jesus and Paul and it tells us something. Jewish piety and reverence for God's transcendence prevented them from uttering the divine name, YHWH, that God had revealed to Moses at the burning bush. Instead, if they were reading aloud in the synagogue and the sacred name occurred in the text, they would paraphrase. They would read not "YHWH" but "Adonai," the Lord. Similarly, to show the same reverence when speaking about divine activity they would phrase the sentence in the passive voice: not "God did it" but "it was done," with the clear implication of divine agency. Thus when Paul quotes a phrase that says of Jesus that "he was raised" we are dealing with this reverential passive. The voice of the verb tells us that God is its agent; God, Paul is saying, raised Jesus.

Notice, second, that the verb is not being used in its literal sense. If you are dead and someone literally raises you, they have not really done you much good. All they have done is relocate your corpse from one position to another, higher one. In various places the New Testament uses two different Greek verbs to speak of resurrection. One is the verb for waking someone from sleep. The other verb designates what you do when a little child is about to fall; you catch the child and set her on her feet again. But Jesus was not asleep, nor had he tripped. He was dead. Hence neither verb is being used literally by the New Testament when it is a matter of resurrection. The verbs are being used metaphorically.

So with this phrase Paul is saying that God did something to Jesus, and he is expressing what God did with a metaphor. This use of metaphor has to be the case for at least two reasons. First of all, Jesus was dead. Where are you when you are dead? Your body, of course, is easy to locate. But your body is now simply a corpse. So where are you? The answer, I would suggest, is nowhere, no–where. Once you are dead, you are no longer able to be located by some set of coordinates within the world of space and time. Space and time define matter, and whatever death may bring, it severs you from the material. Since, however, all our experience occurs within the world of space and time, our language corresponds to that world. Hence to speak of matters outside that world, to speak of an event that occurs on the other side of death, we can only stretch and twist our this-worldly language to make it fit. We have to use our language metaphorically.

There is a second reason as well for Paul to speak metaphorically. "He was raised" implies that God is the agent. The word "God," however, points to a transcendent mystery of infinite intelligibility, truth, goodness, and beauty. The reality of God is literally unimaginable. All images are material, with spatial and temporal dimensions. God, however, is not defined or bounded by space or time, and so we can speak of God only by using our ordinary language in special ways. Since, then, "he was raised" refers to an event on the other side of death whose agent is God, it refers to a literally unimaginable reality of which Paul and the tradition he is quoting, in order to say anything at all, have to speak metaphorically.

Can we nonetheless determine the meaning of Paul's metaphor more precisely? Left to our own resources, we would have a hard time. By sheer speculation we might come up with any number of possible meanings, but speculation by itself is a poor tool for investigating the meaning of a specific text. Possible interpretations, no matter how brilliant, do not thereby become probable. Ingenuity alone does not mean they in fact pertain to the text.

Fortunately, Paul himself helps us out. Later in the same chapter, in verse 35, he raises the question we are dealing with. What does it mean to be raised from the dead? What is it like? "But someone will ask, 'How are the dead raised? With what kind of body do they come?'"

Paul's first answer to this question, in the next verse, is the kind of response that ensures that the questioner will never speak up again. It is the kind of answer that, if a teacher used it, would guarantee that no one in the class would ever raise a hand again. Paul's response? "Fool!" he roars. Why does he respond this way? Why "fool!"? Notice how the question is phrased. It asks for an explanation: "how?" and it asks for a picture: "with what kind of body?" The question is asking for what you cannot have, a picture of what it is like to be raised from the dead. It asks for an image of what is literally unimaginable. Hence Paul's roaring response: "Fool!"

Still, Paul does not leave matters there. Without supplying a picture, he proceeds to say something definite about what being raised from the dead is like. Using the analogies of a seed and how what is planted differs from what comes up (in verses 36 to 44) and of a change of clothing (in verses 53 and 54), he sets up a series of contrasts between our experience now and in the risen state.

In setting up his contrasts Paul begins by reminding us first of all of something that is negative about our experience now, in this life. For instance, little though we like to think about it, we all know that sooner or later, some day or another, each of us has to die. The shadow of mortality falls across all our hopes and plans. Life, it is said, is a fatal disease. Death lies in everyone's future. So what is it like to be raised from the dead? Cancel that experience of mortality. Remove the shadow that hangs over all our moments, sweep away its uncertainty, anxiety, and fear: "this mortal body puts on immortality" (v. 54).

Similarly, not only do our present days all lead to death, but with death comes corruption. Someday our eyes will close, our breathing will stop, and soon thereafter, despite the mortician's best efforts, a set of chemical processes too disgusting to detail will set in. Not only are we mortal, we are corruptible as well. But raised from the dead? "What [the seed] is sown is perishable, what is raised is imperishable. It is sown in dishonor, it is raised in glory. It is sown in weakness, it is raised in power" (vv. 42-43).

What is being raised from the dead like? Without offering a picture, Paul uses the indirect route of a double negative to say something definite in answer to this question. Think, he says, of what is negative about our existence now. For example, to be alive now is to be mortal and corruptible. Now, Paul says, cancel that. Being raised from the dead negates everything that is negative about our experience now. Being raised from the dead means liberation from everything that in this present life is unfree; it means healing of all that is not whole.

One of Paul's contrasts, however, seems to give us a picture after all. In verse 44, using the analogy of the seed that is sown perishable, dishonorable, and weak, but raised imperishable, glorious, and powerful, Paul continues: "It is sown a physical body, it is raised a spiritual body. If there is a physical body, there is also a spiritual body." With this contrast Paul seems to be inviting us to imagine two kinds of body, made out of different kinds of stuff. Is this the case?

The Greek terms can help our inquiry. The word translated as body is *sōma*. The two adjectives that Paul uses are *psychikos*, here translated as "physical", and *pneumatikos*, spiritual. *Sōma*, however, does not simply designate the thing you weigh on a scale. In Paul's use of the term it means you and everything you need to be yourself. If you stop to think about it,

your body is not just a thing. It is a medium, that through which you become present to yourself and to others. Further, *psychikos* ("natural," or
"physical") and *pneumatikos* ("spiritual," or "filled with air/breath/spirit"—
think of the Michelin tire man!) do not designate kinds of stuff, physical
quantities. In Paul's use they are moral and religious terms. To exist as a
sōma psychikon is to exist apart from God's Spirit, subject to forces that
would separate you from God, others, and your own self. To exist as a
sōma pneumatikon is to possess from God a principle of life that overcomes those forces, that frees one and makes one whole. In other words,
the contrast Paul is drawing in order to clarify what he means by being
raised from the dead is not a contrast between two kinds of stuff. He is not
saying that at present we are made of natural, physical stuff but then we
shall be made of something lighter and airier. Rather, as with his other
contrasts, Paul is contrasting two ways of being, our present condition
with its negativities and down sides, and another way of being that is freed
of all that is negative now.

We can return to the question with which we began. When he quotes a
creedal formula that says of Jesus that "he was raised," is Paul saying that
the same thing happened to Jesus as in the stories of the official's daughter, the widow's son, and Lazarus? Is he saying that Jesus was brought
back to life, that his corpse was resuscitated? The answer is clearly no. In
those stories the people who had been raised from the dead came back to
the same way of existing as before. Lazarus could have caught a cold and
died again the next day. This is not what Paul is saying about Jesus.

"He was raised." God rescued Jesus from death and brought him to a
way of being with God as a *sōma pneumatikon*, one who is filled with
God's Spirit, in a way that fulfills Jesus in his humanity, liberates him
from all that in this life works to make human beings unfree, heals all that
makes human beings less than whole. This real though literally unimaginable event transforms Jesus in a final and definitive way. Jesus had proclaimed the nearness of the coming of the kingdom of God, the nearness
of a God who as Abba heals, liberates, and fulfills. Being raised from the
dead, Jesus experienced the fullness of the kingdom of God. Paul is speaking, then, not of the resuscitation of a corpse, but of what scholars call eschatological, that is, final and complete transformation.

"He Appeared"

Besides documenting belief in Jesus' resurrection, the tradition Paul
quotes also offers an answer to the question of how anyone knew about it.
"He appeared." The Greek verb is *ōphthē*, a form of the verb to see. It can
also be translated as "he was seen," or "he manifested himself," or "he

made himself to be seen." As with "he was raised," we want to bring into more precise focus just what Paul is affirming when he quotes this phrase. Second, we want to notice how the meaning of the phrase opens up a further question, really a whole can of worms, although we shall have to postpone answering that further question till later in our treatment of the resurrection when we get beyond asking why the data are the way they are and come to our third major question, why there are any data at all. Only when we get to the issue of historicity will we be able to close off the question that the meaning of the phrase we are now working with will, as we shall see, raise.

Words get their meaning from how people use them, and it is this prior usage that a dictionary tries to capture. Dictionaries mirror usage more than they dictate it. Now the Bible is a much-studied book, and two of the tools that scholars have devised for studying it are called "concordances" and "lexicons." Long before computers became available to simplify the task, scholars had identified every important word that appears in the Bible. Then, for each word, they went through the Bible, book by book, chapter by chapter, verse by verse, in the original languages, listing every time that word appeared. Putting the words into alphabetical order, they then published the results in a concordance. For each significant word in the Bible, a concordance allows you to quickly review how that word has been used and how, like a snowball, it has picked up connotations and nuances in the course of its use. This latter kind of analysis is published in the lexicons.

To determine just what Paul means by *ōphthē* we need to assemble the lexicographical data (the lists in the concordance plus the analysis in the lexicon). What associations has this form of the verb "to see" acquired by the time it shows up in Paul's letter? One place that the word occurs is in the context of divine self-disclosure or epiphanies. Think, for example, of the story of the burning bush when God discloses the divine name to Moses and commissions Moses to lead God's people out of slavery in Egypt (Exodus 3). In that context there are four relevant elements to the lexicographical data. First, the recipient of the disclosure is someone with a prior involvement with the one disclosing and also comes out of the experience with a sense of mission, a job to do. Second, the initiative in these events lies with the one who does the disclosing. Moses, for instance, did not sneak up on the burning bush and overhear YHWH. The entire event took place at YHWH's initiative. Third, such events constitute God's revelation. Fourth (to return to the recipient of the disclosure) the recipient has an experience that includes a visual component.

If these are the lexicographical data, they help us fill out the meaning of what Paul, citing his tradition, is saying. On one or more occasions Jesus, now raised from the dead, took the initiative in disclosing himself to persons who had a prior involvement with him. When they received this revelation their experience included a visual component, and they emerged from the experience with a sense of mission.

The meaning of the phrase, then, is relatively simple. How, on this account, did anyone come to know about Jesus' resurrection? "He made himself to be seen" by certain people who already had been involved with him, and this disclosure was revelatory for them and conferred on them a mission, a job to do.

So far, so good. Notice, however, that the lexicographical data also suggest a further question. To make it concrete, imagine that you can bundle a TV network news team with all their equipment into a time machine and transport them back to one of the revelatory events listed in Paul's passage. Given the meaning of *ōphthē,* can we expect that this news team will be able to capture the risen Lord on film and tape? Or suppose some passerby happened on the scene as the risen Lord manifested himself, say, to Cephas. Will that passerby also have seen Jesus, now raised from the dead?

Media people are reputed to be a secular, nonreligious lot. A passing stranger would probably never even have heard of Jesus. In neither case is there a prior involvement with Jesus. Furthermore, according to the lexicographical data, those who do see the risen Lord receive a mission from him. There are no neutral witnesses. Hence it appears that *ōphthē* contains an ambiguity. What is one to think of the visual component of the experience of the recipients of Jesus' self-manifestation? If seeing him is restricted to those with a prior involvement, to those whom he chooses, if all those who do see him come out with a sense of mission, what would anyone else have seen?

One author, Gerald O'Collins, whose summary of the lexicographical data (in *The Resurrection of Jesus Christ* [Valley Forge, PA: Judson Press, 1973], 8) we have been using, poses the question we are raising. In the next breath, however, he says that the question is unimportant. What is important, he states, is to be persuaded that Jesus' followers really encountered him. Fine, but what about the question? Another scholar, again noting the question that emerges, points out that the risen Jesus is an "eschatological" reality, so naturally our ordinary language breaks down in dealing with him. True, but does this really meet our question? For the moment, having clarified what Paul means when he cites the tradition that the risen Lord appeared and affirms this of himself as well, we can simply note that the phrase raises a further question. What is the objectivity of the visual component of the experience of those to whom Jesus manifested himself?

According to our earliest relevant data, Jesus "was raised on the third day in accordance with the scriptures," and "he appeared." Notice how bareboned the earliest data are. Apart from the names of those to whom Jesus appeared they offer no details about these events. There is no indication of where Jesus appeared. There is no indication of what anyone may have said on these occasions nor of how anyone may have felt about what was happening. Nor do the earliest data say anything about an empty tomb. If, however, Paul and the tradition he cites provide none of these details, the gospels provide an abundance of further relevant data, and to these we turn next.

An Empty Tomb

Beginning with the earliest gospel, Mark, we find in its final chapter (16:1-8) something that Paul did not mention.

> When the sabbath was over, Mary Magdalene, and Mary the mother of James, and Salome bought spices, so that they might go and anoint him. And very early on the first day of the week, when the sun had risen, they went to the tomb. They had been saying to one another, "Who will roll away the stone for us from the entrance to the tomb?" When they looked up, they saw that the stone, which was very large, had already been rolled back. As they entered the tomb, they saw a young man, dressed in a white robe, sitting on the right side; and they were alarmed. But he said to them, "Do not be alarmed; you are looking for Jesus of Nazareth, who was crucified. He has been raised; he is not here. Look, there is the place they laid him. But go, tell his disciples and Peter that he is going ahead of you to Galilee; there you will see him, just as he told you." So they went out and fled from the tomb, for terror and amazement had seized them; and they said nothing to anyone, for they were afraid.

With that the gospel of Mark originally ended, at verse 8. As we shall see, the rest of the chapter, verses 9 to 20, were added later, after the other gospels had been written. If we focus for the moment on this original ending of Mark our question at present is still: what are the data? And if the data are going to speak to us, if they are not going to just sit there as black squiggles on a white page we have to ask some questions. So as we turn from Paul to the gospels, we can play reporter. As we approach Mark's story and then the others we can ask the kind of questions a reporter asks: who, what, when, where, how, and why. (Raymond E. Brown provides helpful charts of the results of these questions in *The Virginal Conception and Bodily Resurrection of Jesus* [New York: Paulist, 1973], 100, 118.)

When? Mark supplies various indications of time. "[T]he sabbath was over," so it is past sundown on Saturday. Mark makes this more specific in the next sentence: "Very early on the first day of the week, when the sun had risen."

Who? Mark names three women: Mary Magdalene, Mary the mother of James, and Salome.

Why? Mark tells us why these three women are out and about so early on a Sunday morning. They have purchased spices in order to anoint the body of Jesus.

Visuals? When the women arrive at the tomb, they find (very conveniently) that the stone sealing the tomb has already been rolled back. Furthermore, they see a youth dressed in white, sitting inside on the right.

Audio? The youth makes a well-mannered three-part speech. First he addresses the women's feelings. He tells them to remain calm, not to be overcome by awe and wonder. Second, he explains why the tomb is empty. Jesus has been raised. Third, he gives them a job to do. They are to go and tell the (male) disciples that Jesus is going before them to Galilee, and there, as he had said earlier, they will see him.

Reaction? The women's response to the good news of the resurrection is a downer. Overcome with fear, they run away and tell no one (leaving one to wonder how the author of Mark knew about all this in the first place).

Matthew (28:1-9) follows Mark in narrating this tale of the empty tomb, though he changes some of the details. Salome drops out of the picture, leaving Mary Magdalene and "the other Mary." They simply "went to see the tomb," not to anoint the body. At the end of the scene, after they have heard the three-part speech, their reaction is tempered: "So they left the tomb quickly with fear and great joy, and ran to tell his disciples."

Beyond these details Matthew introduces one major change into the story. Whereas in Mark when the women arrive at the tomb the stone is already conveniently rolled back, Matthew turns the opening of the tomb into a dramatic scene that almost overpowers the whole story. In his version when the women arrive at the tomb a spectacular show begins.

> And suddenly there was a great earthquake; for an angel of the Lord, descending from heaven, came and rolled back the stone and sat on it. His appearance was like lightning, and his clothing white as snow. For fear of him the guards shook and became like dead men.

Luke's version of the empty tomb story (24:1-10) sticks with Mark regarding the women's purpose in visiting the tomb: "[they took] the spices that they had prepared." The number of women swells: Joanna replaces Salome and there are unnamed others as well. As in Mark the stone is already rolled back when they arrive at the tomb though the youth, who in Matthew became an angel, has now become "two men in dazzling clothes." The most notable change in Luke's version is in the speech the women hear:

> "Why do you look for the living among the dead? He is not here, but has risen. Remember how he told you, while he was still in Galilee, that the Son of Man must be handed over to sinners, and be crucified, and on the third day rise."

Luke has dropped the first and third parts of the speech, keeping only the explanation of why the tomb is empty. Whereas in Mark and Matthew Galilee is mentioned in the third part of the speech in connection with a mandate to send the disciples there to see Jesus, here it is folded into a reminiscence of something Jesus had said there earlier. With regard to the women's reaction to all this, Luke simply has them return and report it all "to the eleven [=the twelve minus Judas] and to all the rest."

The Fourth Gospel also narrates the empty tomb story, but in a way that exemplifies the difference between John and the synoptics. In John 20:1-18 Mary Magdalene finds the tomb empty "while it was still dark" and immediately reports this to Peter "and the other disciple, the one whom Jesus loved." Peter and this other disciple then come to the tomb, find it as Mary said, and go home again. Mary lingers on. Looking into the tomb, she sees two angels in white who ask her why she is crying. Turning around she sees Jesus, whom she takes for the gardener, and he asks her the same question. She answers,

> "Sir, if you have carried him away, tell me where you have laid him, and I will take him away." Jesus said to her, "Mary!" She turned and said to him in Hebrew, "Rabbouni!" (which means Teacher). Jesus said to her, "Do not hold on to me, because I have not yet ascended to the Father. But go to my brothers and say to them, 'I am ascending to my Father and your Father, to my God and your God.'" Mary Magdalene went and announced to the disciples, "I have seen the Lord"; and she told them that he had said these things to her.

Having turned from Paul to the gospels, we have found data on something that Paul had not mentioned, Jesus' tomb being found empty by Mary Magdalene, alone or with others, early Sunday morning. We also find differences from gospel to gospel in how the story is told. With regard to time, for instance, it is already light in the synoptics, but in John it is "still dark." With regard to who is involved, Mary Magdalene is the constant. In John she is alone; not so in the synoptics. Mark and Luke assign the women a purpose, namely to anoint the body, which Matthew drops and John also fails to mention. With regard to what the women see, Matthew stands out like a sore thumb. Whereas the tomb is already open when the women arrive in Mark, Luke, and John, Matthew provides a grand tomb-opening scene, with an earthquake, an angel, and guards who are flattened by what occurs. Still, Matthew's angel then recites the same speech as in Mark, whereas in Luke that speech is severely edited and in John the speech is delivered by Jesus himself and concerns ascending to the Father. Finally, with regard to the women's reaction Mark stands out as one-sided and stark. In Mark, having heard the good news of the resurrection, the women are overcome with fear, flee, and tell no one. Matthew makes them both fearful and overjoyed, while in Luke they simply go and tell. In John, Mary Magdalene tells the disciples about the empty tomb before she has grasped its meaning; her first reaction is to wonder where whoever took Jesus' body had put it.

At this point our next question is forcefully emerging. Given what the data are, why are the data the way they are, namely, with all these discrepancies? Before we can turn to that question, however, we should note that the gospels offer further relevant data. All four gospels as they now stand, after they narrate the finding of the tomb, also pick up the tradition that we found in Paul and narrate stories in which the risen Lord appears. We need to become familiar with these as well.

Easter Appearances

Beginning with the original ending of Mark we saw that chapter 16:1-8 told of the finding of the empty tomb and concluded with the women's reaction; it narrated no appearances. There may, however, be at least a reference to the appearance tradition in verse 7 when the youth tells the women to tell the disciples that Jesus is going before them to Galilee, and there they will see him. While some scholars think this is a reference to the parousia, the second coming of Jesus, others think it alludes to the tradition of Easter appearances.

Matthew 28 narrates two appearances of Jesus. In the first he appears to the two women as they are leaving the tomb area on their way to carry the angel's message to the disciples (28:9-10). Notice what a dinky and, in a way, insulting appearance it is. "Suddenly Jesus met them and said, 'Greetings!' And they came to him, took hold of his feet, and worshiped him." And what does Jesus have to say to them on this momentous occasion? He simply repeats what the angel had just told them to do. "Then Jesus said to them, 'Do not be afraid; go and tell my brothers to go to Galilee; there they will see me.'" And that's it.

Second, whether or not Mark 16:7 referred to an appearance in Galilee, Matthew certainly takes the message at the tomb in that direction and supplies one. Between the appearance to the women on their way back from the tomb and the final scene of his gospel he provides a followup on the guards whom we last saw flattened at the tomb (28:11-15). They report back to the chief priests and the elders who bribe them to spread a story that Jesus' body had been stolen. Next Matthew has the risen Jesus appear and found the Church:

> Now the eleven disciples went to Galilee, to the mountain to which Jesus had directed them. When they saw him, they worshiped him; but some doubted. And Jesus came and said to them, "All authority in heaven and on earth has been given to me. Go therefore and make disciples of all nations, baptizing them in the name of the Father and of the Son and of the Holy Spirit, and teaching them to obey everything that I have commanded you. And remember, I am with you always, to the end of the age (28:16-20).

There, with Jesus as the new Moses once again on a mountain with his disciples, Matthew ends.

In Luke 24 the women go directly from the tomb and report to the apostles, who find their story nonsense (24:9-11). Peter, however, goes out to the tomb by himself and returns amazed (24:12). There follows Luke's first appearance story, in which a disciple named Cleopas and another disciple are joined by Jesus while they are en route to the village of Emmaus, seven miles from Jerusalem (24:13-33). Noting that "their eyes were kept from recognizing him," Luke introduces the scene with a note of irony. Jesus asks the two what they had been talking about, and Cleopas's reply begins with a question. He asks Jesus, "Are you the only stranger in Jerusalem who does not know the things that have taken place there in these days?" Luke's reader, of course, is well aware of Jesus' central role in those events. In explaining to Jesus what had happened, Cleopas's words reflect two early ways in which Jesus' followers had thought of him. He was "a prophet mighty in deed and word before God and all the people" who had raised people's expectations: "we had hoped that he was the one to redeem Israel."

Once Cleopas completes his tale of dashed hopes and recounts how some of their number had confirmed the women's story of the empty tomb, Jesus chides them for failing to believe the message of Moses and the prophets that it was "'. . . necessary that the Messiah should suffer these things and then enter into his glory.' Then beginning with Moses and all the prophets, he interpreted to them the things about himself in all the prophets." Here we see reflected an early interpretation of Jesus' death, which surfaced as well in our text from Paul, as "in accordance with the scriptures."

In concluding the scene Luke sounds one more theme. As it is getting late, Jesus is invited to stay for dinner with the two disciples and "while he was at the table with them, he took bread, blessed and broke it, and gave it to them." Only then do they finally recognize the stranger with whom they have been conversing. "Then their eyes were opened, and they recognized him; and he vanished from their sight. They said to each other, 'Were not our hearts burning within us while he was talking to us on the road, while he was opening the scriptures to us?'"

In narrating Jesus' appearance to the two disciples on the road to Emmaus, Luke thus emphasizes two theological ideas: Jesus' death happened in accordance with the scriptures, and his disciples recognize him as risen in the breaking of the bread.

The two disciples then return to Jerusalem, but before they can recount their stupendous news to "the eleven and their companions" they are first told that "the Lord has risen indeed, and he has appeared to Simon!" (24:34). Even as Paul's text listed the appearance to Peter first, it seems important to Luke as well to give it priority over other appearances.

After narrating the appearance to Cleopas and his companion and mentioning an appearance to Peter, Luke tells the tale of one final appearance "while they were talking about this" (24:36-49). Jesus appears among them and after he has wished them peace his first order of business is to prove he is not a ghost. To this end he invites them to touch him, "for a ghost does not have flesh and bones as you see that I have." To clinch the matter he asks for something to eat and consumes a piece of baked fish. Next he repeats the first theme of the Emmaus story, that his death and resurrection occurred to fulfill what was written in Moses, the prophets, and the psalms. From this theme he segues neatly into a commission founding the Church:

> "Thus it is written, that the Messiah is to suffer and to rise from the dead on the third day, and that repentance and forgiveness of sins is to be proclaimed in his name to all nations, beginning from Jerusalem. You are witnesses of these things. And see, I am sending upon you what my Father promised; so stay here in the city until you have been clothed with power from on high."

In Luke the apostolic mission is to spread the message of *metanoia*/forgiveness. But since Luke will also tell the story of the conferring of the Holy Spirit at Pentecost in his next book, the Acts of the Apostles (Acts 2:1-41), here he has the disciples wait in Jerusalem until they receive power from on high. His gospel ends with the ascension (24:50-53). Jesus leads the disciples out to Bethany, and "while he was blessing them, he withdrew from them and was carried up into heaven." Returning to Jerusalem, the disciples spend their time praying in the Temple.

This brings us to John 20. As we saw, John weaves an appearance to Mary Magdalene into his recounting of her discovery of the empty tomb.

Then, the same evening, as the disciples are hiding behind locked doors for fear of the Jewish leadership, Jesus stands in their midst and, as in Luke, wishes them peace. He shows them his hands and side and they respond with joy. Finally he commissions them:

> "Peace be with you. As the Father has sent me, so I send you." When he had said this, he breathed on them and said to them, "Receive the Holy Spirit. If you forgive the sins of any, they are forgiven them; if you retain the sins of any, they are retained" (20:21-23).

Recall that in Luke, Jesus had to go through quite a bit of trouble to convince the disciples that he was not a ghost. Matthew struck a similar note at the beginning of his Church-founding appearance scene on the mountain in Galilee: "When they saw him, they worshiped him; but some doubted" (Matt 28:17). John 20 now devotes a separate story, centered on the disciple Thomas, to the theme of doubt (20:24-29). Thomas, one of the eleven, is absent in John's narrative of the appearance Sunday evening in Jerusalem. Told about that appearance, Thomas retorts with bravado: "Unless I see the mark of the nails in his hands, and put my finger in the mark of the nails and my hand in his side, I will not believe." A week later Jesus again appears behind locked doors and invites Thomas to do precisely what he had said. Thomas responds: "My Lord and my God!" It is unlikely that this is an expletive. Rather, it is one of only three texts in the New Testament where Jesus is called God. The story ends with a punch line: "Blessed are those who have not seen and yet have come to believe." Two lines later the chapter ends, and those two verses appear originally to have ended the gospel as a whole as well:

> Now Jesus did many other signs in the presence of his disciples, which are not written in this book. But these are written so that you may come to believe that Jesus is the Messiah, the Son of God, and that through believing you may have life in his name (20:30-31).

Nonetheless, someone added chapter 21 to John, and it also narrates an appearance of Jesus. Seven of the disciples have fished in the Sea of Tiberias all night with no luck. At dawn Jesus tells them where to cast their net, and as it fills with one hundred fifty-three fish they recognize him and Peter jumps into the water to reach him. Jesus feeds them a breakfast of bread and fish and then three times asks Peter whether he loves him, each time telling Peter to feed his flock.

At this point we can bring in the longer ending to the gospel of Mark, chapter 16:9-20. Like John it presents a first appearance to Mary Magdalene, proceeds to a commissioning of the eleven that echoes Luke and John in its setting, Matthew and Luke in its wording, and concludes with the ascension.

If Paul supplied our earliest relevant data on the origin and meaning of belief in Jesus' resurrection, the gospels add further data on the empty tomb and appearances of the risen Jesus. If the data on the empty tomb abound in discrepancies, so also do those we have just reviewed, the gospel stories of Jesus' Easter appearances. Where, for instance, did Jesus commission the Church? Matthew would place this event on a mountain in Galilee, while all the Easter events in Luke and John occur in and around Jerusalem. Notice also that the words with which the risen Jesus commissions the Church vary from gospel to gospel. In Luke, further-more, the disciples are told to wait until they receive power from on high while in John 20 the Holy Spirit is conferred on them. Finally, both Luke 24 and John 20 insist on the bodiliness of the risen Jesus. This emphasis is absent from Matthew and Mark and seems to contradict the interpreta-tion of "he was raised" as a real but unimaginable eschatological transfor-mation that we worked out in dealing with Paul. Now that we have reviewed the data, our next question is clear. Why are the data the way they are?

Chapter Nine

Why Are the Data the Way They Are?

We began our study of christology with the question of the historical Jesus, using a historian's lens to view Jesus' ministry and death. But the story of Jesus extends beyond his death, and so we have moved on to a new question. We are presently trying to understand the origin and meaning of Christian belief in the resurrection of Jesus. To that end we have just surveyed the data supplied by the New Testament.

Paul provided the earliest batch of relevant data with the traditions he quotes in 1 Cor 15:3-8. Although the letter was written around 56 C.E. the material Paul cites goes back more than a decade and a half earlier, perhaps to within three years of Jesus' execution. We focused first on the statement that "he was raised," arguing that Paul means by this phrase not the resuscitation of a corpse but a real, though literally unimaginable, eschatological transformation that is, for Jesus, the definitive fulfillment of his central theme, the coming of the kingdom of God. Second, we also worked out what Paul means by "he appeared," drawing on the lexicographical data on the phrase and noting that if its meaning is in one sense clear the phrase also raises a further question about the objectivity of the visual component implied by the verb.

Moving from Paul to the gospels we encountered in Mark 16:1-8 a story about women finding Jesus' tomb empty on Easter Sunday morning. While all four gospels tell the story, they differ from one another on points both small and large. Notably, in John it is still dark when Mary Magdalene visits the tomb. In Matthew the tomb is opened in the presence of both the women and some guards who have been posted there. Luke severely edits the speech delivered by the heavenly messengers at the tomb.

In Mark the women react in a peculiarly negative fashion to the good news of the resurrection.

The gospels also abound in stories about appearances of the risen Jesus, and again these stories differ in both detail and on major points. Where, for example, does Jesus commission the Church, Galilee or Jerusalem? What commission does he entrust to it? What of the bodiliness with which he appears, especially in Luke 24 and John 20?

Given all these differences among the data the question emerges: Why are these data the way they are? On the way to our answer to this question we shall first review two other responses, one of which we have already seen and both of which we find inadequate, and then we shall work out a third.

One answer to our question was proposed by Hermann S. Reimarus, whom we encountered at the very beginning of our overview of the Old Quest for the historical Jesus. Reimarus, we recall, had come up with a Davidic-Messianic interpretation of Jesus' message and a view of Jesus himself as a failed religious and nationalistic revolutionary. Christianity, Reimarus argued, was not what Jesus had intended. Jesus' goal was the restoration of David's kingdom. But when Jesus failed, his disciples wanted to keep a good thing going. Plucked from nowhere, they enjoyed the status they had acquired in Jesus' movement.

So, having spiritualized Jesus' preaching of the kingdom and explained away his death as salvific, they clinched matters by making up the story of the resurrection. On Reimarus's account, Christianity is based on a fraud perpetrated by Jesus' followers. But, he notes, they did a poor job. Their resurrection stories contradict one another left and right. If the gospel writers were witnesses in a courtroom the discrepancies in their testimony would get them thrown out.

Against Reimarus and throughout the Old Quest mainline Christians continued to argue as they had for centuries for the historical veracity of the gospels. Already in the second century a pagan named Celsus had attacked Christian belief in Jesus' resurrection using arguments like Reimarus's, and counterarguments like those forged by the great third-century theologian Origen served modern Christians as well. Look, they said, at who wrote the gospels. Why would the apostles and evangelists be willing to endure persecution and even die as martyrs for something they knew to be untrue? The fidelity of their lives and deaths, they argued, secures the trustworthiness of the witness of the gospel writers.

Hence, from this viewpoint it becomes possible to compose a comprehensive life of Jesus by stitching together into one grand narrative all the material found in all four gospels. With regard to the Easter narratives the data can be harmonized to give an account of Jesus' earthly career from

Easter Sunday until his ascension forty days later, a period during which Jesus appeared on various occasions in both Jerusalem and Galilee.

Both Reimarus and this mainline Christian approach have one assumption in common. They assume that the gospels were produced either by eyewitnesses to the events they recount (the apostles Matthew and John) or by witnesses once removed (Mark, who received his material from Peter, and Luke, Paul's traveling companion). Modern biblical scholarship, however, does not share this assumption. As we saw when we began our study of the New Quest, source, form, and redaction criticism propose a more complex account of the composition of the gospels. On this account, our data are not the way they are because of a clumsy fraud, nor because of differences of perspective among reliable eyewitnesses. Rather, the gospel writers composed their narratives a generation and more after Jesus' execution, drawing on material that previously circulated in oral form.

As the material we have surveyed emerges from the oral tradition into the gospels it is shaped by three factors. Each gospel writer is a creative theologian, and so the material will reflect the theological viewpoint of the redactor. Second, early Christian communities were often involved in controversy, and so the apologetic needs of the community for which the redactor writes, their need to respond to objections to their faith, will also influence how the material is shaped. Third, we have seen that Paul presents a tradition about appearances of the risen Lord, while the tradition about the empty tomb first surfaces in Mark. Hence a third factor operative on the New Testament data will be the effort to tie together literarily, in a single story, these two originally independent traditions.

Now if modern biblical scholarship offers this three-part hypothesis, the proof is in the pudding. Do these three factors in fact account for each of the major points of difference that emerged from our survey of the data?

To tackle one of the more complex issues first, we saw that Luke locates the Church-commissioning scene in Jerusalem, as does John 20, while Matthew has it on a mountain in Galilee. Why does Luke do this? Recall that Luke is the first book of a two-volume work, the second being the Acts of the Apostles. One notable feature of Luke's two-volume work is its geographical structure. In the gospel, having been baptized by John and then spending forty days fasting and being tempted in the desert, Jesus begins his ministry in Galilee (Luke 4:13). After five chapters of this ministry Jesus sets out on a journey to Jerusalem (Luke 9:51), arriving there ten chapters later (Luke 19:28).

At Jerusalem he suffers and dies; there his tomb is found empty, he appears to the disciples, and he ascends. Luke's next volume, Acts, begins with the ascension and goes on to narrate the story of Pentecost, the birthday of the Church. From Jerusalem the Church then spreads throughout the Roman empire, and the book ends with Paul in prison at Rome itself.

The overall movement of these two books, then, is first up to Jerusalem and then out from Jerusalem. But if you take out a map and chart the place names mentioned in the ten-chapter journey to Jerusalem, Luke 9:51–19:27, it seems that Jesus is actually doing nothing during this so-called journey that is different from what he had been doing in the previous chapters. This indicates that the author is the one who makes the material in this section into a journey to Jerusalem, though he failed to adjust the geographical indicators accordingly. Perhaps he was himself unfamiliar with them.

We are asking why Luke locates the Easter events in and around Jerusalem, and we have noticed that his two-volume work exhibits a geographical structure in which Jerusalem is central. He makes Jerusalem the goal of Jesus' ten-chapter journey, the place where the saving events of Jesus' death and the resurrection appearances as well as the sending of the Spirit at Pentecost take place, the center from which salvation then spreads out throughout the Roman empire.

Why does Luke shape his work through this geographical structure? It appears that Luke was probably a Gentile writing for other Gentile Christians. Lacking a lived experience of Judaism and coming from a culture that was marked by anti-Semitism, this community ran the risk of truncating the story of God's gracious dealings with humankind. Himself a Jew, Jesus only makes sense in the context of the story of God's dealings with Israel. But Luke's Christians were in danger of losing that context and hence of losing the full significance of Jesus. To counteract that danger Luke reminds them that in God's plan salvation comes to humankind from the Jews. Hence Luke structures his telling of the story so that Jerusalem, the holy city of the Jews, occupies the central place. Jesus' ministry takes him to Jerusalem; it is there that the saving events of Jesus' death, resurrection, and the conferral of the Spirit take place; and from Jerusalem salvation then spreads throughout the Roman empire.

Luke's theological viewpoint explains why he locates the Church-commissioning appearance of the risen Jesus in Jerusalem. Geography becomes for Luke a vehicle of theological symbolism. This also explains why Luke radically edits the speech delivered by one of the heavenly messengers to the women at the tomb. While Luke's source, Mark, has the messenger tell the women to tell the disciples that Jesus is going ahead of them to Galilee and that they will see him there, Luke turns all this into a reminiscence of something Jesus had said in the past in Galilee. Why? Because Luke is not going to have any appearance in Galilee. Everything in his story will occur in and around Jerusalem and so, as a consistent author, he edits out any reference to a future appearance in Galilee.

Matthew, however, both preserves this element of the messenger's speech at the tomb and proceeds to locate his major Church-commissioning appearance on a mountain in Galilee. Does this mean that, unlike Luke, Matthew has taken care to get the facts of the matter straight? Not necessarily. Notice first of all that Jesus appears on a mountain in Galilee. When we were dealing with the implications of the response of conversion that Jesus sought to evoke during his ministry, we explored Luke 6:20-49. At that time we noticed that Luke cast this material as a Sermon on the Plain, unlike Matthew, who presented much of the same material as a Sermon on the Mount. We suggested then that this was not a matter of differences in factual accuracy, so that one of the evangelists has the facts straight and the other does not, but a matter of differing theological symbolisms. Matthew, we suggested, was picturing Jesus as the new Moses, and so had him deliver the new Law on a mountain.

If Matthew's use of a mountain in his Church-commissioning scene reflects this symbolism, why Galilee? First, of course, there is the reference to Galilee in his source, Mark. But second, the context of Matthew's community also comes into play. Scholars commonly suggest that Matthew's community had recently been excommunicated by those Jewish leaders who, after the fall of Jerusalem and destruction of the Temple in 70 C.E., were shaping the future of Judaism under the new conditions established by these traumatic events. If Judaism had previously been broad and diverse enough to embrace within itself Jesus' disciples, the fall of Jerusalem called for a tighter and stricter self-definition. Excluded from the synagogue, Matthew found himself contending with this newly emergent Judaism as both they and his own community laid claim to the title of being the true Israel.

This tension and hostility explain why, in Matthew, the Pharisees are painted in such negative colors. The Pharisees represent the predecessors of those who had just excluded Matthew's community. For a similar reason Jerusalem has a negative value for Matthew that it does not have for Luke. From his perspective it was there that, when the Messiah had finally come, the Jewish leadership rejected and killed him. Galilee, on the other hand, had a different significance. Historically the area had been subject to mass deportation and repopulation under foreign occupiers. As a result, if you were from Galilee your Jewishness was somewhat suspect. Indeed, in the 1930s some German scholars under the influence of Nazi ideology tried to argue on this basis that Jesus was not a Jew. At any rate, given this historical background Galilee was known as "Galilee of the Gentiles."

In Matthew's perspective those Jews who had excluded his community as well as their predecessors had thereby lost out, so that salvation was passing from them to the Gentiles who were becoming part of Matthew's community. Hence Matthew has the risen Jesus commission the Church not in Jerusalem but on a mountain in Galilee. This symbolizes his theological viewpoint, conditioned by polemic exchanges with the contemporary Jewish leadership.

The same circumstances illumine Matthew's major innovation in the empty tomb story as well. Instead of the stone being already rolled back when the women arrive as in Mark, in Matthew there is an earthquake, an angel descends and opens the tomb, and the guards pass out from fear. Those guards, posted by Pilate at the request of the chief priests and the Pharisees (Matt 27:62-66), appear only in Matthew, as does the follow-up to the empty tomb story. When the women leave the tomb area the guards go and tell the chief priests what had happened. After the chief priests had

> assembled with the elders, they devised a plan to give a large sum of money to the soldiers, telling them, "You must say, 'His disciples came by night and stole him away while we were asleep.' If this comes to the governor's ears, we will satisfy him and keep you out of trouble." So they took the money and did as they were directed. And this story is still told among the Jews to this day (Matt 28:12-15).

Matthew has an apologetic purpose in retelling the empty tomb story. His opponents are saying that the tomb was empty because Jesus' disciples had stolen the body. Matthew retells the story in a way that counters the charge; he has the tomb opened in the presence of witnesses and he lays the origin of the objection to bribery by his community's opponents.

Thus far we have accounted for the discrepancy between Luke and Matthew regarding the location of the Church-founding commission by appealing to the theological viewpoint expressed in their respective symbolic geographies. Luke centers his two-volume work, and all the resurrection events, in Jerusalem as a way of reminding his largely Gentile community that in God's plan salvation comes from the Jews. Matthew, on the other hand, chooses Galilee to symbolize how, given the obdurateness of those fellow Jews who oppose him, salvation is passing to the Gentiles. Closely connected with the geographical symbolism of each author's appearance narrative has been, in each case, a major modification of the empty tomb story as well.

We still need to clarify two further features of the empty tomb narratives. In John, we saw, it is "still dark" when Mary Magdalene arrives at the tomb. To understand this we can refer back to the prologue to John's gospel. We dealt with this text before when we were exploring what a high, descending approach to christology involved. We saw then that John's prologue presents Jesus as identical with the preexistent divine

Word who was with God in the beginning. This same text also appeals to primal imagery of light and darkness to frame the story of Jesus:

> He was in the beginning with God.
> All things came into being through him,
> and without him not one thing came into being.
> What has come into being in him was life,
> and the life was the light of all people.
> The light shines in the darkness,
> and the darkness did not overcome it (John 1:2-5).

When Mary arrives at Jesus' tomb the risen Lord is not yet manifest, and so it is "still dark."

That leaves one final oddity with regard to the empty tomb story, the women's one-sided and negative reaction in the original ending of the gospel of Mark. "So they went out and fled from the tomb, for terror and amazement had seized them; and they said nothing to anyone, for they were afraid" (Mark 16:8). Mark's audience is likely also to have been afraid if, as some scholars suggest, the gospel was written for a community facing persecution of the sort described in chapter 13:

> They will hand you over to the councils; and you will be beaten in synagogues; and you will stand before governors and kings . . . . Brother will betray brother to death, and a father his child, and children will rise against parents and have them put to death; and you will be hated by all because of my name. But the one who endures to the end will be saved (Mark 13:9-13).

Mark uses irony as a means of encouraging this community to persevere in their faith. Throughout his gospel the male disciples are portrayed in most unflattering terms. Consistently they fail to understand Jesus, and at the end they let him down. The women fare better. They stick with Jesus when the men have abandoned him and see to his burial. But then at the very end, just when the resurrection has been announced to them, they also blow it, "for they were afraid." But each time in Mark's story that Jesus' disciples' fail to understand, the community listening to the story does understand. And if the women fail at the end, Mark's community need not fail. Portraying the shortcomings of first the disciples, then the women, is Mark's way of encouraging a fearful community. They can do better.

So far we have seen that the redactor's theological viewpoint explains why Luke locates his Church-commissioning appearance of Jesus in Jerusalem and why he edits the heavenly messenger's speech at the tomb accordingly. Matthew's theological viewpoint leads him to locate his Church-commissioning appearance in Galilee, while allied apologetic concerns prompt him to present a dramatic opening of the tomb in the presence of witnesses. Our hypothesis has also explained why, in John, it is still dark when Mary Magdalene arrives at the tomb, and why Mark's women react so one-sidedly and negatively to the good news of Jesus' resurrection.

The words with which the risen Jesus commissions the Church also deserve attention. In Matthew, on the mountain in Galilee to which the eleven had gone at Jesus' command,

> Jesus came and said to them, "All authority in heaven and on earth has been given to me. Go therefore and make disciples of all nations, baptizing them in the name of the Father and of the Son and of the Holy Spirit, and teaching them to obey everything that I have commanded you. And remember, I am with you always, to the end of the age" (Matt 28:18-20).

In Luke, Jesus appears to a group including the eleven and others, among them Cleopas and his companion, in Jerusalem on Easter Sunday night. In the course of explaining how he fulfills the Scriptures he also commissions his followers:

> And he said to them, "Thus it is written, that the Messiah is to suffer and to rise from the dead on the third day, and that repentance and forgiveness of sins is to be proclaimed in his name to all nations, beginning from Jerusalem. You are witnesses of these things. And see, I am sending upon you what my Father promised; so stay here in the city until you have been clothed with power from on high" (Luke 24:46-49).

As in Luke, in John Jesus appears among the disciples in Jerusalem on Easter Sunday night.

> [Jesus] said to them again, "Peace be with you. As the Father has sent me, so I send you." When he had said this, he breathed on them and said to them, "Receive the Holy Spirit. If you forgive the sins of any, they are forgiven them; if you retain the sins of any, they are retained" (John 20:21-23).

Notice that in both Matthew and Luke the mission is universal. In Matthew the eleven are to "make disciples of all nations," and in Luke the eleven and those with them are witnesses to a message about *metanoia* and forgiveness that is to be preached in the name of Jesus the Messiah "to all nations."

The universality of the mission in these discourses becomes significant if we recall a fact from the history of the early Church. We learn from both Paul and the Acts of the Apostles that the question of universality set off the first major controversy among Jesus' followers. Were they to require full adherence to Judaism, including circumcision for males and observance of the kosher (dietary) laws, or not? Now if Jesus had left clear instructions on this question it never would have arisen. But the discourses we are examining show no trace of the issue. For that reason it seems that they date from a time when the controversy had already been settled.

It is also clear that in Matthew's discourse the risen Jesus speaks Matthean, in Luke he speaks Lukan, and in John he speaks Johannine. That is, the discourses manifest the typical theological concerns and vocabulary of the respective redactors. As they stand, then, these discourses do not originate in someone's transcriptions of what the risen Jesus said on various occasions when he appeared. Rather, like much else in the New Testament Easter material, they reflect the theological viewpoint of the respective redactors.

Finally, in our survey of the relevant data we noted something new in Luke 24 and John 20. In both of these sources there is an insistence on the bodiliness of the risen Jesus. This emphasis is absent from Matthew and Mark. It also seems to contradict our interpretation of Paul's confession that "he was raised" refers to eschatological transformation and not physical resuscitation. Yet Luke's emphasis is very clear. The risen Jesus stands among the disciples on Easter Sunday night and wishes them peace.

> They were startled and terrified, and thought that they were seeing a ghost. He said to them, "Why are you frightened, and why do doubts arise in your hearts? Look at my hands and my feet; see that it is I myself. Touch me and see; for a ghost does not have flesh and bones as you see that I have." And when he had said this, he showed them his hands and his feet. While in their joy they were disbelieving and still wondering, he said to them, "Have you anything here to eat?" They gave him a piece of broiled fish, and he took it and ate in their presence (Luke 24:38-43).

That piece of broiled fish severely tested the ingenuity of theologians in the Middle Ages. They believed that being raised from the dead meant that you had all your organs, but that you no longer used them. Heaven was not a place where you ate or engaged in sex. But in that case, what happened to that piece of baked fish?

At any rate, the emphasis on bodiliness is no less clear in John 20 when, a week after Easter, the risen Jesus calls Thomas's bluff: "Put your finger here and see my hands. Reach out your hand and put it in my side. Do not doubt but believe" (John 20:27).

Why do we find this emphasis on the corporeality of the risen Jesus in Luke 24 and John 20? Remember first of all what we said about Luke and his community when we were asking why he locates all the Easter events in and around Jerusalem. Luke, we suggested, was a Gentile Christian writing for other Gentile Christians, none of whom had first-hand experience of Judaism. While the Christian movement had begun as a sect within

Judaism, by the time of Luke's gospel it was moving away from its origin within Judaism and in danger of losing touch with its Jewish roots.

Furthermore, Gentile Christians were likely to share the philosophical assumptions common to the Hellenistic culture of the Roman Empire. One such assumption has to do with our makeup as human beings. Recall, for example, Plato's image of our humanity. One part of us, reason, is like a charioteer trying to control the other part, our body and its passions. Hellenistic anthropology, the view of our humanity common to Greek-inspired culture, was dualistic. It saw us as composed of two different parts. Reason comprised our spiritual part, while passion, emotion, and the body belonged to our material part. Of these two parts one, the spiritual, was good, and the other, the material, was bad. The conflict between them comprised the human predicament.

This Hellenistic anthropology stands in conflict with how the Bible views our humanity. On the biblical view God created human beings in God's own image, and having created human beings "God saw everything that God had made, and indeed, it was very good" (Gen 1:31). As the bumper sticker has it, "God doesn't make junk."

Still, as the Christian movement moved into the world of Hellenistic culture it was likely to take over that culture's assumptions and values without realizing what was happening. When that occurred, the stage was set for the emergence within Christianity of the movement called Gnosticism. Its name comes from the Greek word *gnōsis*, which means knowledge. This many-shaped movement almost swamped the Christian communities of the first two centuries. Accepting the Hellenistic analysis of our humanity, some Gnostic teachers regarded the creator God of the Bible as a deluded intermediary being. The real, ultimate God could not be responsible for anything so vile as matter. Gnostics also taught that the solution to the human predicament lay in knowing that our real nature is spiritual and that some day we shall be released from matter and ascend to the realm of spirit. Ethically, this led Gnostics in two directions. Some embraced a strict asceticism, trying to live now as though they did not have bodies. Others, assured that their final destiny was in the realm of spirit, reasoned that what they did now made little difference. Hence they felt free to party, party, party.

Gnostics also proposed various versions of a myth of a heavenly redeemer. According to this myth one of the inhabitants from the realm of spirit came down to redeem us by reminding us of our real, spiritual nature. In a Christian version, Gnostics of course cast Christ in this role of heavenly redeemer. Their aversion to matter led them to what is called docetism in their picture of Jesus. They found it inconceivable that a heavenly being could really involve itself with something so disgusting as the human body. Therefore, they taught, Christ only appeared to have a human body; he was never really made of the same stuff as we. Hence the word docetism, from the Greek word meaning to appear or seem. In another version they taught that the heavenly Christ temporarily occupied the body of the man Jesus. When Jesus was arrested, Christ bailed out. One text pictures Christ standing by at the crucifixion and laughing at the error those who executed Jesus were making.

Against this background the concerns that Luke 24 and John 20 are addressing come into focus. They want to make it perfectly clear that Christ, the redeemer, is one and the same Jesus whom the disciples knew and followed during his lifetime and who was crucified. They also want to affirm the goodness of all God's creation, especially the human body. To make these points against the dualistic anthropology of Hellenistic culture and its Gnostic ramifications Luke 24 and John 20 use picture language. They picture the risen Jesus as somehow corporeal, as touchable and able to eat. Even within their picture language, however, they also make the point that Jesus' humanity has been transformed. For all its corporeality, their picture of the risen Jesus does not present him as simply come back from the dead, as resuscitated. Someone who had been resuscitated could not appear suddenly among a group who huddled, as in John 20, behind locked doors.

This consideration of why Luke 24 and John 20 emphasize the corporeality of the risen Jesus covers the last of the major points of difference we discovered in our survey of the gospel data. We have verified the usefulness of the hypothesis suggested by modern biblical research. Differences among the Easter narratives in the gospels are indeed explicable in light of the theological viewpoints and apologetic concerns of the redactors.

One further factor in shaping these narratives remains. Our first witness to a tradition about appearances of the risen Jesus to male disciples was in 1 Cor 15:3-8. Mark 16:1-8 registered a tradition about women finding Jesus' tomb empty. The gospel writers then faced the task of joining these two originally separate traditions literarily into a single, smoothly-flowing narrative. How does this task shape the data we have been studying?

Mark 16:1-8 narrates the discovery of the empty tomb. The original ending of the gospel of Mark narrated no appearances of the risen Jesus. Does it exhibit any familiarity with the appearances tradition? Verse 7, in which the youth tells the women to tell the disciples to go to Galilee to see Jesus, may well allude to the appearance tradition though some scholars think it refers instead to Jesus' second coming at the end of the world.

Matthew 28 follows Mark in narrating the finding of the tomb. It also narrates a Church-commissioning appearance in Galilee. In between these two narratives, by way of a connection, it presents an appearance of the risen Jesus to the women as they leave the tomb area. We have already noted what a disappointing and in a way insulting appearance this is. It does, however, link the two traditions by associating women with the appearance tradition.

Luke 24 knows nothing of an appearance to the women. In Luke they go and report to the disciples. We learn from the two disciples on the road to Emmaus that "some of those who were with us went to the tomb and found it just as the women had said, but they did not see him" (Luke 24:24). Thus Luke ties the male disciples into the empty tomb scene. Finally, John 20 has it both ways. After Mary Magdalene finds the tomb empty, Peter and the beloved disciple check it out, and then the risen Jesus appears to Mary.

In summary, why are the data the way they are? The differences among them do not stem from a clumsy fraud or from the various perspectives and better or worse memories of eyewitnesses. Rather, we have suggested, the data as we have them have been shaped by the theological viewpoints of the respective redactors, by the apologetic concerns of early Christian communities, and by the need to tie together literarily the originally independent traditions about women finding the tomb empty and Jesus appearing to male disciples.

Chapter Ten

Why Are There Any Data At All?

We are exploring the origin and meaning of Christian belief in the resurrection of Jesus. Thus far we have ascertained what the relevant data are and explained why, given the discrepancies the data exhibit, the data are the way they are. At this point we can move on to a further question: Why are there any data at all? That is, what happened to give rise to belief in Jesus' resurrection?

The tradition Paul cites in 1 Corinthians 15 gives us one answer. It states flatly of Jesus that "he appeared." Starting with Mark, the gospels offer a second answer as well. When some women found Jesus' tomb empty, a heavenly messenger told them that he had been raised. Since these two traditions originally existed separately we need to consider each in turn.

The Empty Tomb Tradition

We can begin with the empty tomb tradition. Our first step will be to determine more precisely what we are asking about. The earliest version of the tradition that we possess shows up in Mark. As it stands the story has been shaped by the redactor. We have already suggested, for example, that the women's negative and one-sided reaction at the end of the incident results from the redactor's aim of encouraging his community in the face of persecution. Given that explanation, we can remove the way the women react in Mark from what we are presently asking about.

In other words, if Mark has souped up the empty tomb tradition for the purposes of his gospel we are now in the process of stripping his version down in order to arrive at the basic model. Then we shall be in a position to ask why that basic model exists.

To continue, let us recall the motive Mark assigns the women for being up and about so early Sunday morning. They bought spices in order to anoint Jesus' body. But, one can ask, would they really find a spice shop open that early? Furthermore, does the account of Jesus' burial in Mark 15:45-47 leave the impression that anything was left undone? Did Jesus' body still need to be anointed? Finally, a different kind of observation: In that climate, at that time of year, what shape could the women expect the corpse to be in? Would it not be too far gone to be anointed? For reasons such as these it seems likely that the women's motive in Mark's empty tomb story derives from the redactor. It is the redactor's way of stitching the empty tomb tradition onto the passion narrative, and a somewhat clumsy way at that. Perhaps for this reason Matthew omits it.

Finally, the women encounter a youth sitting inside the tomb. The youth's role in the story is to clarify the meaning of what the women discover, and the white robe in which Mark clothes him identifies him as a heavenly messenger. Despite the current rage for angels, if not God, that has swept through some sectors of American popular culture, the introduction of a heavenly messenger as interpreter of an event can be regarded as a literary device not uncommon among biblical authors.

Once we strip down Mark's version of the empty tomb story in this fashion we arrive at an original kernel of the tradition that turns out to be quite similar to what we find in John 20:1. Very early in the morning on the first day of the week Mary Magdalene, alone or with others, visited Jesus' tomb and found it empty. This stripped-down version of the tradition is what we are now asking about. Our question is, why does this tradition exist? What happened to generate it?

Notice first of all that the witnesses to the empty tomb are women. Earlier in our inquiry, when we were looking into the significance of the people with whom Jesus chose to associate, we learned a bit about women's place in first-century Judaism. The situation of women then was very restricted. For one thing, their word was not valued in a court of law. This fact tells in favor of the historical value of the empty tomb tradition. In that culture, if you were making the story up and wanted it to be believed, you would supply better witnesses than women. So if the tradition in fact puts women forward as the witnesses to the empty tomb this is likely to be because those who related the tradition were stuck with an awkward fact. Knowledge of the empty tomb in fact came from women.

Next, imagine the circumstances under which Jesus' disciples first proclaimed his resurrection in Jerusalem. Would their movement ever have gotten off the ground if their preaching could have been falsified? What would have happened if their opponents could have pointed to an obviously full tomb? The existence of the Christian movement at Jerusalem, it would seem, presupposes an empty tomb.

Finally, even those who would have an interest in denying that Jesus' tomb was empty in fact admit it. Of course they also propose their own explanation of why it was empty, as we learned from Matthew 28. Granting that the tomb was empty, those to whom Matthew is responding circulated the story that Jesus' disciples had stolen the body.

For reasons such as these a great number of New Testament scholars hold that the empty tomb tradition exists because basically that is what happened. It is highly probable, historically, that very early in the morning, etcetera.

Call this Position One. There is also, however, a Position Two, diametrically opposite to the position we have just laid out. On this view the empty tomb tradition is a relatively late legend. Why did it come into being? It originated as a graphic vehicle for proclaiming Jesus' resurrection. Those who support this view point out that our earliest data in Paul say nothing about the empty tomb. The tradition first surfaces in the second generation of the Christian movement with the writing of the Gospel of Mark sometime around 70 C.E. Furthermore, when the legend does appear in Mark, the thrilling high point of the scene comes clearly in 16:6 when the youth tells the women: "Do not be alarmed; you are looking for Jesus of Nazareth, who was crucified. He has been raised; he is not here. Look, there is the place they laid him." That is, in Mark the story does in fact serve to proclaim Jesus' resurrection.

Position Two regards the empty tomb tradition as a late legendary invention. This position is bolstered by a historical argument that Jesus' actual tomb was either nonexistent or unknown. This argument, as proposed by Hans Grass (brother, for those who are up on the contemporary German novel, to Günther Grass, author of *The Tin Drum*) and more recently by John Dominic Crossan, begins by reviewing the gospel accounts of Jesus' burial. Each of the gospels tells the story of Jesus' burial in a tomb donated by Joseph of Arimathea. Who was Joseph of Arimathea? According to Mark's account he was "a respected member of the council, who was also himself waiting expectantly for the kingdom of God," and he "went boldly to Pilate and asked for the body of Jesus" (Mark 15:43). In Matthew "there came a rich man from Arimathea, named Joseph, who was also a disciple of Jesus" (Matt 27:57). Luke tells us that "there was a good and righteous man named Joseph, who, though a member of the council, had not agreed to their plan and action. He came from the Jewish town of Arimathea, and was waiting expectantly for the kingdom of God" (Luke 23:50). Finally, according to John, "Joseph of Arimathea, who was a disciple of Jesus, though a secret one because of his fear of the Jews, asked Pilate to let him take away the body of Jesus. . . . Nicodemus, who had at first come to Jesus by night, also came, bringing a mixture of myrrh and aloes, weighing about a hundred pounds" (John 19:38-39).

In the gospels, then, Jesus is buried by Joseph of Arimathea. Joseph starts out in Mark by being a member of the Jerusalem Jewish leadership group, the Sanhedrin, but he is nonetheless a virtuous Jew. In Matthew he also becomes a disciple of Jesus; John presents him similarly, but improves the story by making his discipleship secret and associating him with Nicodemus. On the position we are reviewing, the starting point for the development of the figure of Joseph of Arimathea in the gospels can be found in an item of information provided by Acts 13:27-29. According to that text, "[t]he residents of Jerusalem and their leaders," having gotten Pilate's permission to have Jesus killed, then "took him down from the tree and laid him in a tomb." Thus, on this account, the gospels improve upon Jesus' having been buried by the leaders of the Jews at Jerusalem when they give one of those leaders a name, insure his virtue despite his membership in the Sanhedrin, and even make him a disciple of Jesus, albeit a secret one.

Furthermore, if Joseph is a fictional character what happened to Jesus' corpse? Would the Jewish leadership, a group hostile to him and the instigators of his death, have furnished him with a tomb? Would Jesus not have suffered the common fate of executed criminals, his dead body being dumped over the city wall onto the garbage heap in the valley of Gehenna? In that case there is no empty tomb because there is no tomb at all. (Archeology, however, has provided counterevidence to this line of thought. A tomb has been discovered dating to the time of Jesus whose inhabitant bears the marks of crucifixion. Clearly not all executed criminals were tossed over the wall.) John Dominic Crossan suggests reticence. We must be content to admit that we, like Jesus' disciples, do not know about Jesus' tomb. For Crossan those who cared about Jesus, his disciples, did not have access to information about where his body was, while those who knew, the Roman contingent assigned to execute and dispose of him, did not care.

Asked whether the empty tomb tradition is historically probable, proponents of our Position One answer with a resounding yes. Those who espouse Position Two, however, respond with an equally resounding no. That leaves one further logical possibility: not a firm yes nor yet a clear no, but an answer of maybe, maybe not. We can call this Position Three, and we find one version of this position in Edward Schillebeeckx's monumental *Jesus. An Experiment in Christology* (New York: Seabury, 1979).

Schillebeeckx takes a form-critical approach to the empty tomb narrative. Form critics, we recall, seek to identify the units of oral tradition upon which the gospel writers drew and then proceed to determine the literary genre of each unit and the original setting in which it functioned. With regard to the literary genre of the empty tomb tradition, Schillebeeckx's suggestion is a mouthful. He proposes that the empty tomb tradition started out as what he calls an aetiological cult legend. That is, the original purpose of the empty tomb story was to explain (aetiology) why people were engaging in a religious practice (cult). The practice in question would have been the custom of keeping vigil in Jerusalem at a tomb held to be that of Jesus. If someone were to ask why Jesus' followers were gathering there to sing and pray through the night, the empty tomb story would explain that this is where, very early in the morning, etcetera.

But did it happen? Calling something a legend says nothing one way or the other about its historical status. Some legends are built upon a historical nucleus, others are not. What about the empty tomb?

On the one hand, the tradition goes back to before the destruction of Jerusalem in 70 C.E. It is very old, and it clearly predates the gospel of Mark. This factor certainly counts in favor of the historicity of the story. On this point Schillebeeckx clearly differs from the proponents of Position Two.

On the other hand, not all the tombs in Jerusalem during Jesus' time contained bodies. Some, Schillebeeckx suggests, were built simply as monuments. New Yorkers are familiar with the ornate tomb, located on Riverside Drive, of Ulysses S. Grant, winning general for the Union side in the Civil War and later president. Even if Grant's descendants carry out their threat to move his remains elsewhere, Grant's tomb will remain as a landmark. It will continue to be Grant's tomb even without Grant. Perhaps, Schillebeeckx speculates, the tomb at which Jesus' followers gathered was such a memorial. Given that possibility, the available evidence regarding the empty tomb tradition is not compelling one way or another. In the absence of sufficient evidence to make a firm historical judgment, on historical grounds the best position on the historicity of the empty tomb tradition would become a maybe. Or maybe not.

We have been exploring the question of the origin of the empty tomb tradition. Having stripped down the earliest version of the tradition we possess, Mark 16:1-8, we have discovered in the scholarly literature three quite different positions on its historicity that cover the logical possibilities: yes, no, and maybe. We need to add two footnotes to this discussion.

First, we have seen that proponents of Position One adduce cogent arguments for the historicity of the empty tomb tradition. They do not, however, believe that this amounts to proof for Jesus' resurrection. Even within the gospel narratives the meaning of the empty tomb is unclear until either an angel (synoptics) or Jesus himself (John) intervenes to interpret it.

Mary Magdalene's first reaction (in John) is to wonder where those who removed Jesus' body put it. Of itself an empty tomb is an ambiguous phenomenon. Its real significance only becomes clear in light of belief in Jesus' resurrection. Position One, then, presents the fact of the empty tomb as a sign to be read by people of faith, not as proof to compel that faith.

Second, Positions Two and Three imply a notion that seems somewhat odd the first time you encounter it. At least some of the scholars who argue for Position Two, and certainly Edward Schillebeeckx, are devout, convinced Christians who believe firmly in Jesus' resurrection. They believe that God raised Jesus. They do not, however, regard the empty tomb as an indisputable fact. It follows that, for them at least, belief in Jesus' eschatological transformation does not necessarily entail the disappearance of his corpse from the tomb. From this perspective, belief in Jesus' resurrection would not be affected one way or another if his bones were to be discovered tomorrow.

The Appearances

Whatever position one takes about the origin of the empty tomb tradition, scholars do not propose that the empty tomb tradition accounts for the rise of belief in Jesus' resurrection. Our attention turns, then, to the appearance tradition. Here, in contrast to Mark 16:1-8, we have no need to strip down the earliest data. In 1 Cor 15:3-8 Paul cites a creedal formula that affirms of Jesus that "he appeared/manifested himself (*ōphthē*) to Cephas." As we saw, Paul appends to this a list of other recipients of appearances of the risen Lord: the Twelve, more than five hundred brethren, James, the apostles. Finally, Paul also claims a place for himself among these witnesses to the risen Jesus.

In its earliest form the appearance tradition simply affirms *ōphthē* and gives Peter a priority among recipients of the appearances. We find echoes of that priority throughout the gospel narratives as well: in Mark 16:7 ("But go, tell his disciples and Peter that he is going ahead of you to Galilee. . . ."); in Luke 24:34 ("The Lord has risen indeed, and he has appeared to Simon!"); in John 20:3-10, when the "beloved disciple" arrives first at the tomb but waits for Peter to go in ahead of him; and in John 21:15-19, when the risen Jesus tells Peter three times to feed his flock.

Appealing to the lexicographical data to specify what Paul means when he cites *ōphthē* we found him to be affirming that on the occasions listed the risen Jesus took the initiative in manifesting himself to people who had had a prior involvement with him, people whose experience of this revelatory event included a visual component and who emerged from it with a sense of mission. We also noted that the lexicographical data raise a further question. Given the lack of any neutral witnesses to appearances of the risen Jesus, what objectivity is to be attributed to the visual component of the experience? What kind of "seeing" are we talking about if it is instigated by the risen Jesus and is only experienced by people with prior involvement with Jesus who subsequently devote their lives to promoting his movement?

Two observations can serve to set up our question of the origin of the appearance tradition. First, it seems likely that Jesus' disciples experienced his arrest and execution as a catastrophe. As the Emmaus story in Luke puts it, "[W]e had hoped that he was the one to redeem Israel" (Luke 24:21), but that hope had been dashed. From the disciples' viewpoint Jesus' execution meant the end of his movement. Second, however, there is the fact that Jesus' movement revived. Shortly after Jesus' execution these same disciples are found confidently proclaiming his resurrection.

An obvious question arises from these two facts. What happened to turn the disciples around? Clearly, it can be argued, it would take a powerful experience to account for the radical change in the disciples. Add to that a particular consideration. What the disciples proclaim is precisely Jesus' resurrection. In Judaism, however, resurrection functions within the framework of apocalyptic as a hope for the entire people, or at least for the righteous among them. The Judaism of Jesus' day has no notion of the resurrection of a single individual. Yet while nothing in their background supplied them with this notion, this is precisely what Jesus' disciples proclaim. Where else would they have gotten the idea if they had not in fact encountered him? What the New Testament suggests, namely a real encounter with the risen Jesus, thus serves to explain what turned the disciples around.

Could this encounter have been some sort of vision induced by the disciples' psychological state? Against this idea is the last point we mentioned, the novelty of the idea of the resurrection of a single individual. Nor do the gospel data on the disciples' condition indicate anything other than sober acceptance of Jesus' fate. Nothing indicates the conditions under which something like wish-fulfillment, for example, might produce a vision.

Furthermore, the New Testament itself distinguishes appearances of the risen Lord from subsequent visions. This can be seen in Paul, for example. Paul recounts a mystical experience of rapture (2 Cor 12:1-2), but this is different from the experience that qualified him to add himself as the last link in the list of witnesses to appearances of the risen Jesus.

Finally, it is improbable that the same psychologically induced visionary experience would occur among so many people; Paul lists Peter, the

Twelve, more than five hundred, James, the apostles, and himself. Doubly improbable is a psychological chain reaction that would have extended over several years.

What about the visual component of the experience? On the one hand the seeing in question has unique aspects. It results from an initiative of the risen Jesus and it is restricted to those who have a prior involvement with Jesus and emerge with a sense of mission. This is not simply your ordinary, garden variety seeing of what is simply out there in plain view for anyone to take a look at. On the other hand it is real; it is not to be explained psychologically.

In sum, at the origin of the appearance tradition lies a real encounter with the risen Jesus. That encounter involves an experience of seeing him that, though unique and mysterious, is also real. It can in no way be explained as the result of psychological factors operative on the disciples to produce a vision.

We can label the account of the origin of the appearance tradition that we have just worked out Position One. As with the empty tomb tradition, the scholarly literature yields a Position Two as well. Position Two agrees that the appearance tradition stems from a real encounter or encounters with the risen Jesus. It agrees as well that Paul's *ōphthē* describes that encounter as an occasion on which the recipients of the risen Jesus' self-manifestation underwent an experience with a visual component. It disagrees with Position One regarding the status of that visual component. If the seeing involved is not ordinary, publicly accessible seeing, then Position Two suggests that one should call a spade a spade. One is indeed talking about a vision, and visionary experience is, at least in principle, explicable by the discipline of psychology. One recent proponent of this position, Gerd Luedemann (*The Resurrection of Jesus: History, Experience, Theology* [Minneapolis: Fortress Press, 1994]), suggests that, specifically, the psychology of mourning is a fruitful area to consult.

If both positions agree that the disciples really encountered the risen Jesus and that the encounter included a visual component, they disagree on what is required for the encounter to be real. In Position One if the experience of seeing the risen Jesus were to have a psychological explanation, the encounter would not be real. Psychology would have explained the encounter, and with it the basis of Christian faith, away. Critics of Christianity from Celsus in the second century to D. F. Strauss in the nineteenth, for whom the appearances were mere hallucinations, would have the final word. Any psychological explanation reduces the appearances to something less than a real encounter.

This is not so for Position Two. Take a parallel case, they might suggest. Interview the participants at a Christian liturgy. In their coming together, in their reading the Scriptures, and in their praying over and then eating the bread and drinking the wine, they will say, they encounter Jesus. "Really?" you ask. "Really," they answer.

Concentrate for a moment on the bread and wine. If you run a chemical analysis of them before, then during, then after a liturgy, will that analysis detect any difference? No. Does that invalidate the faith of the liturgical community that that bread and wine have really become Christ's body and blood? Again, no. But the reality of Christ's presence is not subject to verification through an empirical, chemical analysis. The objectivity of the claim that Christ is present and bodied forth in the eucharistic elements differs from the objectivity of statements made on the basis of the empirical natural sciences. The conditions for verifying faith statements are different from the conditions for verifying empirical scientific statements. They are different kinds of statement and hence the objectivity that attaches to each is different. This does not mean that one kind of statement is merely subjective while the other is objective. Both can be objective, both can claim to affirm what is really the case.

Christians believe it to be objectively the case that the risen Jesus can use the gathering of his followers, the proclamation of the Scriptures, and the thanksgiving celebration with bread and wine as media through which to manifest himself. So also, proponents of Position Two might argue, can the risen Jesus have used a psychogenic vision to manifest himself to his disciples.

Positions One and Two differ, ultimately, along the same lines as the two understandings of miracle that we explored earlier differ. For Position One either there is a real encounter with the risen Jesus or the appearance is just a vision. For Position Two a both/and approach prevails. There is a real encounter, mediated by a vision that is, from one angle, probably psychogenic. These differences lie on a philosophical level. They focus on the philosophical issues of what is required for a real encounter and on the nature of objectivity. Position One requires the objectivity of miracles and of appearances of the risen Jesus to be the kind that is certified by the empirical natural sciences. Position Two distinguishes that kind of objectivity from the objectivity that belongs to the truth of faith.

Apart from this sharp philosophical difference Positions One and Two agree that at the origin of the appearance tradition lies a real encounter with the risen Jesus and that *ōphthē* describes that encounter as involving a visual component. There exists as well a Position Three. It also traces the appearance tradition to a real encounter with the risen Jesus, but it does not read *ōphthē* as literally descriptive of that encounter. Once again we can find Position Three laid out in Edward Schillebeeckx's *Jesus. An Experiment in Christology.*

Schillebeeckx notices how heavily the gospel appearance narratives are shot through with the theology of the early Church. He also notices that in those narratives the disciples are conveniently grouped together when the risen Jesus appears to them. This raises a question. Did not the disciples scatter in reaction to the fiasco of Jesus' arrest and execution? In that case, what would have brought them together again?

Taking his lead from the priority accorded Peter in the Easter traditions that we noted above, Schillebeeckx surmises that after Jesus' execution Peter experienced guilt for having let Jesus down. This, however, was only the starting point for a process in which both memory and new experience played a role. Peter remembered, for instance, that the night before he suffered Jesus had not acted as though his impending death meant that his entire ministry had been a waste. Rather, right up until the end, even in the face of impending death, Jesus continued doing what he had been doing all along, celebrating meals with his disciples in anticipation of the coming of the kingdom of God. Peter further remembered the God disclosed in Jesus' ministry, a God who as Abba was pure positivity, infinitely accepting, freeing, and making whole. Jesus' death did not negate the reality of that God. Thus it occurred to Peter that Jesus' death did not necessarily mean that everything was over.

In addition to the insight sparked by memories of Jesus' last evening and of his central theme, Schillebeeckx speculates, Peter also found peace. He experienced forgiveness for having let Jesus down. But dead people have no power to forgive. This forgiveness was an experience of Jesus as not dead but alive in a new way. Thus, through this process of memory and the new experience of forgiveness Peter underwent a conversion. From feeling guilty and thinking that all was at an end he found himself in a new solidarity with Jesus and Jesus' mission.

Seeking out the other disciples, Peter shared his experience with them. After working through their doubts and discussing the matter together they also came to share in Peter's experience. They too found themselves in a new solidarity with a Jesus newly alive and present to them in the gifts of peace and forgiveness. With that shared conversion, the Church was born.

In that case, however, why does the early tradition that Paul cites say *ōphthē*, with its implication of visual experience? Schillebeeckx suggests that this language reflects the usage of Hellenistic Jews in speaking of the conversion of a Gentile to Judaism. Such a Gentile, one might say, "saw the light." Or along the same lines, "The Law/Torah manifested itself to him." Thus, Schillebeeckx says, *ōphthē* reflects a literary device current among Hellenistic Jews to express what happens in a conversion process. In the conversion of Peter and the rest of the disciples, the risen Jesus indeed manifested himself to them. This need not imply a visual experience, whether unique and mysterious or psychogenic.

The earliest witness to appearances of the risen Jesus comes from 1 Cor 15:3-8. We have been asking how that tradition began, what happened to set it off. Prescinding from Reimarus's fraud theory and similar approaches we have surveyed three positions on this question. All agree that at the basis of the appearance tradition, and hence at the origin of Christian belief in the resurrection of Jesus, lies a real encounter with him. They differ, however, on how that encounter occurred. Did Peter and the others really see Jesus, albeit in a unique and mysterious fashion? Or was the visual component of their experience a psychogenic vision? Or, finally, did they encounter him through the medium of a conversion process such as that reconstructed by Schillebeeckx?

The differences among these positions are not differences between Christian faith and the lack of it. All three positions agree on the reality of the encounter with the risen Jesus. Their differences lie on the level of philosophical and historical issues.

This can be seen clearly in the follow-up to the publication of Schillebeeckx's *Jesus*. The book won him a free trip to Rome, but not a very enjoyable one. He was summoned to the Vatican to clarify some of the positions he proposed in his book, including his position on the origin of the appearance tradition that we have just reviewed. The process called for him to dialogue with three examiners. One, a Jesuit professor at the Gregorian University in Rome, had reason to take offense at an unflattering comment in one of Schillebeeckx's footnotes. Another, Albert Descamps, was a biblical scholar, bishop, and rector of the Catholic University of Louvain in Belgium.

Descamps had already published a review of Schillebeeckx's book. In that review (in *Revue Théologique de Louvain* 6 [1975] 213-225) Descamps expressed disagreement with Schillebeeckx's proposal that the origin of the appearance tradition lay simply in a conversion process. In Descamps' opinion, a visionary experience (Position Two) was historically probable. But having registered this disagreement, he hastened to clarify its status. Schillebeeckx's position, he stated, was wholly compatible with Christian faith. The disagreement between them was a matter, not of faith, but of historical judgment.

Apparently Descamps' judgment carried the day in the interview at Rome. Schillebeeckx went home again with no official censure having been imposed. At the same time Descamps' opinion made an impression on him. In his *Interim Report on the Books Jesus and Christ* (New York: Crossroad, 1981), Schillebeeckx responds to many of the critics of the first two volumes in what he projected as a three-volume project. Descamps is one of the few to whose criticism he accedes. By so doing he shows that Positions Two and Three are not incompatible. At the same time he makes clear that the origin of Easter faith lay in a religious experience on the part of Jesus' disciples, a gift of God's grace, not in some brute fact that physically imposed itself upon them.

Chapter Eleven

Sin, Biblically Speaking

Our investigation of the origin and meaning of Christian belief in the resurrection of Jesus has taken us on a lengthy tour. In order to assemble the relevant data we began with 1 Cor 15:3-8, noting how very old the traditions Paul cites in that passage are. We paused to clarify what precisely Paul means by the phrases "he was raised" and "he appeared." Regarding the former, "he was raised," we worked out a notion of eschatological transformation. The latter, "he appeared," opened up a further question about the objectivity of the "seeing" implied by the verb.

Next we moved on to the closing chapters of the four gospels and played reporter. As we encountered first a narrative about the finding of the empty tomb and then appearance narratives, the questions we posed brought into sharp relief the differences among these data. Notably in John's telling of the empty tomb story it is still dark when Mary Magdalene arrives at the tomb. In Matthew, differently from the other three gospels, the stone is not already rolled back when the women arrive. Instead Matthew provides a grand tomb-opening scene, complete with earthquake, angel, and guards. Luke, we found, severely edits the heavenly messenger's speech at the tomb, and Mark provides the women with a strangely one-sided and negative reaction to the good news of the resurrection. Turning to the appearance narratives we noted differences in where the Church-commissioning appearance is located, in what words the risen Jesus uses in commissioning the Church, and in how Luke 24 and John 20 emphasize the risen Jesus' bodiliness.

These differences among the data called for explanation, and we turned to modern biblical scholarship for assistance. Three factors, we hypothesized, shaped the data as they emerged from the oral tradition into the written gospels. Each redactor molds the material to express a particular theological viewpoint. Further, the communities for which the gospels were written were embroiled in controversy, and so there was a need to respond to objections brought against Christian belief by their adversaries. Finally, if the appearance tradition and the empty tomb tradition originally circulated separately and independently from one another, the redactor faced the task of uniting them literarily into a single gospel narrative. Armed with this three-part hypothesis we put it to work, showing that it provides a better explanation of the state of the data than competing hypotheses like Reimarus's fraud theory or the traditional harmonizing approach.

In a third step we moved from the question of why the data are the way they are to the modern historical question: Why are there any data at all? Given the originally independent status of the two traditions that comprise the data, this question bifurcated. What happened to give rise to the empty tomb tradition? And what happened to give rise to the appearance tradition? In each case we found a spectrum of positions in the scholarship on these historical questions and we laid out the contours of each position.

Raised From the Dead—So What?

This brings us to a fourth and final question regarding belief in Jesus' resurrection. Bluntly put, so what? Is Jesus' resurrection simply one of the odd facts that Christians happen to believe and other people do not? Raised from the dead—how strange! Send it in to *Ripley's "Believe It or Not!"* Or is there more to the matter than this? Is it even possible, as Christians claim, that Jesus' resurrection impacts the life of every human being who ever lived?

To get started on this question, we should notice that we are not asking about belief in resurrection in general. We are concerned with belief in the resurrection of Jesus. Now within any narrative each part gets its meaning in the context of the whole. That applies to the story of Jesus. In that story the meaning of Jesus' resurrection does not stand apart from the life he lived and the death he died, even as the meaning of his life does not stand apart from the death in which it issued or from his resurrection. The same holds for his death as well. The relationship among Jesus' life, death, and resurrection is a circular one, each feeding into and drawing its significance from the others to compose a single whole.

In order to honor this principle we need to revise and expand our question. If it is belief in the resurrection of Jesus of Nazareth that we are asking about, our question becomes this: Given the life, death, and resurrection of Jesus, so what?

There is a traditional, one-word Christian answer to this question: salvation. Salvation in turn implies something from which one is saved, namely sin. Traditionally, salvation from sin is the answer to our so-what question, the question of what difference Jesus' life, death, and resurrection make.

The words, however, are one thing, the reality those words intend to communicate another. In today's culture there is a good chance that the words of the traditional answer to our question communicate very little of the reality the traditional answer had in mind. Words like salvation and sin have lost much of their currency. They do not belong to the public discourse of our common living. If we use them at all we probably do so in the private corner of our lives to which our culture relegates religion. Churchgoers may use the language of sin and salvation on Sundays, but it does not show up in the newspapers, in the world of commerce or politics, in foreign affairs—in short, in what counts as the real world.

Our culture tends to reduce religion to a private matter, an individual leisure-time activity for those who like that sort of thing. In this context the meaning of traditional religious language is likely to drift. That language is now likely to communicate a diminished and distorted understanding of what was traditionally meant by the assertion that through Jesus' life, death, and resurrection God has saved the world from sin. What, if anything, do the terms salvation and sin mean to people today? Is salvation just a matter of my "getting to heaven?" Does sin have to do mostly with sexual matters?

Our wager is that, given the situation of religion and religious language in our culture, the terms salvation and sin need to be reconstructed. Traditionally, salvation is the divine solution to sin. Therefore on the premise that the structure of the solution must in some way correspond to the structure of the problem we shall begin with the latter.

We begin with sin. Our reconstruction of the meaning of this term will move through four steps. First, we want to devote this chapter to sketching a biblical understanding of the term. What does the Bible mean when it talks about sin? In the next chapter, once we have obtained a general understanding of the term "sin" from the Bible, we can ask concretely what the reality of sin looks like today. Given the biblical definition, what is the dominant form of that reality in late-twentieth-century North America? Third, we can then ask what tends to happen to religion in a context characterized by that dominant contemporary form of sin. Last, we can also bow in the direction of the traditional categories in which Catholics were taught to think about sin. How do those categories relate to the understanding of sin we have been working out?

Genesis 3

First we want to sketch a biblical understanding of the term sin. While it would be easy to spend an entire semester on the topic we have to settle for a lot less. We can at least examine one biblical text that has had an enormous influence on Western culture. That text is the story of the fall found in Genesis 3.

The text begins with a conversation between "the serpent" and "the woman":

> Now the serpent was more crafty than any other wild animal that the Lord God had made. He said to the woman, "Did God say, 'You shall not eat from any tree in the garden'?" The woman said to the serpent, "We may eat of the fruit of the trees in the garden; but God said, 'You shall not eat of the fruit of the tree that is in the middle of the garden, nor shall you touch it, or you shall die.'" But the serpent said to the woman, "You will not die; for God knows that when you eat of it your eyes will be opened, and you will be like God, knowing good and evil."

The serpent proves persuasive, and the dastardly deed is done:

> So when the woman saw that the tree was good for food, and that it was a delight to the eyes, and that the tree was to be desired to make one wise, she took of its fruit and ate; and she also gave some to her husband, who was with her, and he ate.

There follows the first game ever of hide and seek, as God calls Adam and Eve on the carpet for disobeying.

> Then the eyes of both were opened, and they knew that they were naked; and they sewed fig leaves together and made loincloths for themselves. They heard the sound of the Lord God walking in the garden at the time of the evening breeze, and the man and his wife hid themselves from the presence of the Lord God among the trees of the garden. But the Lord God called to the man, and said to him, "Where are you?" He said, "I heard the sound of you in the garden, and I was afraid, because I was naked; and I hid myself." [God] said, "Who told you that you were naked? Have you eaten from the tree of which I commanded you not to eat?"

Our hero ducks the charge, trying to lay the blame first on God for creating his wife, and then on his wife for giving him the fruit:

> The man said, "The woman whom you gave to be with me, she gave me fruit from the tree, and I ate." Then the Lord God said to the woman, "What is this that you have done?" The woman said, "The serpent tricked me, and I ate."

The consequences follow, first for the serpent:

> The Lord God said to the serpent, "Because you have done this, cursed are you among all animals and among all wild creatures; upon your belly you shall go, and dust you shall eat all the days of your life."

So if your children ask you why snakes don't have legs, Genesis 3 gives you the aetiological legend. Presumably, the story seems to imply, snakes stood upright prior to the encounter with the woman. The curse on the serpent continues:

> "I will put enmity between you and the woman, and between your offspring and hers; he will strike your head, and you will strike his heel."

Next comes the woman's turn:

> To the woman [God] said, "I will greatly increase your pangs in childbearing; in pain you shall bring forth children."

So if the Lamaze instructor talks about "discomfort" during childbirth, don't believe it. Anyone who has been there knows that Genesis 3 has it right—the word is pain! God's address to the woman continues, laying out further disastrous consequences of the fall: "yet your desire shall be for your husband, and he shall rule over you."

Next comes Adam's turn: "And to the man [God] said, "Because you have listened to the voice of your wife . . . ." So what was the original sin? (Clearly this text was written by a man.)

> "Because you have listened to the voice of your wife, and have eaten of the tree about which I commanded you, 'You shall not eat of it,' cursed is the ground because of you; in toil you shall eat of it all the days of your life; thorns and thistles it shall bring forth for you; and you shall eat the plants of the field. By the sweat of your face you shall eat bread until you return to the ground, for out of it you were taken; you are dust, and to dust you shall return."

This text reflects no notion of an afterlife. In Jesus' day it provided the Sadducees with a basis for their position against the Pharisees and other Jews who hoped for resurrection. The story winds down:

> The man named his wife Eve, because she was the mother of all living. And the Lord God made garments of skin for the man and for his wife, and clothed them. Then the Lord God said, "See, the man has become like one of us, knowing good and evil; and now he might reach out his hand and take also from the tree of life, and eat, and live forever"—therefore the Lord God sent him forth from the garden of Eden, to till the ground from which he was taken. [God] drove out the man; and at the east of the garden of Eden [God] placed the cherubim, and a sword flaming and turning to guard the way to the tree of life.

As the novelist Tom Wolfe says, you can't go home again. Here we have been ever since, barred from paradise, eating bread by the sweat of our faces.

In order to get this text to talk to us it will be helpful to know something about its literary and historical context. We are in the book of Genesis, the book of beginnings, the first book of the Bible and the first book as well of that section of the Bible known as the Pentateuch. These five books, made up of Genesis, Exodus, Leviticus, Numbers, and Deuteronomy, are deemed especially significant by the Jews, who refer to them as the "Law" or "Torah."

Who wrote the Pentateuch? Traditionally it was ascribed to Moses himself—even though the Pentateuch includes an account of the death of Moses (Deuteronomy 34). Source critics now regard the five books as we possess them as the final version of a document that underwent three major revisions. Our Pentateuch is like the top layer of an archeological dig. By digging down, archeologists discover layers that mark progressively earlier settlements on the same site. In like fashion the Pentateuch seems to be the final version of an original document that was then revised and expanded three times. The original writer is referred to by the letter J, the first letter in German of the word YHWH, this writer's usual name for God. After the J writer, or Yahwist, came the E writer. So named because he used the general term Elohim to refer to God, the E writer wove into J's document traditions from the northern kingdom. Then came D, the Deuteronomic historian. Finally, in the 6th century B.C.E. the P writer added material that reflects the interests of a priestly group.

Genesis 3, it turns out, belongs to the original version produced by the Yahwist. When did this author, the J writer, operate, and what was he up to? Scholars trace the Yahwist's document to the tenth century B.C.E. Under Kings David and Solomon, Israel's initial experience of monarchy was also in many ways the high point. From having been nomadic herdsfolk, the Israelites now possessed their own land. They were settling down to farming, and because the territory they occupied lay on trade routes they enjoyed as well the further prosperity that mercantile activity brought in. David had conquered Jerusalem, the last stronghold of the Canaanites, whom the Israelites were displacing on the land, and he made it his capital city.

These social, political, and economic shifts set the stage for cultural developments as well. While nomads told their folk tales around the campfire, the Israelites now began producing a written literature. As wandering herders dwelling in tents they had carried their sacred objects from place to place. Now Solomon could embark on an architectural program whose centerpiece was a magnificent temple dedicated to YHWH.

The rise of this prosperous new monarchy also raised a question. Who are we? Every people and every nation draws the sense of identity that binds it together from some story of the founding events that brought it into being. Americans celebrate the Boston Tea Party and Bunker Hill, the French, Bastille Day. So also the new kingdom of Israel experienced a need for a story of the founding events that gave it its place in the universe.

This is where the J writer comes in. In response to this need he drew upon ancient traditions to forge for Israel a religious-national epic. This epic embraced three stages. In the first, most immediate stage the Yahwist reached back as far as Moses and the exodus from Egypt. Who are we? We are what God had in mind when God raised Moses up to lead us out of slavery in Egypt, when God made a covenant with us at Mount Sinai and led us through the desert before giving us possession of this land.

But not all the twelve tribes of Israel had shared the experience of slavery in Egypt. In order to function as the story of all Israel the narrative needed to be expanded. Hence the J writer takes it back a second stage. Each tribe had for its mythic ancestor one of the twelve sons of the patriarch Jacob, and so the Yahwist draws upon these traditions as well. When God raised up Moses and led the people into a land flowing with milk and honey, God was fulfilling what God had had in mind centuries earlier when God first called Abraham to leave his native land and follow where God would lead him. From Abraham came Isaac, then Jacob, and then Jacob's twelve sons, proto-ancestors of the twelve tribes.

Finally, to clinch matters, in a third and final stage the J writer takes the story all the way back to recount how God created the universe in the beginning. This move conspired on a grand scale with the other two to meet the new Israelite kingdom's need for the story that conferred its identity. Who are we? In all modesty, we are what God had in mind when God created the universe, blessed be God!

If the J writer is composing a religious-national epic to ground the identity of the new kingdom, Genesis 3 forms part of a cycle of stories within that epic. The stories in this cycle function as a kind of meditation on the human condition. The cycle includes, after the story of Adam and Eve and the fall, the story of Cain and Abel (Genesis 4), the Great Flood (Genesis 6–8), and the Tower of Babel (Genesis 11).

In order to understand Genesis 3 we need to put it back into the context of this cycle to which it belongs. In that context we can ask three questions. First, what was on the J writer's mind? What aspects of life in the kingdom of Israel was he wrestling with? What dimension of human experience comes to expression in these stories? Second, and very briefly, we can also ask why the J writer expresses his subject matter the way he does. Why does he employ these specific stories? Finally, what sense does he make out of his subject matter? What interpretation of it does he offer? With this third question we shall have arrived at our goal, namely a biblical understanding of the term "sin."

First, then, what aspect of human experience comes to expression in these stories? Recall Adam's response when God calls him on the carpet. "Don't blame me. She made me do it." What we have here is a disruption, a distancing between husband and wife. Where there should be oneness, harmony, mutuality, we find instead alienation. Nor is this simply alienation between a husband and a wife. These are epic-sized, mythic characters. Adam is not just someone named Adam. As his name in Hebrew indicates, he is The Man. Similarly, Eve stands for The Woman. What we have here is an expression of alienation between husband and wife, and more generally between male and female.

In Genesis 3 that alienation receives a specific shape. As part of the fallout from her disobedience Eve is told that Adam shall be her master. Domination of husbands over wives, of men over women, replaces mutuality between them. If human beings were created male and female in the divine image (Gen 1:27), that image is distorted with the loss of equality between them.

Notice also the reason Adam gives for hiding from God. He was afraid and hid, he says, because he was naked. But was he not naked before he ate the forbidden fruit as well? So what is different? What is different is the shame Adam now experiences at exposing his nakedness. Here we find alienation and dehumanization in another form, within the human being. Now the human being experiences alienation from his or her own nature, and in this instance from his or her sexuality. Once again what should be a relationship of oneness and harmony is disrupted and distorted. Human sexuality, a source of energy for appreciating and relating to others, becomes a power within and yet over against Adam. And for Eve it becomes a source of subservience. As the text has it, it is her urge for her husband that renders her submissive to his mastery.

Notice also what happens to the garden. The ground is cursed and resists Adam's effort to wrest a living from the plants of the field. In place of his previous idyllic existence Adam will have to earn his bread by the sweat of his face until he returns to the dirt from which he was taken. Adam and Eve now find themselves alienated from external nature, from an environment that in the wake of their failure to obey God's command has grown hostile to the human.

We are asking what aspect of human experience the J writer is dealing with in the cycle of stories that starts with Genesis 3. Thus far we have noticed how various forms of alienation come to expression in the Adam and Eve story, alienation between husbands and wives, between men and women, between human beings and their own nature (especially their sexuality) and between human beings and external nature, the environment. In each case a relationship of oneness and harmony is disrupted, dimming and distorting the image of God that humans were created to show forth by their full humanity.

The cycle continues into the next generation with the story of Adam and Eve's sons, Cain and Abel. Cain is a farmer, his younger brother Abel a shepherd. When God looks with favor on Abel, who had offered in sacrifice to God one of the best firstlings of his flock, Cain grows resentful. Luring his brother out into a field he attacks and murders him.

Here we have an expression of alienation within the family, between brothers, sibling rivalry grown murderous. Not only that, but once again we are dealing with larger than life characters. Cain is The Farmer; Abel represents The Herdsman. The common good calls for an intelligent division of labor in society. Cooperation among groups with different skills will ensure that the needs of all are met. Instead we find that alienation poisons the system. Specialized groups seek their own good at the expense of others. Suspicion and hostility divide society into antagonistic classes, and violence follows.

The dynamic we have been tracing undergoes one more expansion in the story of the Tower of Babel. In their pride human beings, having discovered how to make bricks, decide to build a single city and, within it, a tower that reaches to the sky. But clustering within a single city contravenes God's command to fill the earth, and so God foils their project by confusing their speech. Whereas hitherto all spoke a single language, they now find themselves unable to communicate. Alienation has now spread out onto the international level, dividing one people from another, nation from nation.

Thus far we have been asking what is on the J writer's mind in this cycle of stories that functions as a meditation on the human condition. The answer that has been emerging is the experience of alienation and dehumanization as a dynamic and expanding process. The stories trace that process as it expands from alienation within individuals, between the sexes, and between human beings and the environment, through alienation between the groups in society to alienation on the level of nations.

To grasp the function of the story of the Great Flood within this cycle we need to move somewhat into our second question, namely, why does the J writer express his material the way he does? Why does he tell these specific stories? Water was an ambiguous phenomenon for desert nomads like Israel's tribes. On the one hand it signified life itself as they traveled from oasis to oasis in search of sweet, drinkable water. On the other hand, the desert was riddled with *wadi*s, gullies that in a sudden storm became raging torrents capable of sweeping herdsfolk and their animals to their death. In addition, the ocean was an awesome and fearsome sight for nomads. Whereas people like the coastal-dwelling Phoenicians might react to the sight of the sea by knocking down trees to build a ship in order to see where they might get to, wandering herders shared none of this enthusiasm. Israelites felt no inclination to become sailors.

In the story of the Great Flood the depravity of humankind leads God to cleanse away the corruption of the earth with forty days and forty nights of rain. The waters rose higher and higher until

> all the high mountains under the whole heaven were covered; the waters swelled above the mountains, covering them fifteen cubits deep. And all flesh died that moved on the earth, birds, domestic animals, wild animals, all swarming creatures that swarm on the earth, and all human beings. . . . Only Noah was left, and those that were with him in the ark (Gen 7:19-23).

The rising flood waters harken back to the first line of Genesis:

> In the beginning when God created the heavens and the earth, the earth was a formless void and darkness covered the face of the deep, while a wind from God swept over the face of the waters (Gen 1:1-2).

Prior to God's creative activity the earth is a watery chaos, dark and desolate, incapable of supporting human life or the network of life on which human life depends. Creation, in this story, consists of God progressively ordering the primal chaos, establishing the conditions necessary for human living.

Against this background the story of the Great Flood shows where the process of alienation and dehumanization set in motion in Genesis 3 heads. It heads toward the undoing of creation, the destruction of the order required for human living, the resurgence of the desolate watery chaos that preceded God's creative ordering activity.

So far we have been suggesting that the J writer's theme is alienation and dehumanization as a dynamic, expanding process. At its extreme that process heads toward the undoing of God's creation, toward a chaos in which life, especially human life, cannot survive. As for the second question, why these particular stories, we have suggested that the Great Flood draws on the symbolism water exercised for nomadic herdsfolk. That is, the material the J writer employs reflects his historical and cultural background.

This latter factor also explains why, in the Adam and Eve story, the serpent is cast in the role of tempter, and why, in the Cain and Abel story, Cain plays the role of bad guy. The ancient world did not neatly distinguish science, technology, philosophy, ethics, and religion. It all came as a package. Hence when Israel began settling down to farming they had to learn about seeds and weather, crop cycles and rainfall. Each year the earth burst forth in spring's fertility, bore summer's crops, wound down in autumn and seemed to die off in winter. Hence in order to insure a successful startup again in springtime you had to do what the gods had done in the beginning, when they first established the cycle. What had the gods done? The sky god had rained down upon the earth goddess, rendering her fertile. Therefore each spring, at the New Year's festival, the king had to assume the sky god's role and engage in sacred intercourse with a temple priestess.

As Israel settled down to farming it was likely to take up the nature religion, based on the cycle of the year, of their predecessors the Canaanites. Israel was likely to bid adieu to YHWH, who had guided them in their wanderings, and take up with other gods. Hence not everything about life in the new monarchy under David and Solomon was a plus. Some hankered for the good old days in the desert when Israel had been footloose and faithful to YHWH.

In this context the serpent, a phallic symbol, alludes to Israel's temptation to take up the nature religion that went with farming. So also Cain, the farmer, is the bad guy while Abel, the herdsman, enjoys YHWH's favor. The stories with which the Yahwist expresses his theme reflect the particular conditions of the day.

Finally, what sense does the J writer make of his theme? What interpretation does he offer of the dynamic, expanding process of alienation and dehumanization that he finds all about him? First of all, this state of affairs is contrary to what God intended for human beings. As contrary to God's will it constitutes sin. What did God intend? According to the story, God placed human beings in a garden, in Paradise. That is what God intended for them. Secondly, how did things get this way? Where did sin come from? It is a human product. By their choices human beings do this to themselves and to each other. Human beings create the dynamic, expanding process of alienation and dehumanization that penetrates individuals, couples, families, classes, and nations. Third, this is what it means to sin against God. People rarely climb the highest mountain in order to shake their fist directly in the Almighty's face. Rather we sin against God by sinning against ourselves, by sinning against our humanity and the universe with which we are vitally and wholly connected. Last, in this sense sin is its own punishment. Alienation really alienates. Dehumanization really dehumanizes. Disrupting the order God provided for our flourishing, we mar and distort the image of God that is our true identity. We make ourselves less than fully human.

Chapter Twelve

Sin Today?

Biblically we can say that the term "sin" points to the reality of a dynamically expanding process of alienation and dehumanization. Calling that reality by the term sin interprets it as contrary to God's will. It is a human product; we sin against God by sinning against our own humanity. In that sense sin is also its own punishment.

This biblical notion of sin is also fairly general and abstract. But while the notion of sin may be abstract, the reality is always concrete. Because it is concrete the reality of sin is also historical. It will take different shapes from age to age. At the time of the J writer, for instance, the Israelites were tempted to abandon YHWH for the fertility gods of Canaan. That is not our precise problem today.

Given the concrete and therefore historical character of the reality of sin we can ask what the dominant form of that reality looks like today. What shape does sin take in late-twentieth-century North America? Our response will lay out an idea that we shall call the "dialectic of enlightenment." Then, once we have worked this out, we can ask further what role religion is assigned in that context. Finally we shall pause to relate all of this to the traditional categories in which sin was spoken of as either original or personal, as mortal or venial.

The Dialectic of Enlightenment

In order to grasp the dominant form of sin today we want to explore a notion called the "dialectic of enlightenment." The analysis that goes into this notion can be found in two sources. On the one hand it can be traced to the work of a Canadian philosopher and theologian named Bernard Lonergan. Many consider Lonergan one of the three or four most important thinkers in the Roman Catholic Church in this century. The analysis we are drawing upon comes from a book of his entitled *Insight: A Study of Human Understanding* (New York: Philosophical Library, 1957). Oddly enough, practically the same analysis can also be found in the work of a couple of maverick Marxist German Jewish thinkers named Max Horkheimer and Theodor Adorno. They belonged to the founding group of the Frankfurt Institute for Social Research, and they co-authored a book whose title, *Dialectic of Enlightenment* (ET New York: Herder and Herder, 1972), we are using to sum up the idea of the contemporary form of sin that we want to explore.

To outline where we are heading, our treatment of this contemporary form of sin will move through two steps. In a first step we want to suggest that the impact of the Enlightenment upon the culture in which we live was to leave a hole in the middle of our cultural doughnut, as it were. In a second move, having suggested what in fact fills that hole, we want to add a series of four ifs, ands, and buts about that situation. That series in turn will give us an answer to our question: what does sin look like in our situation today?

First, then, a major influence upon the culture in which we live was the Enlightenment. This was a broad cultural movement in the eighteenth century that took as its aim the basing of our communal and individual living on reason. This harmless-sounding aim gave the Enlightenment the character of a liberation movement. Politically it meant liberation from all irrational forms of authority. The Enlightenment challenged the idea that heredity—belonging to the right family—qualified someone to rule over other people. This seemed irrational. Politically the Enlightenment was a movement toward democracy, self-government by reasonable people. Religiously, Enlightenment thinkers also sought liberation from what they regarded as the irrational exercise of authority by Christian Churches that, in their perception, told people what to think and forbade them to ask why. Religiously the Enlightenment pushed a so-called natural religion or religion of reason, the worship of a supreme being who rewarded the good, punished evil, and whose existence was self-evident to all rational minds. Reason was to provide the basis for our living.

Second, in the course of the Enlightenment something happened to reason itself. There are different ways of understanding human reason and how it works. The goal of the Enlightenment, to base our living on reason, implied one particular understanding of reason. On that understanding reality itself is rational. There is an order to the universe and human beings have the ability to figure out what this order is and to live accordingly. This was an understanding of reason that emerged in ancient Greece. It was shared by many Christian thinkers of the Middle Ages and it was taken for granted as well by the early Enlightenment thinkers when they sought to substitute reason for religion as the basis of our individual and communal living.

In the course of the Enlightenment this understanding of reason dissolved. David Hume argued that we only really know for sure what our senses tell us. The order of the universe, however, is not something we can perceive with our senses. If we nonetheless cannot help thinking in terms like causality, that is only because our minds are structured that way. Immanuel Kant then concluded that all we ever know is how things appear to us, not how they are in themselves.

In a series of developments from Hume to Kant the older understanding of reason dissolved. What took its place in modern culture was the idea of scientific reason. On this view the human mind is operating the way it should when it follows the procedures of classical empirical natural science. This scientific knowing begins by observing things as they appear to us and it verifies its hypotheses about those things again by observation. Thus knowing begins and ends with sense perception. We can trust what we can observe and measure.

Scientific reason arrived on a wave of success, and its contribution to our world has been stupendous. Our understanding of ourselves and our place in a still evolving universe has advanced in gigantic leaps over the past two centuries. Science has put its understanding to work delivering the means to accomplish feats that formerly were the stuff of fantasy. We can prowl about the ocean floor, we can fly, we can walk on the moon. Our lives have grown longer, and we enjoy an abundance of goods that earlier civilizations could not even imagine. The advance of modern science and the technology it has spawned is one of the great adventures of human achievement.

Notice also the limits within which scientific reason works. It deals with what can be observed and quantified. It tells us how things work and suggests what we can do with that understanding. It gives us facts and possibilities. What science as science rules out, however, is the question of what we should do. Science as science does not indicate which of the many possibilities it creates we should pursue. Should-questions have to do with values, and on the modern understanding of reason values are not a matter of hard, scientific knowledge. Science, in the accepted cultural understanding, is objective, but values, in that understanding, are a subjective matter. Their lack of objectivity means that tolerance becomes the ideal, acceptance of what each individual decides works for himself or herself as long as those choices do not impinge on others and their freedom.

This commonly accepted understanding of science and its objectivity leaves us with a split between fact and value, objectivity and subjectivity, hard knowledge and personal preference. That split, in turn, leaves us with a hole at the center of our cultural doughnut.

In the Middle Ages, for better and for worse, religion filled that center. Religion made the world go round. It provided the sacred canopy that legitimated political, social, and economic living in the world of Christendom. In the sixteenth century, however, the Protestant Reformation split that world into rival factions, each claiming exclusive possession of the sacred canopy, and after the wars of religion decimated Europe, Enlightenment thinkers turned from religion to reason as a shared center for common life. They effectively dislodged religion from that center.

But reason, as we saw, turned into scientific reason, and scientific reason is not up to the job that the Enlightenment wanted reason to take on. Because scientific reason systematically prescinds from questions of value it is too narrow to replace religion at our cultural center as what makes the world go round.

In that case, what has replaced religion at the center of our cultural doughnut? If it is not religion that makes our world go round, and surely not reason, then what does serve that purpose for late-twentieth-century North America?

To answer this we should back up and take account of another factor besides the Enlightenment that has a lot to do with the shape of the modern world. That additional factor is the industrial revolution. Clearly the industrial revolution has had a hand in drastically changing the face of the earth.

As it emerged it seemed that the industrial revolution was working hand in glove with the early Enlightenment as a liberation movement. If, in the Middle Ages, you were born to parents who were serfs on someone's estate no one had to ask you what you were going to be when you grew up. You knew clearly what life lay before you. Like your parents, you also would be a serf—as would your children, and theirs as well. The same principle determined membership in the guilds. How did you get to be a baker, or a smith? Again the answer is heredity. Traces of this system remain in the last names some of us carry. Heredity, in the Middle Ages, was the primary principle of social organization.

That changed with the industrial revolution. Instead of being whatever it was that you were born to, you now took a job. Perhaps you signed a contract. You became an employee. Your employer freely hired you and you freely accepted a job. Thus the industrial revolution, by breaking heredity as the principle of social organization and replacing it with a freely chosen contractual arrangement, worked with the early Enlightenment in promoting liberty. No longer doomed to remain what you were born, you now freely chose your place in society, and you were free to better yourself by advancing economically.

The self-understanding of the industrial revolution took the form of an economic theory classically articulated by Adam Smith. Classic capitalist theory appeals to two factors in its account of a healthy economy. Add free competition to supply and demand and the result will be a self-regulating market. This is the economic theory that provided the self-understanding of the industrial revolution and the social revolution that went with it.

Notice, however, a couple of ifs, ands, and buts about the new freedom to freely contract for one's place and to better oneself. The first is somewhat abstruse, hard to get hold of. Proponents of classical capitalist theory put that theory forth as though it had the same status as the law of gravity, as though it were a sort of natural law of the economy. This claim rested on an error. Whereas the regularities captured in the laws of classical physics are simply a given, that is not true of economic systems. Unlike gravity, economic systems are human products, created by human intelligence and subject to human responsibility. To claim natural necessity for an economic system, to claim that an economic system must work the way the theory postulates, is to remove that system from the sphere of human responsibility. Such a claim endows that system with an authority as irrational as any of the political absolutisms from which the early Enlightenment sought liberation.

Hence our first if, and, and but. To what extent is the new freedom that comes with the industrial revolution a freedom to submit to an economic system that, by its claim to operate by natural necessity, imposes itself with an irrational authority?

This point may be abstruse but its consequences are very concrete. If classical capitalist theory enjoys natural necessity, then the economic sector of society is autonomous, following its own laws. To violate those laws for reasons of morality is to allow extraneous factors to interfere with the natural working of the economy. Hence no restraints are to be placed on competition, and labor has no rights. To suggest otherwise is to contravene the ironclad laws of the economy.

It turns out that to claim natural necessity for Adam Smith's theory is not only a mistake, but it is a mistake that serves the interests of the winners in this economic system. The irrational authority of the system relieves them of the burden of ordinary morality or concern for any good but their own advantage.

A second if, and, or but. The industrial revolution succeeded in increasing human productivity many times over. With that increased productivity has come a flow of goods that makes possible a standard of living unheard of in previous history. The key to this spectacular success is mass production whereby both goods that are produced and the process of producing them are rationalized into standardized, interchangeable parts and standardized, repetitive steps.

The outcome is an enormous gain in efficiency. Imagine what it would be like if when you wanted a car the only way to obtain one would be to have the owner of the local auto shop build it from scratch. Take away standardized components and process, and how long would it take to build a car? How many cars would be on the road? Increased efficiency is obtained by moving the production of goods out of a piecework context and onto an assembly line. This yields an enormous improvement in the material conditions under which we live our lives.

It also suggests a question. The appropriate criterion for evaluating a system of mass production is the mechanical criterion of efficiency. Has the success of this method of production also generated a new image of what it is to be human? In a society that has enjoyed the material benefits of the industrial revolution, has the mechanical criterion of efficiency also become the effective human ideal? Does such a society measure the worth of human beings by their efficiency, efficiency in production, sales, or management? Is efficiency the ideal that determines how human beings are rewarded for the contribution of their labor and establishes their place in society? Does lack of efficiency consign people to a permanent underclass? Does loss of efficiency relegate people to a human junk pile? Has the industrial revolution tended to effectively reduce human beings to the level of mechanical components in a system of production and consumption of material goods?

Third, how have developments in the economic sector affected the political sector? Good government, to put it very generally, is a matter of intelligent and responsible management of both problems and opportunities. Has the model of mass production, with its promise of efficiency, penetrated the process of governing and distorted it? Have problems and opportunities been reduced to standardized stereotypes, for each of which there exists a preset routine of steps to be followed? In place of intelligence and responsibility do we instead get bureaucracy, standardized procedures administered according to the book by faceless, interchangeable bureaucrats?

Furthermore, once the political sector is held accountable for the economic well-being of society, does this introduce a bias into the political sector in favor of the dominant economic powers? Does it become self-evident, as one of President Eisenhower's cabinet officers said many years ago, that "What's good for General Motors is good for the country"? Does this mean that no matter which political party is in office, government tilts toward the interests of the major economic players?

Also with regard to the political sector, has political office become a commodity to be sought by reducing the office-seeker as well to a commodity? In place of proven competence do the dynamics of the advertising industry take over to package candidates, matching them to the expectations uncovered by market research on the electorate?

Third, then, we can ask to what extent the development of mass production within the economic system has extended into the political sector with effects that distort and pervert the process of governing. Does it promote bureaucracy in place of intelligence and responsibility? Does it tilt government toward the interests of the dominant economic powers? Does it reduce the electoral process to the dynamics of an advertising campaign?

Fourth and finally, we can also ask whether there is not a tendency on the part of the economic sector to spread out and rationalize every conceivable aspect of our human living as a commodity in the production of which a profit is to be had. For instance all of us have bodies, and our bodies naturally come in various sizes and shapes. On the other hand there exists an industry that constantly bombards us with images of what stereotyped, standardized bodily shape is acceptable, and so we spend billions of dollars each year doing violence to ourselves in order to make our bodies conform to these images.

Similarly, we are social beings who find our identity in relationship with others. Some relationships become romantic, and some of these relationships find expression in physical intimacy. Under the right circumstances all of this is, as God says in Genesis 1, very good. It also provides the basis for an industry that tells us that interpersonal fulfillment can be guaranteed if one will only purchase certain exotic products and follow certain techniques made available in specialized, not-for-minors literature. Even our most intimate interpersonal relationships, this industry tells us, can be reduced to techniques and instruments that can be mass produced in order to turn a profit.

To take another example, modern means of production allow for the enjoyment of leisure time; no longer is every available minute taken up in providing the material goods necessary for physical survival. At the same time technology has made available a wealth of possibilities for using this leisure time. Television channels broadcast twenty-four hours a day. Compare this with the opportunities available to rural communities a century ago when the arrival of the circus or a traveling theater troupe was more like an annual event. Compared to earlier generations we are blessed with more leisure and greater opportunities for its use.

What determines which shows in fact appear on television? "Sweeps week" only intensifies what goes on all year, the race among networks for ratings. The shows that survive this competition are those that attract the widest possible audience because this audience appeal is the basis on which they can charge advertisers for air time. Hence when one turns on the television in one's leisure time one encounters entertainment geared to attract the largest possible audience. This means that the lowest common denominator, sometimes said to be the eleven-year-old mentality, is functioning as our cultural norm.

We are asking whether we do not experience a tendency on the part of the economic sector of our society to expand into every nook and cranny of our lives. Do we find a tendency to reduce every conceivable aspect of our humanity—for instance, our bodies and how we adorn them, our relationships, our leisure time pursuits—to a standardized, interchangeable stereotype on the basis of which goods can be sold and a profit turned?

To the extent that the answer to this question and to the previous three questions that we raised is yes, to that extent we find concretized the notion of a dynamic, expanding process of alienation and dehumanization. If what has replaced religion at the center of society and culture is an economic system in which profit is the ultimate good, if we are subject to a system that reduces us to our economic significance as producers and consumers, then in those dynamics we find the dominant contemporary form of the reign of sin in late twentieth century North America.

The Enlightenment began as a liberation movement. Dislodging religion from the center of the culture that succeeded Christendom, it failed to establish reason in its place. Neither religion nor reason makes our world go round. What does perform that function, we are suggesting, is an economic system in which profit is the ultimate aim. Left unchecked, that system will claim to operate by natural necessity and thus endow itself with an irrational authority. It will redefine human beings in terms of the mechanical criterion of efficiency, it will pervert the political sector, and it will rationalize every aspect of our human living as a commodity. To the extent that all of this occurs, the Enlightenment, from having begun as a liberation movement, turns into the opposite. This process of beginning as one thing and turning into its opposite is the meaning of the term dialectic. This dialectic of enlightenment, we are suggesting, constitutes the dominant form of sin in our situation today.

The Role of Religion

What happens to religion in a society characterized by the dialectic of enlightenment? What role or function does such a society assign religion? In considering this question we want to draw upon some ideas proposed by a sociologist, Peter Berger.

First we should recall that the United States presented a novelty when it drew up a constitution guaranteeing freedom of worship and forbidding the establishment of an official state religion. Historically religions have tended to be coterminous with national identity. There is no need to ask what religion the ancient Hebrews practiced. In the fourth century

Christianity succeeded paganism as the official religion of the Roman Empire. Even when the Reformation split Christendom, the expectation that religious identity and political allegiance were one held sway. *Cuius regio, eius religio* (whose the region, his the religion) was the principle that gave us Catholic Bavaria but Protestant Prussia, for example.

In this context the United States presented a novelty when it separated church from state. Religion lost its traditional monopoly, as it were. It also lost its traditionally guaranteed constituency. Church membership no longer came automatically with birth in a given geographic area. No longer established by the state, religion became a matter of voluntary association.

In this new situation, where does religion now fit in? First, there is a difference between the United States and a country like France. The French revolution targeted both the monarchy and the monarchy's ally, the Church. Hence the modern French republic underwent an actively anti-religious stage in which the clergy were persecuted and religious orders banned from the country. The American revolution entailed no such religious purge.

In contrast to a country like France, in the United States religion still belongs to our public rhetoric. In this respect we retain vestiges, traces of the old monopoly system. For example, whereas popes anointed emperors, we elect presidents—but at the swearing-in ceremony presidents take their oath on a Bible and in the presence of a representative selection of clergy. Similarly the houses of Congress support chaplains who open their sessions with a prayer and the military commission clergy to serve as officer-chaplains. On our money we proclaim that "In God we trust."

Religion still belongs to our public rhetoric. At this level, however, it tends to be decorative, a vestige of the old monopoly system. The Senate may open with a prayer but then it gets down to its real business, and determining God's holy will for the United States does not often show up on its agenda. Our money may proclaim trust in God but Wall Street seems to operate on other principles.

In the private sector, however, religion continues to thrive. Crassly put, the market for religion is a thriving enterprise in American society. Equally crassly, one may therefore ask what needs generate this market. What are the needs that religion meets?

Two such needs come to mind. First there seems to be a human need to think of oneself as upright, decent, moral. That need, however, can be extraneous to one's work experience. Indeed, it can even be an impediment. After all, the business of business is business. Hence there arises the notion of private virtue, the virtues that characterize a godfearing American. One is faithful to one's spouse. One is responsible in caring for one's family. One keeps one's lawn cut. Notice that these are virtues that pertain to family and neighborhood, to what one does in one's leisure time. They allow one to think of oneself as a good, moral person, even if in the world of work, after all, one has to be realistic. Religion, we might suggest, receives the assignment of fostering this private virtue.

Second, human beings also seem to experience a need to be accepted simply for who they are. This is a need for community. On the other hand the operative criterion in the public sector, in the world of work, is efficiency. Work may also bring with it collaboration and camaraderie, but should one's efficiency slip other dynamics take over. Hence religion receives another assignment, namely to provide people with an experience of community apart from their efficiency and its accomplishments, an experience of being accepted simply and unconditionally.

We are suggesting two needs that contribute to explaining the continued vitality of religion in a society in which religion has become a matter of voluntary association. Religion is not, of course, the only candidate to meet these needs. One may also find community and a sense of moral uprightness by joining a hiking club or any of a variety of other options. But these two needs do seem to constitute the market in which religion competes, and successfully.

In a word we are suggesting that religion tends to be assigned a therapeutic role in our society. Religion is to assist people to meet in the private sector needs that are bypassed or even denied in the public sector, namely a need to identify oneself as morally upright and a need to experience community. Furthermore, to the extent that religion simply accepts this role and allows itself to be defined by it, to that extent religion becomes an agent of sin. It takes on a role of adjusting people to a public sector to which morality is more or less irrelevant, a secondary consideration, and in which people are essentially defined by the mechanical criterion of efficiency. Adjusting people to the kind of society and culture generated by the dialectic of enlightenment, religion becomes part of the problem. It gets co-opted. It becomes, to that extent, an agent of sin.

Traditional Categories

Thus far we have identified sin with a dynamically expanding process of alienation and dehumanization, and we have suggested that the dialectic of Enlightenment may capture the dominant form of that process in our situation. At this point we want to pause to relate this development of the meaning of sin to the traditional categories in which Catholics have been taught to speak of sin. Those categories are four in number. All sin is first of all either original or personal. Original sin is inherited from Adam and

Eve; personal sin is one's own contribution. Personal sin in turn falls into two further categories. One commits a mortal sin when the matter is grave, one knows what one is doing, and one freely does it. A mortal sin deprives one of sanctifying grace. Should one die in this state, one would spend eternity in hell. Venial sin is anything less: either the matter is less grave, one's awareness faulty, or one's consent incomplete. Venial sin sends one to purgatory on the way to heaven.

What is meant by original sin? Where did this doctrine come from and what sense does it make? The doctrine of original sin affirms that there is an objective reality, sin, that is passed on from generation to generation, so that it is true to say that to be born into this world is to be born into a state of sin. The phrase "original sin" itself does not show up in the Bible; the doctrine is a post-biblical development.

The notion of original sin received an impetus in the third century with the growth of the practice of infant baptism. Baptism, which had previously been administered to adults, had always been understood to entail the remission of sins. In the case of infants, however, the question arose: what sin can one so young have committed? In this light a passage from St. Paul stood out which, in the Latin version, spoke of Adam "in whom all sinned" (Rom 5:12).

Next the doctrine of original sin took a further jump in the fifth century when St. Augustine entered into controversy with an Irish monk named Pelagius. Pelagius recommended a severe life of asceticism through which one could hope to gain heaven. His focus was on our obligation to keep the commandments. Prior to his conversion, however, Augustine had experienced his own inability to keep God's commandments. He emphasized the need for God's grace, won for us by Christ's death. On his view Pelagius rendered Christ's coming superfluous; Christ became at best a source of good example. To explain our need for grace Augustine developed further the idea of an inherited sin passed down from Adam. This inheritance left the human race a *massa damnata,* a condemned crowd, of whom only a few could expect to be saved.

Augustine's own history of sexual addiction prior to his conversion led him to associate the transmission of original sin with the sexual intercourse of parents, and Thomas Aquinas systematized this view in the thirteenth century, drawing on the best available science of the day, Aristotelian biology. This was pre-seventeenth century science, science under a metaphysical umbrella. Metaphysically, everything is composed of form and matter. Form is the active principle that makes something to be what it is. Matter is the passive principle that receives and individuates the form, giving you this instance of what the thing is. Moving into biology, in the conception of a human being, form, the active principle, is donated by the father, while matter, the passive principle, is supplied by the mother.

By way of digression, notice two corollaries of this science. First with regard to sexual ethics it follows that while it is natural for the husband to be active in carrying out the marital act the woman ought to be passive. Any activity on her part would be unnatural and hence immoral. Second, if the form makes the thing to be what it is, and if the form is donated by the father, notice what the ideal outcome is. In the ideal the offspring should be male. Females, according to this science, are defective males, born because the father was insufficiently macho or because of some other defect in the process.

With regard to original sin it also follows for St. Thomas that this is a father's gift to his offspring. Hence the importance of the virginal conception of Jesus. Since Jesus was born of a virgin, there is no question of his having been exposed to original sin.

From the thirteenth century we move to the sixteenth and the Council of Trent, at which the doctrine of original sin became a defined dogma of the Catholic Church. In this context the doctrine is actually an optimistic statement. According to the Reformers, Luther and Calvin, original sin left human nature totally depraved and capable of no good. The Catholic version of original sin held us to be, as the song in *West Side Story* has it, merely deprived and not depraved.

This is the background from which the Catholic dogma of original sin emerged. According to that dogma there exists an objective reality, sin. That reality is passed on from generation to generation. To be born into this world is to be born into a state of sin. In addition to the basic dogma there is also the question of how the transmission of original sin takes place. As we saw, Augustine and then Thomas thought of this in biological terms. On the other hand, Thomas' biology is clearly outdated.

If we drop the biological model for understanding the transmission of original sin we can make a fresh start in asking whether the dogma makes any sense. For openers, notice the difference between, on the one hand, a rock or guppy, and, on the other, a baby human. A rock is a rock is a rock. The biography of a rock, even your pet rock, won't be a bestseller. Similarly for a guppy. Its life cycle is fairly tightly predetermined. In contrast to these a human being is very incomplete at birth. In at least one sense our humanity is not a given but a task, something to be achieved in the course of our lifetime. In this sense being human is something you can do better or poorly, more successfully or less successfully.

Second, like it or not, we are very dependent beings from the outset. Recall our brief dip into developmental psychology when we were trying to understand the idea of conversion as transformation on the level of spontaneous felt meaning. We noted that during our first three months there is not a thought in our heads. We are small bundles of needs and affects. But even if we are not thinking, there is being imprinted on us what kind of a universe it is into which we've been pushed and pulled. To the extent that our nurturer does a good job we are learning to trust that it is good to be here, that this universe supports us and cares for us. But nurturers have agendas of their own that get in the way. In the extreme, Mom may be an addict or, as the news of late has made us aware, worse. The point is, to the extent that there is something distorted in the nurturer that is going to have an impact on the infant's development and give that child an agenda of her own to deal with. Psychologists have traced neuroses and psychoses through several generations of a family.

So if there is a sense in which becoming human is a task with which we are born rather than simply a given, the kind of nurturing we receive has a lot to do with our odds of success. Distortions in the nurturer are likely to be imprinted on the infant as well.

The situation into which we are born includes more than the nurturer. For instance each of us is born black, white, red, yellow, or some combination thereof. That is, each of us is qualified by race. And of itself that makes no difference. We are all equally human. But that "of itself" is enormously abstract. Concretely it makes a great deal of difference whether you are born black or white in this country. Whatever your racial background, you are born into a situation shot through with a history of racism. And whether you are born white, black, or whatever, that history will affect how you develop as a human being.

Perhaps this is the point of the dogma of original sin. To be born into this world is not to start off with a *tabula rasa*. To be born into this world is to be born into a situation that is, among other things, shot through with dehumanizing dynamics. Racism is one. Consumerism, we have suggested, is another. Dynamics like these do not simply remain outside us. To the extent that they shape the structures of our society, to the extent that they become part of the assumptions of our culture, they become part of the identity we acquire as we are raised in this society. We internalize them and make them our own.

Original sin designates the dynamics of alienation and dehumanization in so far as they inform the situation into which we are born and into which we are socialized. Insofar as those dynamics are there before us we are not guilty of original sin. But as we in fact internalize the disvalues of our culture and begin acting on them the process continues and spreads. We then become agents of sin. To original sin we begin adding our personal contribution.

The concept of mortal sin recognizes the reality of our responsibility for the person we make ourselves to be. At the limit it is possible for us to render ourselves radically incapable of relating in trust and love to God, others, or ourselves. Perhaps you can think of a character in literature or the movies who seems to have reached this state. Such extreme isolation, in which others are never more than things to be manipulated, would signal the death of our humanity. Venial sin in turn designates the lesser choices that, though falling short of this effect, head us in the same direction.

Chapter Thirteen

Salvation from Sin: The Law of the Cross

Our fourth and final question about the origin and meaning of Christian belief in Jesus' resurrection was "so what?" Because we are asking precisely about Jesus' resurrection and not about resurrection in general we broadened our question to include also the fuller context of his resurrection provided by the life Jesus lived and the death he died. Given the life, death, and resurrection of Jesus, our question then became "so what?"

There is a traditional Christian answer to this question: salvation from sin. It is not clear, however, that the language of that answer any longer communicates what it was intended to convey. Hence we have embarked on a process of reconstruction, attempting to get hold of the reality that the traditional language originally engaged. On the premise that the structure of a problem in some way sets up the structure of its solution, we began with sin. From Genesis 3 we drew a biblical understanding of the term as pointing to the reality of alienation and dehumanization as a dynamic, expanding process. Next, because of the general, abstract character of that definition, we further asked what shape that process takes today. By way of an answer, we explored the notion of the dialectic of enlightenment. Noting how the dynamics of that dialectic can spread out and co-opt even religion, we then paused to ask how the understanding of sin we have been working out relates to the traditional categories whereby sin is either original or personal, and personal sin is either mortal or venial.

With this understanding of sin we are ready to turn from the problem to its solution, salvation. The Christian tradition affirms that through the life, death, and resurrection of Jesus God has provided salvation from sin. To understand what this means and how it works we want to borrow another page from Bernard Lonergan. Besides writing the book *Insight,* which we drew upon in our analysis of the contemporary shape of sin, Lonergan also taught theology for many years at the Gregorian University in Rome. He published his course in christology under the title *De Verbo Incarnato* or, in English, *On the Incarnate Word* (Rome: Pontifical Gregorian University, 1964). The book basically follows the "high, descending" approach to christology typical of textbooks of the period. What interests us at present is the final three theses in which Lonergan takes up the question of how Jesus, the Word incarnate, fulfilled his mission and saved the human race from sin. We are especially interested in Lonergan's final thesis in which he goes beyond the traditional theological treatment of this matter.

Three Theses

Thesis fifteen is the first of the three theses that Lonergan devotes to what is called soteriology, the study of Christ's work as savior (*sōtēr* = savior in Greek). In this thesis Lonergan simply demonstrates that the New Testament in fact teaches that through Jesus' life, death, and resurrection, God has saved the world. According to the New Testament, Christ is the mediator of salvation. To establish his point Lonergan piles up citations showing the various images and concepts through which the New Testament expresses this belief: Christ gave his life as a ransom; he underwent his passion and death on account of sins and on behalf of sinners; as our High Priest he poured forth his blood as a sacrifice; his obedience was meritorious; as risen Lord he exercises power; and he intercedes for us as the eternal priest who stands before God pleading on our behalf. Through this wealth of images and metaphors the New Testament affirms salvation through Jesus' life, death, and resurrection.

Thesis sixteen moves from salvation as a fact affirmed by Scripture to the traditional understanding of that fact. In the eleventh century, in a work entitled *Cur Deus Homo (Why God Became Human),* Anselm of Canterbury had introduced the theory of satisfaction. How does Christ's death save us? For Anselm sin disrupts the order of the universe, the beautiful harmony of all things that constitutes the honor of God, their creator. Furthermore, as an offense against the infinite God sin has an infinite quality to it. Since human beings are the originators of sin, human beings are the ones who ought to restore the order of the universe and, in addition, they should make up to God for their offense against God.

Because of the infinite quality of that offense, however, human beings cannot do this. Hence, Anselm reasons, a God-man is required, who as God can do what as human he ought to do. But what does any human being, even Jesus, have to give to God that he or she does not already owe to God? Only something above and beyond what is already owed God can serve to make satisfaction for the offense of sin.

For Anselm, death is the result of sin. Since Jesus alone of all the human race is sinless, he was not bound to die. Hence what Jesus can offer to God that he does not already owe God is his death, and since Jesus is the God-man his death has the infinite value required to match the infinite weight of sin. In freely offering his life to God, Jesus makes satisfaction for sin.

Thomas Aquinas had refined Anselm's novel theory and integrated it with traditional biblical and patristic views of Jesus' saving death as re-demptive and as a sacrifice. Whereas Anselm had defined satisfaction in terms of offering the one offended something over and above what was al-ready owed, Thomas shifted the accent. For him we satisfy for an offense by offering the one offended something that he or she loves more than they detest the offense. If we apply this to Jesus' death, what makes that death count as satisfaction is, for Thomas, the love and obedience to God that it expresses.

In 1870 the First Vatican Council had been ready to define satisfaction as a dogma of the Church when political events in Italy caused the coun-cil to be suspended indefinitely. In thesis sixteen Lonergan clarifies the meaning of this traditional doctrine. Negatively it does not mean that Jesus' death saves us as payment of the penalty for sin in our place. Neither Anselm nor Thomas, nor the Catholic tradition in general under-stands satisfaction in terms of penal substitution. Nor does the doctrine of satisfaction mean that Jesus' death was a sacrifice that appeased God's wrath. God does not take pleasure in innocent suffering. Rather, a correct understanding of the theory of satisfaction finds its key in an analogy with the sacrament of reconciliation. Through this analogy Jesus' death comes into focus as an expression of his revulsion at sin and love for God—not as an instance of divine child abuse!

In thesis seventeen Lonergan goes beyond scriptural imagery and the traditional theory of satisfaction. Teaching in a Roman seminary, he could assume Christian belief on the part of his audience. Hence if thesis fifteen demonstrated that the New Testament affirms something, Lonergan could expect his audience to accept as true what the New Testament affirms. Thesis fifteen functioned to establish the fact that through Jesus' life, death, and resurrection, God has saved the world from sin. Thesis seven-teen now asks what sense that fact makes. What sense does it make that God would save the world precisely that way rather than some other?

Lonergan's procedure here resembles that of modern science. Scientists recognize that things do not have to be the way they are. The universe might have developed otherwise. But given the universe that has in fact de-veloped, given that things are the way they happen to be, what sense do they make? In more formal terms, what is their immanent intelligibility? For example, it happens to be the case that apples fall from trees. Does the universe absolutely have to be that way? No. But given that it is that way, what sense does it make? With regard to falling objects, the answer is the law of gravity. The law of gravity expresses the immanent intelligibility of a contingent matter of fact.

So, Lonergan asks, given a universe in which God saves through the life, death, and resurrection of Jesus, what sense does that make? What is the immanent intelligibility of that contingent matter of fact?

The Law of the Cross

In response Lonergan proposes something that he calls the law of the cross. The law of the cross, he suggests, expresses the intrinsic intelligibility, the what-sense-it-makes, of the many New Testament affirmations, with their varied imagery, of salvation through Jesus. If the New Testament supplies the fact, the law of the cross supplies the intelligibility of that fact.

In form the law of the cross is a three-step principle of transformation: Something somehow turns into something else. After laying out what those three steps are, we shall need to back up and make sense of them, one after the other. The law of the cross goes as follows:

> First, sin incurs the penalty of death.
> Second, this dying, if accepted out of love, is transformed.
> Third, this transformed dying receives the blessing of new life.

Now what does Lonergan mean? Notice first of all that the language of the law of the cross is close to the language of Scripture. It is poetic and evocative rather than technically precise. For example, in the first step death does not mean simply the moment when the waves go flat on the brain monitor. Besides that physical event there are many situations that we can aptly call situations of death for human beings. Think, for example, of what two people locked in a sincerely hate-filled marriage are doing to themselves and to each other. Death does not seem too strong a term for what they are doing to their humanity.

Again, what is happening to a child born and raised in a neighborhood where jobs are nonexistent, school is irrelevant, and the only signs of success—big cars, flashy clothes, heavy jewelry—come through the market for drugs and sex? What kind of life can that child aspire to? And, literally, what happens to his or her life-expectancy?

Or what sense does it make that in this country a small proportion of the world's population is consuming a large proportion of the world's resources while at the same time other people starve to death? And at the same time our government pays farmers not to grow their crops.

Why do these situations exist? They result from human shortsightedness, self-interest, and stupidity. Sin is a human product. The first step of the law of the cross simply sums up the understanding of sin we have developed thus far. To verify it, you need only to read the newspaper. Turn on the TV. Look in the mirror. Sin incurs the penalty of death. Alienation really alienates, dehumanization really dehumanizes.

Transformed Dying

The second step: This dying, if accepted out of love, is transformed. Before we try to figure out how this second step works, two preliminary comments are in order.

First, this step, the second step in the law of the cross, is where Christianity differs from a number of other classical responses to the problem of evil, the phenomenon of sin. Arnold Toynbee was a historian who wrote on the grand scale, tracing the origin, rise, flourishing, and decline of major civilizations. He labeled one classic response to sin "new soil" movements. The idea behind this response is that the present situation is hopelessly corrupt and messed up. Yet if we can find a number of similar-minded people and get away from here we can make a fresh start and do it right this time, creating a society of justice and peace. This idea was clearly operative in the early years of the United States, which identified itself as the "new world" in contrast to the decadence and corruption of Europe. The same mindset continues to function today. What is the solution to the problem of evil? Start a commune on a farm in upstate New York.

Similar to "new soil" movements is revolutionary anarchism. The analysis of the present as corrupt is the same, but instead of getting away to start over the solution in this case is to remain in place and tear it all down. Make room for a fresh start by first destroying all systems and institutions. This is a modern version of ancient New Year's rituals. We referred to rituals like these when we were working on Genesis 3, and they also survive in our own culture in Mardi Gras celebrations. In these ancient rituals, once a year all institutions are put on hold. This allows society to plunge back into the primal chaos from which the humanly-ordered world emerged. Once a year political authority and family structure take a break while a king of fools presides over orgiastic merrymaking in the streets.

Unlike "new soil" movements or revolutionary anarchism, Christianity does not believe that making a fresh start is the answer. Getting away from it all or pulling it all down will not eradicate original sin. In terms of the biblical story, you cannot go back to the garden. You cannot undo the Fall. But if evil cannot be eradicated, it can be transformed.

A second preliminary comment on this second step of the law of the cross is a warning. Unless this step is understood correctly, one is likely to end up with the nineteenth-century German philosopher Friedrich Nietzsche. Nietzsche despised Christianity as a religion of the weak, a religion for the world's doormats, people who fairly begged to be walked on. In Nietzsche's view Christianity and its talk of love created a community of passive victims who got off on suffering and abuse. This critique finds an echo among feminist authors today. They can point out how Jesus' example has been used to encourage women to accept abuse from their spouses and, more generally, to submerge their personalities in order to meet the demands of childrearing and serve their husbands' needs. Men have used Jesus' example to keep women in their place—the place, that is, that men want them in. If, as we suggested when we were dealing with the dialectic of enlightenment, religion can be coopted by sin, Nietzsche and contemporary feminists alert us to one way in which that perversion of religion has at times operated.

The second step of the law of the cross states that the dying that results from sin, if accepted out of love, is transformed. This step involves three components. First, there is the dying that results from sin. Second, there is the activity that transforms the dying. Finally, there is the transformed dying.

We can clarify this first of all by seeing how it works out in the case of Jesus. Initially his death is one more instance of the first step of the law of the cross. Sin leads to death. During Jesus' ministry, by his parables, by his healings and exorcisms, by his associations, Jesus contradicted the expectations concerning the coming of the kingdom of God entertained by the elite among his fellow Jews. As we saw, he subverted a world in which it was self-evident that some people deserve to enjoy status and wealth to the exclusion of and on the backs of others. Calling that world into question, he evoked hostility from those who enjoyed its benefits and in that hostility they revealed their true colors. They acted out the dehumanization operative in the narrowness and distortion of the worlds they constructed. Acting out the violence embedded in those worlds, they grew murderous. Sin leads to death, and people whose identity is defined by their status and wealth grow violent in defending the system that favors them. Initially, then, Jesus' death results from one more spin of the ever-expanding cycle whereby sin leads to death. Dehumanized people act out their loss of humanity and reveal what lay beneath the facade of status, wealth and respectability by inflicting violence on others.

The story of Jesus' arrest places him in an extreme situation where only two options are available. Option one: Play the game according to the normal rules. Be realistic. Do the practical thing. Meet hostility with hostility, violence with violence. Do whatever it takes to survive. Give the dynamic, expanding process of dehumanization and alienation another spin. Option two: Refuse to be whittled down to that game on those terms. Refuse to continue the spiral of hostility and violence. Set up a dead end for that expanding process even if it costs you your life.

What might motivate Jesus to choose option two? At least two factors come into play. First of all, continuing the spiral of alienation and dehumanization, giving the cycle of sin and death a further spin, was incompatible with responding to ultimate reality as a God who is Abba. Faithfulness to his relationship with the one he called Abba forbade option one. Second, option two would also represent a choice to throw something different into the historical pot. It would demonstrate other possibilities than the same sad, vicious old thing. This is a matter of responsibility for other human beings and for the difference one's life makes to the future course of history. It is a matter of the solidarity of all human beings with one another.

Rather than continue the expanding process of sin, Jesus short circuits it in his own person. Jesus, it seems, accepted dying out of love for the one he called Abba and out of a responsible love for all his fellow human beings. By this active refusal to play the normal game, Jesus' dying was transformed. Instead of being one more instance of the tired tale of sin and death his dying became an affirmation that some things are more important than saving one's skin. His dying became a statement that faithfulness to God and to other human beings is more important even than physical survival. His dying became an act of love for the God he called Abba and for the family into which all human beings are bound.

The law of the cross has a third step: This transformed dying receives the blessing of new life. This third step of the law of the cross is clear in the story of Jesus. As the ancient tradition has it, "he was raised." God rescued Jesus from death and brought him into a closeness to God that heals all that in this life needs healing, that liberates from all that in this life works against our freedom, that fulfills a humanity called to be the image of God. Resurrection means that for Jesus the kingdom has come with eschatological fullness.

Notice, however, the practical twist that resurrection has within the story of Jesus. To put the matter negatively, in that story resurrection does not function first of all to answer the question whether there is life after death. Resurrection is not meant first of all to calm our egos, to reassure us that dying is no big deal, that we can expect to survive and save our skin after all.

Rather, within the story of Jesus resurrection says something about our living here and now. According to the normal standards of this world Jesus was a loser. Love everyone? Claim nothing as your own? Look where it got Jesus. What could be more impractical? After all, he ended up dead. Within the story of Jesus, however, resurrection says that such practicality does not have the final word. Resurrection says that living as Jesus lived, the enormously impractical lifestyle sketched in the Sermon on the Plain, and dying as Jesus died, out of faithfulness to God and to other human beings, is from a God's-eye point of view what human living is all about. Thus within the story of Jesus resurrection says something about our human living here and now, this side of death.

This transformed dying receives the blessing of new life. In a sense you can say that Jesus already received this blessing on the cross. Dying on the cross, Jesus reached the fullness of authentic human living. Accepting the cross, Jesus experienced what it means to love God and to love one's fellow human beings with all one's heart and all one's strength. The Fourth Gospel makes this point when, in sharp contrast to Mark and Matthew, it pictures Jesus' death scene, his being lifted up on the cross, as his exaltation and enthronement. It is precisely on the cross, by his choice to accept the death that sin metes out rather than expanding it, that Jesus transforms that dying into a source of new life.

Given a world characterized by sin, the only way to the fullness of authentic human living is through death to all that makes us unfree and less than whole, to all that makes us less than the image and likeness of God. If the law of the cross is clear in the story of Jesus, Christians believe it is also part of everyone else's story as well. Perhaps two examples can make this clearer.

First, a good number of years ago there was a psychiatrist in New York whose office was in a brownstone on a fashionable street just above Greenwich Village. Among this psychiatrist's patients was one of New York's finest, a policeman. More precisely, this policeman was a lieutenant in the NYPD.

As a lieutenant the policeman made a solid, decent salary. And for a lieutenant in the NYPD that salary was doubled by a system of perks and payoffs. All this allowed the officer a comfortable lifestyle—a nice house out on "the Island", as Long Island is known to New Yorkers, enjoyable family vacations, funds put away for college when the kids got to that age.

So what was our policeman doing visiting a psychiatrist on that street just above the Village? He had a son, a little boy about five or six years old, and that little boy thought his father was God Junior. The uniform probably helped. Often when the lieutenant was shaving in the morning his son would come into the bathroom, lather up, and with his plastic razor join his Dad shaving. It was a guy sort of thing.

What started to happen was that the lieutenant began feeling the difference between what his son saw when they were shaving—his father, the police officer, God Junior—and what he himself saw in the mirror—a cop on the take. That difference did not feel good. How would the boy feel about his father if he really knew? So far, step one: sin leads to death. The lieutenant was taking part in a system that gave him the identity of cop on the take. He was caught up in a dehumanizing and thus sinful dynamic.

So where does the psychiatrist come in? Once the lieutenant became uneasy with what he was doing and with the person he was making of himself, why didn't he just stop, just go clean? Apparently it was not that simple. What would happen to the lifestyle he was providing for his family? Where would he stand with his peers? The system that was making him a cop on the take had enormous power. The moment of insight into the contrast between his son's vision of him and what he saw in the mirror was compelling. But following up on it meant entering a process that felt very much like dying. Freedom from the system and for his own best self meant dying to that in himself which gave the system power over him.

What might motivate him to undergo that dying? Love for his son came into play, as well as, ultimately, a healthy self-love that would not settle for the identity of cop on the take. Through these loves the dying that buying into the system was bringing about was changed. From dying to his own humanity by becoming a cop on the take he began the painful process of dying to those things in himself that gave that system its power over him. Undergoing that second, freely accepted entry into dying expressed and acted out those loves. That transformed process of dying was what brought the lieutenant to the psychiatrist's brownstone office. The outcome? Eventually freedom and a more authentic self, a more genuinely human life. The dying transformed by loving acceptance receives the blessing of new life.

Another example. During the winter on college campuses people scurry from building to building. They do not linger outdoors. With spring, however, things change drastically. On warm days malls become beaches, and you see something that you missed when people were rushing through the cold. Couples emerge. Young men and young women stroll across campus holding hands or arm in arm. Or these days it's also young men and young men, young women and young women—whatever. It's the nineties. Anyway, in spring couples are once again seen on campus, and it's a lovely thing.

Still you need not be a total cynic to suspect that not every one of these couples is engaged in a healthy, growth-producing relationship. At least occasionally someone is the user and someone is the usee. Sin leads to death. Something distorted and dehumanized in a person gives him or her a need to manipulate, or control, or in some fashion use another person, reducing her or him to a thing, an object. Sin leads to death.

Presumably, for the person on the receiving end of this treatment it does not feel good. It hurts. But have you ever noticed how often people in that situation hold on to it as tightly as they can? Often enough, the worse it gets, the tighter they cling.

What is the solution? At least a flash of self-love will enable them to see that they deserve better than this treatment. At least a glimmer of healthy self-love will lead them—where? Into a process that again is very aptly described as dying. While it is going on there is no assurance the sun will ever shine again or the birds ever sing. The only way to escape a dehumanizing relationship is to undergo the process of dying to that in oneself that gave the relationship its power over one. The dying, accepted out of love, is transformed. And eventually, one trusts, that transformed dying will receive the blessing of new life. Some day the sun will shine again after all.

The Christian tradition affirms that God wills all people to be saved and that God gives them the grace they need to be saved. Christians know that they are saved from sin by God's love made available in Jesus' life, death, and resurrection, and that their salvation occurs as they follow Jesus through death to new life. But known or not, God's love also operates in the lives of people who never think in these terms. It operates through their authentic human loves, including the love they owe themselves. That same love calls them also to the fullness of life that lies on the other side of death to sin in its many forms.

Salvation, then, occurs in this world insofar as people live the law of the cross. Through the law of the cross people find freedom and wholeness. Besides the dynamic, expanding process of alienation and dehumanization, a different kind of process enters history as well. In this process God's love in its many forms, sometimes explicitly known as such and sometimes anonymously, draws people to follow Jesus through death to life.

Part III

The Christological Process

Thus far we have dealt with two major questions. First we asked what happens when you bring the data available on Jesus, supplied for the most part by the New Testament, into the particular focus provided by the lens of contemporary historical-critical method. This is not the only lens through which those data can be studied nor is it even ultimately the most important one. Still, in our contemporary cultural context the question of the historical Jesus imposes itself as unavoidable. A culture shaped by historical consciousness cannot refrain from asking whether and how events recounted in ancient documents "really happened."

Such a culture has lost what Paul Ricoeur identified as the "first naiveté." If the displacement of that relationship of unproblematic openness to the world of the Bible is experienced by some as a crisis, however, it is also an opportunity. For one thing historians are learning the importance of whose lens is brought to bear on the data yielded by the past. As we shall see, the results of historical-Jesus research provide an important resource for several major currents of contemporary theology.

From the question of the historical Jesus we turned our attention to the closing scenes of the story of Jesus, his death and resurrection. Immersing ourselves in the New Testament data, we have tried to grasp how, according to the account offered by contemporary biblical scholarship, the relevant texts were shaped and formed, and why they came into existence at all. Having probed the origin and development of Christian belief in the resurrection of Jesus, we also raised the pragmatic question "so what?" This question opened onto a very broad vista as we probed what it means to live in a world in which, although sin is a powerful and pervasive reality, God communicates through Jesus the grace that enables people to resist and overcome the death-dealing dynamics of sin.

Our questions thus far have concentrated first on the historical Jesus and then on the origin and meaning of belief in the resurrection of Jesus. By pursuing these two questions we have in a way recapitulated the experience of the first Christian communities. Whichever proposal you accept regarding the origin of belief in the resurrection of Jesus, how the Easter experience happened, the earliest Christians believed themselves to be once again in solidarity with a Jesus they experienced as alive and present to them in new ways. That presence and that solidarity imposed a new task on them.

During his lifetime and now in a new way after his resurrection these Christians found that in their encounter with Jesus they came to a felt grasp of what ultimate reality was like and what human living was about. Ultimate reality was indeed a mystery that could be addressed as Abba, a transcendent mystery whose lived closeness meant healing, liberation, transformation and fulfillment. Through Jesus some of his fellow Jews came to experience the lived closeness of God as Abba, and their conversion or *metanoia* set them on the path of a lifestyle of the sort we saw sketched in Luke's Sermon on the Plain. The love of God poured forth through Jesus empowered people to move in the direction of loving everyone, even those who would ordinarily be considered enemies. It began to free them to claim nothing for themselves but instead to use all they were and had to meet the needs of others. They could make a start at forgiving everyone everything while judging no one but themselves.

This vision of God and human living in response to God had come to Jesus' followers through the impact of his person and activity. After his execution, however, Jesus was no longer accessible in the same manner. During his lifetime he had communicated the values he embodied by preaching about the nearness of the kingdom, by telling parables, and so forth. Now, however, Jesus' followers had a new task. In order to communicate Jesus' impact to others, since he was no longer accessible as he had been, they had to get Jesus into words both for themselves and for others.

Through Jesus they had encountered ultimate reality and discovered God's solution to the problem of evil. Now they had to find the words with which to evoke Jesus' revelatory and redemptive significance. This process of discerning, articulating, and communicating Jesus' impact is what we are calling the christological process.

We shall explore the christological process first in its beginnings, the formative period of the New Testament. As we shall see, the task of this initial period was to tell the story, to create symbolic narratives capable of evoking Jesus' religious significance.

It turns out, however, that the narratives that Christians forged raised further questions regarding Jesus' relationship to the one he had called Abba. Those questions set in motion a process of trial end error that establishes the context in which, in a further chapter, we shall revisit the classical dogmas from which the "high, descending" approach to christology drew its content.

Finally, however, the christological process is unfinished and open-ended. It will need to be performed anew in each generation for as long as people continue to discover in Jesus the meaning of ultimate reality and what human living is about. Hence in a final chapter we shall survey four major issues that constitute the cutting edge along which christology is moving forward at present.

Chapter Fourteen

Telling the Story

The Need for Story

At the outset of the Christian movement Jesus' followers faced the christological task. They had to get Jesus into words. To understand their task somewhat better, think of a couple who have been happily married for a long time. Clearly they know each other very well. Now sit that couple down, give them some writing materials, and ask them to communicate in writing who their spouse is. They are being asked to move from their lived knowledge of who their spouse is, the meaning that their spouse has come to embody for them, to a written expression that will communicate that lived meaning to others. From the meaning that their spouse embodies or incarnates they have to move to its articulation in words.

Now how might our hypothetical married couple proceed? Each might have come up with a lengthy list of facts about the other: date and place of birth, parents, siblings, schools, occupation, etcetera. Memory, however, is a notoriously faulty faculty, and so any list like that would require verification—and, no doubt, correction—by comparison with such relevant documents as birth certificates, diplomas, correspondence, and so on.

But even a correct set of facts would fail to meet the assignment. A list of facts would wholly fail to communicate who this person was in the experience of the other spouse, what his or her personal reality was, what impact he or she made.

Instead, to fulfill the assignment our spouses would have to begin telling stories about each other. They would want to tell when and how they met, what first impression the other made, what their early dates were like and how their courtship went. Stories about their wedding and honeymoon, about what it was like when the children came and about the ups and downs of raising them—all this would be needed to meet the task. Not a set of facts, no matter how accurate, but only narratives would do the trick.

And in this regard it becomes less important that memory is so notoriously faulty because the point of the narrative would not be to convey accurate information but to capture the reality of one spouse for the other. By that criterion even a story wildly inaccurate in its factual details might very well be true. It might be true as an answer to the question originally posed, capable of evoking the significance one spouse had come to have for the other.

So far we have identified a need on the part of early Christians that generated the christological process and we are suggesting the kind of material that would meet that need. The lived impact of Jesus, the meanings and values he incarnated and embodied, would be captured and communicated first of all in stories, narratives that expressed what he came to mean to those who followed him.

Further, the questions to which they found answers in their experience of Jesus were the big questions—what is the character of ultimate reality, what is the purpose of human living? The scope of these questions renders them religious in character no matter what answer one provides to them. This fact in turn qualifies the kinds of narratives that were needed at the outset of the christological process. The primary language of religion is symbol, a meaning-laden image that can integrate heart and head, affectivity and intellect in effectively orienting us to the transcendent mystery to which the word "God" points. Hence the need was for symbolic narratives that would evoke the meaning of Jesus as religious. Another word for a symbolic narrative is myth—not in the sense of something made-up and untrue but, technically and precisely, in the sense of an extended symbolic narrative.

In order to set the christological process in motion the early Christian communities needed narratives, and since Jesus' significance to them was religious in nature they needed symbolic narratives, or myth. One final consideration needs to enter into our account of the genesis of the christological process. Both Jesus and his first followers were Jews. This means that his followers already had a context for making sense of him. They did not have to invent their symbols out of whole cloth. Their Jewish religious heritage provided a basic story line within which to make sense of Jesus as well as a wealthy fund of symbols with which to evoke his significance. At the same time, of course, that heritage would itself be redefined in terms of the one whose meaning it now conveyed. This becomes clear when we examine three very early patterns through which Christians worked out Jesus' significance.

Three Early Patterns

Parousia Christology

A first pattern drew upon Jewish apocalyptic thinking to make sense of Jesus. If Jesus had suffered and died, this was the beginning of the final tribulations that marked the nearness of the end-time. Jesus himself was presently with God, but only for a very short period of time. His second coming, or parousia, was imminent. Indeed, in his very first letter Paul had to assure Christians at Thessalonica that those in the community who died before Jesus' return would not therefore miss out.

> For the Lord himself, with a cry of command, with the archangel's call and with the sound of God's trumpet, will descend from heaven, and the dead in Christ will rise first. Then we who are alive, who are left, will be caught up in the clouds together with them to meet the Lord in the air (1 Thess 4:16-17).

Those still alive would be snatched up, while the dead would be raised.

Upon his return Jesus would be Messiah as well as final judge; by virtue of the latter function he was called "Son of Man," a title drawn from the apocalyptic imagery of the book of Daniel, composed about a century and a half before the time of Jesus. That book pictures Israel's enemies as beasts whose fate is sealed in the court of heaven. In that court

> thrones were set in place,
>   and an Ancient One took his throne,
> his clothing was white as snow,
>   and the hair of his head like pure wool;
> his throne was fiery flames,
>   and its wheels were burning fire (Dan 7:9).

Perhaps this text is the basis for the common image of God as a white-haired old man. As the scene continues, we see

> one like a human being [Aramaic "son of man"]
>   coming with the clouds of heaven.
> And he came to the Ancient One
>   and was presented before him.
> To him was given dominion and glory and kingship,
>   that all peoples, nations, and languages should serve him.
> His dominion is an everlasting dominion
>   that shall not pass away,
>   and his kingship is one that shall never be destroyed (Dan 7: 13-14).

Whomever the author of Daniel had in mind, Christians had no doubt that Jesus was the "one like a son of man," and they looked forward eagerly to the time when, "coming with the clouds," he would establish his everlasting kingship. These apocalyptic-minded followers of Jesus originally prayed in Aramaic, Jesus' native tongue as well, and the New Testament preserves their prayer in that language: "*Marana tha*—Our Lord, come!" (1 Cor 16:22).

Death and Resurrection Christology

A second very early pattern focused on Jesus' death and resurrection. We have already seen one very early witness to this pattern in the tradition Paul cites when, in his first letter to the Corinthians, he reminds them of the gospel he preached among them:

> For I handed on to you as of first importance what I in turn had received: that Christ died for our sins in accordance with the scriptures, and that he was buried, and that he was raised on the third day in accordance with the scriptures, and that he appeared to Cephas, then to the Twelve (1 Cor 15:3-5).

Writing later to the Christian community at Rome, Paul again refers to the basic message that defined his role as apostle, namely

> the gospel concerning his [God's] Son, who was descended from David according to the flesh and was declared to be Son of God with power according to the spirit of holiness by resurrection from the dead, Jesus Christ our Lord (Rom 1:3-4).

In another of his letters Paul quotes an ancient hymn that somewhat amplifies this death/resurrection pattern. Urging the Christians at Philippi to "let the same mind be in you that was in Christ Jesus," he proceeds to cite a hymn to explain what that attitude is. The hymn praises Christ Jesus

> who, though he was in the form of God,
> did not regard equality with God
> as something to be exploited,
> but emptied himself,
> taking the form of a slave,
> being born in human likeness.
> And being found in human form,
> he humbled himself
> and became obedient to the point of death,
> even death on a cross.
> Therefore God also highly exalted him
> and gave him the name
> that is above every name,
> so that at the name of Jesus
> every knee should bend,

> in heaven and on earth and under the earth,
> and every tongue should confess
> that Jesus Christ is Lord,
> to the glory of God the Father (Phil 2:5-11).

This hymn makes sense of Jesus in the context of the story of Adam, the first human being. If Adam, as we saw in Genesis 3, having been created in the image and likeness of God, did indeed think that being equal to God was something to be grasped for, Jesus, although he was in the form of God, did not. Where Adam disobeyed, Jesus obeyed even unto death and, Paul adds, death on a cross. God then rewarded Jesus' faithfulness by exalting him.

Notice how God rewarded Jesus. He gave him "the name that is above every name" so that "every tongue should confess that Jesus Christ is Lord." We saw the Aramaic version of Lord, *"Mar,"* in the prayer of the community whose parousia christology we just reviewed. There it carried the weight of their images of Jesus as Messiah-designate and coming eschatological judge. Even during his lifetime it is likely that Jesus was addressed as *"Mar,"* though with less weighty connotations. In that context it functioned as the simple title of respect due a teacher—more like "Mister" Jesus, or "Sir."

Now, however, we have moved from Aramaic to Greek, and so from *Mar* to *Kyrios*. It happens that *Kyrios* was already a familiar title to those Jews who read their Scriptures in Greek, in the Septuagint version. Where the Hebrew Scriptures read YHWH, the Greek paraphrased the sacred name as *Kyrios*.

In the hymn Paul is quoting, Jesus himself is addressed by the title these Greek-speaking Jewish Christians have been using for God. The hymn indicates that this is not simply a linguistic accident but quite deliberate. As reward for his faithfulness God has bestowed on Jesus God's own name, Lord, and Jesus is to be honored accordingly.

Wisdom christology

A third early Christian pattern draws on Israel's Wisdom literature as a resource for making sense of Jesus. This literature comprises five books, namely Proverbs, Job, Ecclesiastes (Qoheleth), Sirach, and Wisdom of Solomon. While Catholics and Orthodox Christians count all these books as part of the Bible, Protestants do not include Sirach and Wisdom. This difference among Christians reflects the difference between the Septuagint, a Greek version of Israel's Scriptures in use at the time of Jesus and the early Church, and a list of the books of the Hebrew Bible that was drawn up by Jews toward the end of the first century and attained official status. That list reduced the forty-six books found in the Septuagint to thirty-nine, and Sirach and Wisdom were among the books that got dropped.

As a whole the Wisdom literature centers on the practical question of how to live properly in a world created and ordered by God. The books may reflect the milieu of the school at the royal court in Jerusalem as well as ancient tribal and family lore. Much of their material is similar to what can be found in Egyptian, Mesopotamian, and Canaanite texts as well and is likely to have been borrowed and adapted from these neighboring cultures.

In the course of reflecting on how the course of nature and history expresses the divine wisdom from which all things flow, the composers of this literature at points personified God's wisdom, portraying it as though it were a figure distinct from God. This occurs, for instance in chapter 1 of Proverbs, where Lady Wisdom laughs at those who ignore her at their peril. In chapter 8 of Proverbs she recalls how, before God created the universe, God poured her forth, so that she was present when God established the heavens and set limits to the sea. In chapter 24 of Sirach she recounts how, having made her way through the heavens and the abyss, she took up her dwelling with Israel where, indeed, she is identical with the Torah. Finally, in chapters 7–9 of Wisdom she is the shining forth of God's light; she shares God's throne and, in chapter 10, shows herself as savior of the just, God's holy people.

If the author of Sirach could identify the divine wisdom by which God ordered the universe and human living with the Torah, Christians found God's wisdom in Jesus, and so Israel's wisdom literature readily lent itself to the task of articulating Jesus' impact and significance. Thus Paul could write to the Corinthians, ". . . we proclaim Christ crucified, a stumbling block to Jews and foolishness to Gentiles, but to those who are the called, both Jews and Greeks, Christ the power of God and the wisdom of God" (1 Cor 1:23-24).

An ancient hymn cited in the letter to the Colossians, whose authorship is debated (some scholars believe Paul composed it, others a later author), clearly transfers to Jesus the role attributed to Lady Wisdom. The first stanza relates Christ to creation:

> He is the image of the invisible God, the firstborn of all creation; for in him all things in heaven and on earth were created, things visible and invisible, whether thrones or dominions or rulers or powers—all things have been created through him and for him. He himself is before all things, and in him all things hold together. He is the head of the body, the church; . . . (Col 1:15-18a).

A second stanza moves from Christ's cosmic role in creation to his work of reconciliation and redemption:

> he is the beginning, the firstborn from the dead, so that he might come to have first place in everything. For in him all the fullness of God was pleased to dwell, and through him God was pleased to reconcile to himself all things, whether on earth or in heaven, by making peace through the blood of his cross (Col 1:18b-20).

Through this imagery drawn from Israel's reflection on Lady Wisdom, Christians were enabled to express their conviction that in Jesus they had encountered nothing less than the divine wisdom who had established the universe and set its goal.

This wisdom christology is very early. Already the poetry of this early christology carries the themes of preexistence (Jesus' being with God prior to his earthly existence among us) and agency of creation that characterize a high, descending approach to christology. Against this background, the prologue to the Gospel of John will represent no great novelty.

Four Gospels

If, as these three patterns indicate, diversity characterized the earliest Christian communities, that continued to be the case as, with the passage of time, written Christian literature emerged. The earliest gospel, Mark, weaves an apocalyptic tale of the wonderworking Son of God. In its New Testament usage this title is innocent of metaphysical connotations of strict divinity. In the Hebrew Scriptures it had imaged Israel's sense of divine election as a people; Israel as a whole was Son of God. The title designated as well specially commissioned individuals like kings and prophets. In a text we saw above, Romans 1:3-4, Paul could confess that Jesus had been established Son of God at the resurrection insofar as it was then, by pouring forth the spirit of holiness, that like the kings of old Jesus formed his disciples into a people, a new Israel. Thus Mark illustrates how titles like Son of God or Messiah that first referred to Jesus at the second coming or in his risen state came in the gospels to be retrojected onto his earthly career.

Matthew, though literarily dependent on Mark, tells quite a different story. If none in Israel surpassed Moses in authority and closeness to God, Matthew presents Jesus as the new Moses who on the mountain proclaims the new Law and who, again on a mountain, commissions a new and universal Israel with which he will abide until the end of time.

Unlike Matthew, Luke sets Jesus' great sermon on a plain, not a mountain, for in his symbolism the mountain is the place of withdrawal for prayer. And unlike Matthew whose community is steeped in Jewish tradition, Luke needs to remind his community of their Jewish roots, and so he plots his gospel as a steady progress up to Jerusalem, the sacred city of the Jews in which the Church is founded and from which, in the Acts of the Apostles, salvation spreads to the ends of the earth.

Mark, Matthew, and Luke provide variants on the synoptic tradition. John, the last of the gospels, emerges from a complicated process representing an independent tradition, and it composes a unique figure of Jesus. Taking the wisdom tradition a decisive step forward, John presents a Jesus in whom the divine Word, with God in the beginning, has become incarnate, a Jesus whose "I am" sayings echo YHWH's self-expression in the Hebrew Scriptures, a Jesus whose self-manifestation in his risen state evokes Thomas' "My Lord and My God."

Two Infancy Narratives

We noted above that, in a sense, New Testament christology developed backwards. Titles like Messiah and Son of God were first used to characterize Jesus as he would be when he came again at the parousia. Very soon he was also recognized as already functioning as Messiah in his present, exalted state; established as Son of God at the resurrection, he is pouring forth the spirit of holiness that joins his disciples together as a people. Mark's gospel takes a next step when Jesus is declared Son of God by a voice from heaven at his baptism and when he is acknowledged as such again by a Roman soldier at the cross. In the gospels the titles first used to express the identity Jesus would exercise at the second coming come into play to illumine who he already is throughout his public ministry.

Two of the gospels, Matthew and Luke, carry this process a step farther when they preface their narratives of Jesus' ministry with accounts of his conception, birth, infancy, and youth (Matthew 1–2, Luke 1–2). On these accounts it is clear that Jesus is Son of God from the first moment of his human existence. In them the manner in which Jesus is conceived is marvelous. He is conceived of a virgin, without a human father.

As we saw was the case with Jesus' passion, these infancy narratives aim to show that the events they recount took place according to the Scriptures. Raymond E. Brown has written a magisterial study of these narratives, *The Birth of the Messiah* (revised edition Garden City, New York: Doubleday, 1993), that shows how, as gospel accounts, they are shaped by factors whose impact we studied at length in the Easter narratives: each reflects the theological viewpoint of its redactor and apologetic concerns come into play as well.

The two accounts agree on numerous points. Jesus is conceived by the power of the Holy Spirit before his parents, Mary and Joseph, have come together as man and wife. An angel announces his forthcoming birth and what his name will be. His father, Joseph, is a descendant of King David, and the birth occurs in Bethlehem though Jesus will grow up in Nazareth.

The existence of these common points indicates that Matthew and Luke are working with traditional material that predates their gospels. Each of them develops this material in very independent fashion, however. Matthew supplies Jesus with a genealogy that relates him to both David and Abraham. If Matthew's opponents objected to the idea of a Messiah from Galilee this lineage from King David, as well as birth in David's town, would counter their objection. If, further, Matthew has a vision of salvation passing from the Jews to the Gentiles, lineage from Abraham, in whom it was prophesied that all nations would be blessed, would serve to underpin that vision. The tale that Matthew tells sets the infant Jesus forth as the new Moses, whose birth is attended by a slaughter of innocents at the hands of a wicked ruler, and as the new Israel, exiled in Egypt. Like the patriarch Joseph whose career in Egypt was illumined by dreams, Jesus' father Joseph learns in dreams to accept his wife-to-be's child and to seek shelter for his family in Egypt. In Matthew Jesus' beginnings foreshadow his end as both the ruler and the chief priests seek the infant's death. In contrast to these leaders of the Jews it is the Gentile Magi who, following the guidance of a star, recognize the infant and pay him royal homage.

Luke's infancy narrative establishes the overall theme of the gospel that salvation is from the Jews. Absent is the conflict with Jewish leaders that figures so prominently in Matthew. Rather, in Luke figures like Zechariah and Elizabeth, the parents of John the Baptist whom Luke models on Abraham and Sarah, Simeon and Anna, and Mary herself are all pious Jews who welcome the new thing that God has wrought in bringing John the Baptist and Jesus onto the scene. Luke anticipates the themes of the Sermon on the Plain when he has the good news of Jesus' birth announced by an angel to lowly shepherds. This ties in with Mary's prayer, the Magnificat, in which she praises God for the coming of salvation by which the ordinary world in which the mighty rule and the wealthy feast is subverted.

"My Lord and My God"

For Matthew and Luke the story of Jesus' virginal conception demonstrates that, from the first moment of his human existence, Jesus is Son of God, Emmanuel, God-with-us. John's gospel, we have seen, completes the backward extension of New Testament christology. The prologue reaches into eternity to establish a framework for the story of Jesus:

> In the beginning was the Word,
> and the Word was with God,
> and the Word was God" (John 1:1).

It goes on to affirm that the Word became incarnate:

> And the Word became flesh
> and lived among us,
> and we have seen his glory,
> the glory as of a father's only son,
> full of grace and truth (John 1:14).

The same gospel tells the story of doubting Thomas who, when confronted by the risen Jesus, exclaims "My Lord and my God" (John 20:28). Besides these two texts from the Fourth Gospel, one more New Testament passage explicitly speaks of Jesus as God. The letter to the Hebrews cites a psalm to have God say "of the Son . . . 'Your throne, O God, is forever and ever'" (Heb 1:8).

In a way these three texts represent a startling development. Jesus and his first followers were Jews. Within the Roman Empire Jews were regarded as odd and stubborn for clinging to the notion that there was only one God. Daily they prayed the Shema:

> Hear, O Israel: The Lord is our God, the Lord alone. You shall love the Lord your God with all your heart, and with all your soul, and with all your might (Deut 6:4-5).

Given this fervent Jewish monotheism it seems strange that Jesus' followers could come to confess him as divine.

Yet we have also seen that this was no late and erratic development among Christians. Rather these texts bring to culmination a process that we have seen going forth from the earliest christological patterns. In the parousia christology Jesus was expected to exercise upon his return the office of judge, a divine prerogative. In the death/resurrection christology he is pouring forth the spirit of holiness, a gift that texts in the Hebrew Scriptures expected from God in the last days. Again we traced somewhat the development of the title Lord to a point where, in the hymn in Philippians, God has given Jesus God's own name and he is to be honored accordingly. We also saw that John's prologue, while it substitutes God's Word for Lady Wisdom, continues a wisdom pattern that emerged very early among Jesus' followers.

In time the twenty-seven documents eventually canonized as the New Testament took shape. Scattered among them were the elements of a symbolic narrative extending from God's eternity with the Word before creation to the second coming of the Christ and the eternal kingdom it would inaugurate. The hymns preserved in this literature suggest that in liturgical ritual Christians raised their hearts to God and to the central figure of the story of God's creative and redemptive activity, Jesus. This Jesus, memories of whose earthly ministry and fate they shared, they found themselves imaging as sharing God's royal prerogatives, exercising God's functions, bearing God's name. If they followed their Jewish heritage in drawing a sharp line between the transcendent God and all that God created they found themselves imaginatively locating the man Jesus, now raised from the dead, on the other side of that line.

The New Testament provides evidence that in their liturgical practice and its symbolic narrative Christians were broadening the notion of God to include not only the one to whom Jesus prayed but also, somehow, Jesus himself. As Pliny the Younger, a pagan author writing around 111 C.E., would note, these Christians "sing a hymn to Christ as to a god." Thinking out coherently what they were doing was, however, a different matter, and this was a task that the New Testament bequeathed to subsequent generations. To the process of trial and error upon which they embarked we turn next.

Chapter Fifteen

Classical Dogma

Three late New Testament passages refer to Jesus as God. By the close of the New Testament period it was the custom of Christians to sing hymns to Christ as though to God. Doing this, however, is one thing. Thinking out what one is doing is another. The latter task occupied Christian thinkers for several centuries after the formation of the New Testament. It led them through a process of trial and error culminating in the statements of the great councils of the patristic era—Nicea in 325 C.E., and Chalcedon in 451 C.E. As we saw in Chapter One, Chalcedon in turn set the pattern that dominated Christian thinking about Jesus for the next millennium and a half.

To make sense of this phase of the christological process we can begin by taking a long jump forward, from the close of the New Testament to the Council of Nicea. Having recalled what was done at Nicea, we shall then back up in order to figure out why and what was at stake. That will allow us, in the rest of this chapter, to proceed forward to Chalcedon.

The Way To Nicea

First, recall what we said about the Council of Nicea when we were explaining in Chapter One what is meant by a high, descending approach to christology. The Council was summoned by Emperor Constantine. At Nicea the bishops doctored a profession of faith that was already in use by adding several phrases and appending a number of curses. The phrases they added spoke of Jesus as "true God of true God, begotten not made, one in being (*homoousios*) with the Father." All of this was in response to an Egyptian priest, Arius, who apparently taught the opposite of these phrases. The outcome was the dogma of the divinity of Christ.

In order to deepen our understanding of what was going on at Nicea we need to focus a bit more on Arius. Arius, we want to suggest, brought to a head an ambiguity that ran through previous Christian thinking about Jesus. He brought this ambiguity out into the open and resolved it, but his solution was rejected. To understand the dogma of Nicea, then, we need to understand first of all what the ambiguity was that Arius exposed, and we need to understand why his solution was rejected. That is, what was at stake in the dogma of Christ's divinity? What real difference does it make whether one thinks of Jesus as divine or not?

To get hold of the ambiguity that we have been talking about we shall back up from Nicea to the close of the New Testament period. At that point a double task faced the Christian communities. One aspect of the task was cultural. Christianity had begun as a Jewish sect. Recall, for instance, the first of the early christological patterns that we laid out, the parousia pattern. That pattern functioned effectively to convey Jesus' significance within a community who already operated out of a Jewish apocalyptic style of thought. So also did a title like "Messiah." To non-Jews, however, neither an apocalyptic pattern of thought nor the title of Messiah communicated much of anything. Hence, even within the period of the formation of the New Testament, Christians found other patterns as well, while the title Messiah, once translated into Greek as Christ, very rapidly became more of a proper name for Jesus. Already within the New Testament period, the process of articulating Christianity in terms that could communicate with the broader Hellenistic culture of the Roman empire was under way.

We have already mentioned the other aspect of the task facing the Christian community. Besides inculturating themselves in the Hellenistic culture of the empire, Jesus' followers also had to think out what they were doing when they were "singing hymns to Christ as though to God." How was the Christian practice of honoring Jesus as divine compatible with the prayerful conviction of their Jewish heritage that there is but one God? More precisely, the complex question they faced was this: How could the Father be one, the Son another, both divine, and yet there be only one God?

In the course of the first few centuries Christians engaged in a process of trial and error as they faced this double task. In some cases they backtracked from the tension that generated the question at hand. *Adoptionists*, for example, denied the real divinity of Jesus, resting content to view him as a human being whom God favored with an exceptionally rich outpouring of God's spirit. Views like these have been labeled *psilanthropism*, a fancy word whose Greek roots mean "merely human." *Monarchians*, on the other hand, denied that the Son was really distinct from the Father. They believed that while God had been revealed as Father in the history of

Israel, God's revelation in the New Testament was under a different modality, namely as Son. Father and Son were successive modes of the one God's self-revelation in history.

In addition to these ways of relaxing the tension inherent in Christian liturgical practice, another avenue of development also opened up. The image of Jesus as God's *logos* proffered by the prologue to the Fourth Gospel came to the forefront. On the one hand it served to bridge the Jewish and Hellenistic worlds. On the Jewish side, translated as "Word," *logos* resonated with the medium through which God created and interacted with history throughout the Hebrew Scriptures. In Genesis 1 God creates by speaking. For instance, God commands "'Let there be light,' and there was light" (Gen 1:3). Subsequently God guides Israel's history by sending God's word to the prophets. On the Hellenistic side *logos* could be translated as "reason." Hellenistic culture contained a philosophic stew in which bits and pieces of various philosophic schools floated around together. Stoicism contributed the notion of *logos* to designate the principle of order immanent to the universe, the principle of rationality that made the universe an ordered cosmos rather than chaos. Seeds of the *logos*, *logoi spermatikoi*, were contained by each human mind.

With this dual background John's image of Jesus as God's *logos* offered itself as a vehicle for the development of the christological process. A review of that process in three major Christian thinkers will get us back to Arius and the Council of Nicea.

Around the middle of the second century a wandering philosopher from the Near East named Justin set up shop in Rome. Having tried out a number of the philosophies of the day, he had eventually become a Christian. Still he continued to wear the distinctive garb of the philosopher, whose way of life was highly revered in the culture of the Roman empire. On the premise that you defined yourself by what you spent your time on, philosophers, who engaged in contemplation of the eternal and unchanging, were deemed to have chosen the highest human pursuit.

In his desire to commend Christianity to the Romans Justin presented it as the true philosophy. In a culture that despised novelty and prized antiquity he endowed Christianity with an ancient lineage. Christianity, he proposed, was the true philosophy that summed up, corrected, and completed what was found in both the Hebrew scriptures and among the Greek philosophers.

Central to Justin's proposal was the notion of Christ as the *logos*. In the Old Testament God's *logos* was revealed intermittently and partially. Greek philosophy, on the other hand, represented an imperfect human grasp of the divine *logos*. Christianity excelled both of these because it received its teaching straight from the lips of the *logos* who had become human. Christianity thus embraced what was good in both Judaism and Greek philosophy, claiming them as its own while superseding them.

Justin shows how the notion of Jesus as God's *logos* could serve as a bridge to the Hellenistic culture of Rome. Perhaps Justin was too successful. At any rate, a competitor denounced him to the authorities for being a Christian, and Christians now honor him as St. Justin Martyr.

Jumping ahead a century, we come to the figure of Tertullian, a North African, perhaps a lawyer, and the first major Christian thinker to write in Latin. Important for his writings against the Gnostics, Tertullian himself eventually ended up a member of the Montanists, a rigorously ascetic Christian sect.

Tertullian takes up the question that the Christian practice of honoring Christ with divine worship raised, and his answer comes at it from a double angle. On the one hand, what defines God is power, *monarchia*. This divine power belongs properly to the Father. The Father in turn confers on the Son a share in its exercise, but this no more divides or diminishes the divine power than the emperor divides or diminishes his imperial power by appointing a governor. Thus the Father is one, the Son is another, both are divine by exercising the divine *monarchia*, and yet that divine power remains one and undivided.

With regard to the origin of the Son, Tertullian teaches that the Father alone is God from all eternity. What makes him God is that he is made of *spiritus*, divine stuff, the divine form of matter. When the Father decides to create, he first extrudes—the image calls to mind a tube of toothpaste—his *logos*. Through this *logos*, as Scripture says, all else is then created. Once again the Father is one, the Son is another, and both are divine because both are made of *spiritus*, yet there remains only one batch of divine stuff. Notice, however, that while both are divine, the Son or *logos* is not so divine as the Father. The divine power belongs properly to the Father, while the Son receives a share in its exercise and only the Father is eternal.

One more figure will bring us back to Arius. Moving from the Latin West to the Greek East, we encounter Origen, a contemporary of Tertullian in the middle of the third century. The brilliance and novelty of his work as a biblical commentator, apologist, and systematic theologian place Origen among the giants in the history of Christian thought alongside such figures as Augustine, Aquinas, and Luther.

Unlike Tertullian, for whom spirit was simply a fine grade of matter, Origen recognizes the difference between spirit and matter. He recognizes as well that God is spirit, not matter, and that if both Father and Son are divine, then the Son must likewise be eternal. The Son proceeds from the Father eternally in a non-material fashion similar to the way in which an act of willing proceeds from the will. On all these counts Origen represents an advance over Tertullian.

Yet Origen can also say such things as that the Son is Wisdom itself, but the Father is beyond Wisdom, and that the Son does not know the Father the way the Father knows himself. Hence for Origen as for Tertullian both Father and Son are divine, but nonetheless the Son is not so divine as the Father. For Origen, while the Father is divine in himself, the Son participates in the divinity of the Father.

We have been reviewing three early Christian thinkers who take up the image of Jesus as God's *logos*. They use it both to rearticulate Christianity in terms that make sense to the Hellenistic culture of the Roman Empire and to think through the problem of reconciling biblical monotheism with belief in Jesus as divine. What emerges in both Tertullian and Origen (and Justin, too, for that matter) is the idea that while both Father and Son are divine, the Son is less divine than the Father. This idea is called *subordinationism*; the divinity of the Son is subordinate to that of the Father.

The explanation for this trend lies in the philosophic baggage that came along with the Hellenistic notion of *logos* when it was put to use by these Christian thinkers. This philosophic baggage explains how it was possible for Tertullian to think of the Son as divine and yet not eternal. Without reflecting on it, drawing it in with the air he breathed, Tertullian thought in terms of Stoic philosophy, a form of materialism. Thus for him the Son could be divine as long as he was made of *spiritus*, divine stuff.

Hellenistic philosophy, though of a different brand, plays a similar role in Origen. Spontaneously thinking in terms of contemporary Platonism, a form of philosophic idealism, Origen locates God the Father in a realm of total mystery beyond intelligibility and rationality. These come on the scene when from this God there emanates the *logos*. The *logos* is divine by participation in the divinity of the Father but also inferior, a step down.

In both Tertullian and Origen Hellenistic philosophic assumptions have crept into Christian thought unnoticed, and the outcome in each case is subordinationism. This is the situation when Arius arrives on the scene. He was an Easterner, and his background lies in Origen's thought. Subordinationism is the only game in town and Arius blows the whistle on it. Origen saw reality in a very Greek way as a ladder whose top step was God and each of whose steps emanated from the one above and participated in it. Such a view makes God a part of a larger whole, the universe. It loses the biblical insight into God's transcendence, the distance that separates God from all that is not divine. For the Bible, being divine is not a matter of more or less. God is God, and all else is not God but God's creation.

Bringing this insight to bear on Origen's system, Arius could rightly demand that a spade be called a spade. If the Son or *logos* was not fully di-

vine, then it was really not divine at all. The *logos* was God's first crea-
ture, the blueprint according to which God created all else. Not divine, the
logos was a cosmological first principle. Taking on flesh in time, this cosmological first principle was what Jesus incarnated.

For Arius, then, Jesus was not divine. This seemed especially self-
evident to Arius because for him the divine was by definition incapable of
changing, while Jesus clearly moved in the realm of this changeable world
and indeed showed us how to live in such a world. Neither, however, was
Jesus really fully human, since the *logos* functioned in him in place of a
human soul.

Arius thus smoked out the ambiguity that had attended *logos* christologies since Justin Martyr. By rendering the divinity of the *logos* an inferior,
derived divinity, and by introducing degrees of divinity within the
Godhead, Justin, Tertullian, and Origen all smudged the line that divides
the transcendent God from all that is not God. Unnoticed Greek philosophical assumptions introduced subordinationism into the christologies
of Justin, Tertullian, and Origen. This subordinationism reduced the creator God of the Bible to being part of a universe with which, as the first
principle in a series of emanations, he was continuous.

But if Arius' solution was perfectly coherent, it also finally represented
a triumph of Hellenistic thought over Christianity. A non-divine Jesus
might be considered one whom others might more confidently seek to im-
itate, but a major reason for Arius' refusal to consider Jesus "true God of
true God" was his very Greek repugnance to associating the divine with a
world of change. On Arius' solution God was left untroubled in the realm
of divine transcendence when the non-divine *logos* took on flesh.

Nicea rejected Arius' solution. In his divinity, it proclaimed, Jesus is
"true God of true God, begotten, not made, one in being with the Father."
Why? What was at stake in this remote quarrel among ancient thinkers?
What difference does it make today whether one accepts Nicea and its
dogma of the divinity of Christ?

While the bishops gathered at Nicea would not have put it this way,
what was at stake between Arius and Nicea was the structure of Christian
religious experience. We can develop this idea in four steps.

The first step: During his lifetime, and in a different way after the resurrection, some people encountered another human being, a first-century
Jew, Jesus of Nazareth. In their encounter with him they underwent
metanoia, conversion. Thus in encountering this human being, Jesus of
Nazareth, they also encountered the reality of the one true God, the God
whom Jesus addressed as Abba.

The second step: On the basis of this experience (step one) those who
had undergone it could then reflect on what had been happening. What had

been happening was that through Jesus of Nazareth the one true God had been communicating, revealing, giving, expressing God's own self to them.

The third step: In that case, they could proceed to say, with regard to Jesus himself, that this human being was God's self-communication, God's self-expression, God's self-revelation, God's own Word.

The fourth step: Finally, if God really is as God reveals God's own self to be, then Jesus is identical with God's eternal self-communication, self-expression, or Word.

Nicea maintained that the human being Jesus is divine as God's self-expression, as the Word that proceeds from God, as Son of the one whom Jesus called Father. For Arius, however, when we encounter Jesus, we do not encounter God's very own self-expression. Rather we encounter a mythic figure, a cosmological first principle who has taken on a body but is neither divine nor human. This leaves God remote, untouched and untouchable in the infinite distance that separates the unchangeable realm of the transcendent from this world.

What is at stake between Arius and Nicea is the structure of Christian religious experience whereby Jesus is Emmanuel, God-with-us. For Arius that is not true. Before beginning our march forward to Chalcedon, we need to add two footnotes regarding Nicea.

The first footnote is this. If Nicea is the first ecumenical council of the Church, the bishops at the time did not realize this. After all they had no precedent, and the canon law governing councils had not yet been written. Hence it could and did happen that, once the council was over, Nicea's formula of belief was widely rejected. One reason was its use of the phrase "one in being" (*homoousios*) to characterize the relation of Jesus' divinity to that of the Father. Some took it to mean something like what we saw of Tertullian's position, namely that Jesus and the Father were made "of the same stuff," and so they rejected what looked like a claim that God was material and divisible. In the midst of a great deal of political intrigue surrounding the matter, Athanasius, who became patriarch of Alexandria, eventually won over Nicea's opponents.

Athanasius offered an explanation of what it meant to say that the Son was *homoousios* with the Father. It meant that whatever you could say about the Father you could say about the Son and vice versa, except what is proper to being Father or to being Son. Thus if you can say that the Father is eternal, omnipotent, all-wise, so also for the Son. But if you can say that the Son is only-begotten, you cannot say this of the Father. Being only-begotten is proper to being Son.

On Athanasius' interpretation, Nicea's *homoousios* gives you a rule for speaking correctly about God as Father and Son. It does not give you an explanation, much less a picture, of how God can be both Father and Son.

While Christian religious experience leads to that affirmation, it does not penetrate the mystery of God to explain it.

Second, one factor at play in the political intrigue that followed Nicea was the image of ultimate reality that the council proposed. From a political viewpoint the older subordinationism was far more expedient. It solidified the emperor's grip if, just as on earth there was a single absolute ruler to whom all else was subordinate, the same obtained in heaven. Nicea's profession of faith clashed with the imperial system inasmuch as it imaged ultimate reality not as a solitary ruler, but as a communion of equals. Perhaps this discordance with the imperial system explains in part the resistance Nicea initially encountered.

From Nicea to Chalcedon

Our next target is the Council of Chalcedon, one hundred twenty-six years after Nicea. The history leading from Nicea to Chalcedon is complex. We can control it, however, if we think of this period as a ball game in two innings, with a change of roster between innings. When we were introducing the idea of a high, descending approach to christology in Chapter One, we located our teams at Alexandria in Egypt, and Antioch in present-day Syria.

Each had its own team spirit. Alexandria was taken by the fact that with Jesus' coming, God was at work to save the human race. Hence they stressed the oneness of the divine with the human in Jesus, using the language of John's prologue to speak of Jesus in terms of *logos* and flesh. With this emphasis they had a hard time holding on to the fact that Jesus was completely human. This difficulty came fully into the open with a thinker named Apollinaris, who taught that in Jesus the *logos* replaced the human soul. For Apollinaris, Jesus was not fully human. This extreme version of Alexandrian thought was condemned at the second ecumenical council at Constantinople in 381 C.E.

Developing in response to this extremism, Antioch's team spirit was the mirror-opposite of Alexandria's. Focusing on the fact that with Jesus' coming as human we are saved, Antiochene thinkers stressed Jesus' full humanity. The completeness of our salvation depends on the completeness of Jesus' humanity, for if there is something about us that God's Son did not take on, we are not entirely saved. Thus Antiochenes spoke of Jesus in terms of the *logos* and a human being. The difficulty they ran into was in maintaining Jesus' unity as a single person.

Besides these differences in theology, political factors also came into play. Alexandria, a very ancient center of Christianity, regarded itself as second in dignity only to Rome among the churches of the world and as first among the Christian churches of the eastern part of the Empire. The Alexandrian ambition was to see its theology accepted throughout the East. In addition Alexandrians were particularly concerned by developments at Constantinople, present-day Istanbul in Turkey, which had only recently become the second, eastern capital of the Roman empire. From their viewpoint Constantinople was an upstart.

The roster for the first inning of play: At Alexandria the patriarch, or head bishop, was Cyril, at Antioch it was John, and at Constantinople Nestorius. The ball gets thrown out when Nestorius, new to his job, delivers a series of sermons at Christmas time in 428 C.E.

Christians at Constantinople had been quarreling about what to call Jesus' mother. Alexandrians honored her as *Theotokos*, Mother of God. Antiochenes objected: Mary was mother of Jesus' humanity, and to call her Mother of God threatened the integrity of his humanity. As bishop, Nestorius had the job of holding the community together, and so in his Christmas sermons he proposed a compromise: call Mary *Christotokos*, Mother of Christ. But in the course of his sermons Nestorius made it clear that his own thinking was thoroughly Antiochene, and he subjected the notion that God could have a mother to ridicule.

Informed of Nestorius' sermons by his agents in Constantinople, Cyril of Alexandria saw an opportunity to pounce. If Nestorius denied that Mary was Mother of God and recognized her only as Mother of Christ, then, Cyril reasoned, Nestorius must be dividing Jesus into two persons, the divine Son of God and a human Christ; the latter, because of his outstanding holiness, merited to have the Son dwell in him in a particularly full manner. Having sent these accusations of heresy to Rome, Cyril was charged by the pope to clean up Dodge City (in this case, Constantinople).

To this end he sent Nestorius a series of letters, demanding that Nestorius stop dividing Christ in two, give up his Antiochene language about two natures in Christ, and honor Mary as Mother of God. Receiving these letters, Nestorius passed them on to John of Antioch without doing anything else about them. Cyril then convinced the emperor and the bishop of Rome that a council was needed to deal with Nestorius' stubbornness and got one called at the city of Ephesus.

Called into session on June 22, 431 under Cyril's presidency, the bishops at Ephesus listened to a reading of the creed of Nicea. Then Cyril's second letter to Nestorius was read, and the bishops were asked whether it accorded with the faith of Nicea. The answer was a loud yes. Then some of Nestorius' materials were read, with the same question. The answer was a resounding no, and Nestorius was declared deposed, out of his position as patriarch at Constantinople. In addition a canon, or law, was passed stipulating that no one should add to the faith of Nicea.

At the Council of Ephesus the Nicene creed had become the standard for Christian faith, and Cyril's second letter was accepted as an officially sanctioned explanation of that faith. In this way *Theotokos*, Mother of God, came to be solemnly approved as a title for Mary.

Cyril had acted somewhat hastily. Several days later John of Antioch and his group of bishops arrived at Ephesus for the council, only to find out that the show was already over. Angrily they drew up their own profession of faith and, picking up on a phrase in one of Cyril's letters, declared him a heretic. Thus the immediate upshot of the Council of Ephesus was a schism, or split, in the Church in the East. This state of affairs lasted for two years until, under considerable pressure from the emperor, a compromise was reached. Cyril accepted the continuing legitimacy of Antiochene theology and its talk of two natures in Christ, while, after considerable resistance, the Antiochene bishops accepted Nestorius' deposition and exile. The schism formally ended when, in 433 C.E., Cyril sent out a letter entitled "The Heavens Rejoice" into which he incorporated, word for word, a version of the profession of faith drawn up by the Antiochene bishops. With Cyril's letter our first inning ends. Tie score.

The second inning brings onto the field a new roster of players. At Alexandria, Dioscorus succeeds Cyril as patriarch. Flavian holds that position at Constantinople, where Theodosius rules as emperor. The emperor's favorite monk, in fact a head monk or archimandrite, is one Eutyches. At Rome, Leo is pope.

Once again the action begins at Constantinople where, in 448 C.E., the patriarch Flavian is holding a meeting, or synod, with the bishops under his jurisdiction. To Flavian's dismay, while the meeting is underway someone accuses Eutyches, the archimandrite and imperial favorite, of heresy. This puts Flavian, patriarch of the imperial capital in the East, in a no-win situation. He bobs, he weaves, but in the end he is constrained to put Eutyches on trial.

Eutyches represents an extreme version of Alexandrian thought. The phrase into which he sinks his teeth is "after the union, one incarnate nature." The phrase is slippery in both meaning and history. Eutyches gets it from Cyril. At Cyril's hand, "nature" simply means "concrete being," and so the phrase simply says that after the coming together of the divine with the human at the incarnation, Jesus exists as a single, concrete individual. Moving back a step, Cyril thought he had gotten the phrase from Athanasius, the champion of Nicea. In fact, however, the document from which he got it had been written by Apollinaris who, as we saw, denied the completeness of Jesus' humanity. After Apollinaris' condemnation in 381, Athanasius' name had been put on the document to make it more respectable.

Asked to clarify whether he was denying Christ's human nature, Eutyches stubbornly stuck to his phrase. Pushed to accept the letter Cyril had written in 433 C.E. that ended the schism between Alexandria and Antioch and in which Cyril had accepted Antioch's language about two natures in Christ, Eutyches refused. Consequently he was found guilty of heresy.

Flavian then sent the proceedings of the trial to Leo in Rome. Leo approved and composed a document known as Leo's *Tome*, which likewise used the language of two natures to speak of Christ's divinity and humanity.

However, before the return mail could make its way back from Rome to Constantinople, Eutyches took off, finding refuge with Dioscorus in Alexandria. It turns out that through his agents in Constantinople Dioscorus had been stage-managing Eutyches' trial to make sure that his own man, Eutyches, would be condemned. This allowed him to turn to Theodosius, the emperor, and persuade him that since his favorite monk had been condemned for heresy, a council was needed to set matters straight.

Theodosius concurred, and in 449 the meeting was held at Ephesus with Dioscorus presiding. As we shall see, church historians count it not as the Second Council of Ephesus, but as the Robber Synod of Ephesus. At this meeting the pope's legates asked to read Leo's *Tome* and were refused. The proceedings of the trial held by Flavian were read out and the decision was reversed: Eutyches was exonerated. Then they nailed Flavian on a technicality. The Council of Ephesus in 431 had passed a law saying that no one should add to the faith of Nicea. Since Flavian had been using Cyril's letter of 433, "The Heavens Rejoice," as a norm for Eutyches, Flavian was found guilty of contravening Ephesus' law, and hence he was deposed. Nor did Flavian live much longer, having been badly beaten after an encounter with some of Dioscorus' deacons in a dark alley. To wind matters up, Dioscorus also had most of the other Antiochene bishops deposed and replaced with Alexandrians. At this point it looked as though Dioscorus had succeeded in fulfilling Cyril's ambition; Alexandria's would be the only licit theology throughout the eastern part of the empire. At Ephesus Dioscorus hit a grand slam with bases loaded, and victory seemed certain.

Leo, once his legates had informed him of all this, began asking the emperor Theodosius to convene another council in order to undo the irregularities of Dioscorus' meeting, but Theodosius turned a deaf ear. After all, his favorite monk had been rehabilitated and he finally had, so he thought, religious uniformity throughout the eastern half of the empire. So matters continued until the most important animal in the history of Christian doctrine, whose name unfortunately has not been preserved, intervened. One day Theodosius' horse threw him, killing him in the process.

Theodosius' sister Pulcheria ("The Pretty One") followed him on the imperial throne and, marrying a general named Marcian despite a vow of perpetual virginity she had taken earlier, raised her new spouse to the rank of emperor. Marcian and Pulcheria began undoing Dioscorus' mischief, recalling the Antiochene bishops to their episcopal sees, and so Leo ceased calling for a council. Now, however, their royal highnesses decided that the unity of the realm required an end to religious wrangling and that to achieve this a council was in order. With Leo's reluctant assent they called one, first for Ephesus but then, since Marcian was running a war at the time, for his convenience nearer the capital at a town named Chalcedon just across the water from Constantinople.

Sensing that the wind was turning against him, Dioscorus remained ever defiant. As he made his way to Chalcedon he excommunicated Leo. At Chalcedon, however, Dioscorus found himself isolated and abandoned. Leo's *Tome* was endorsed enthusiastically. At first when the imperial couple requested a new profession of faith the council fathers refused, citing the law passed at Ephesus. Their imperial highnesses insisted, however, and a document was drafted. The papal legates objected strongly to what they perceived as an ambiguity in the document, and it was sent back to committee.

The Faith of Chalcedon

What finally emerged runs as follows:

> Wherefore, following the holy Fathers, we all with one voice confess our Lord Jesus Christ one and the same Son, the same perfect in Godhead, the same perfect in humanity, truly God and truly human being, the same consisting of a rational soul and a body, one in being with the Father according to the divinity and the same one in being with us according to the humanity, like us in all things except sin; begotten of the Father before the ages according to the divinity but the same in the last days for us and for our salvation born according to the humanity of Mary the Virgin and Mother of God; one and the same Christ, Son, Lord, Only Begotten, to be acknowledged in two natures, without confusion, without change, without division, without separation; the distinction of the natures being in no way abolished because of the union but rather the characteristic property of each nature being preserved, and coming together into one Person and one subsistence, not as if Christ were parted or divided into two persons, but one and the same Son and only begotten God, Word, Lord, Jesus Christ. Even as the prophets from the beginning spoke concerning him, and our Lord Jesus Christ instructed us, and the Creed of the Fathers has handed down to us.

It will be convenient for purposes of discussion to divide this text in half, with the first part ending at the phrase "Mary the Virgin and Mother of God."

The first part of the text contains what the participants at the council wanted to affirm. Four times over they repeat the teaching of the Council of Nicea, and each time they balance that teaching with an equally strong affirmation of Jesus' complete humanity. Thus if, as Nicea taught, Jesus is "perfect in divinity," he is also "perfect in humanity." If he is "truly divine," he is also "truly human being," and, repeating Constantinople I's rejection of Apollinaris, they spell this out: "consisting of a rational soul and a body." Having balanced Nicea with an affirmation of Jesus' humanity twice, they do it again. They repeat Nicea's "one in being (*homoousios*) with the Father according to the divinity," balance it with "one in being with us according to the humanity," and spell this out with "like us in all things except sin." Finally, if for Nicea Jesus is "begotten of the Father before the ages according to the divinity," he is also "born according to the humanity of Mary the Virgin and Mother of God," and this is "for us and for our salvation."

By thus balancing Nicea's dogma of the divinity of Christ with an equally strong affirmation of his complete humanity Chalcedon at the same time seeks to do justice to the valid emphases of both Alexandria and Antioch. With Alexandria it affirms that Jesus is "one and the same," so that Mary is, as Cyril insisted and the Council of Ephesus taught, rightly honored as Mother of God, while with Antioch it stresses the completeness of his humanity.

The second part of the text introduces some terms that can be of use in thinking about what the first part affirms. Because the first part consists in a series of double affirmations, balancing the teaching about Jesus' divinity with teaching about his humanity, the second part sums these doublets up by stating that he is "to be acknowledged in two *natures*." Having introduced the term, the text immediately sets out to preclude misconceptions.

With Antioch it reaffirms the integrity of the divine and the human in Jesus: Jesus' two natures are "without confusion, without change." What is human about Jesus remains fully human, and so also for the divine. They do not get mixed up with one another, nor does one change into the other. Jesus is not a hybrid, a third kind of being that would result from blending the divine and the human together.

With Alexandria the text reaffirms the oneness of the divine and the human in Jesus. If in encountering Jesus you only encounter a human being, you have not encountered his whole reality. Fully human, Jesus is at the same time wholly Word and Son of God. That is, the two natures are "without division, without separation."

After again restating the integrity of each of the natures, the text introduces a second term. Having consistently spoken of Jesus as "one and the same," the text affirms that Jesus' two natures come "together into one *Person* and one subsistence." From the Greek word for person, *hypostasis*, Chalcedon's teaching has become known as the dogma of the hypostatic union.

We can conclude our examination of the faith of Chalcedon with three comments. First, Chalcedon clearly teaches that Jesus is fully and completely human. This is the obvious thrust of the four statements with which, in the first part of the text, it reaffirms and then balances the teaching of the Council of Nicea.

Second, Chalcedon strongly rejects any notion that Jesus is partly human and partly divine. This is not what its language about two natures means. Jesus is not a hybrid, made out of two kinds of stuff. It is the one Jesus, a fully human being, who is at the same time wholly divine as God's Word of self-expression, as Son of the Father.

Third, as was the case with Nicea, Chalcedon affirms that the human being, Jesus, is nothing less than Emmanuel, God-with-us. It does not satisfy the tendency to want to be able to imagine how one and the same can possess two natures, nor does it offer an explanation. Rather it presents the dogma of the hypostatic union as a restatement of the mystery of God's graciousness brought about and made known through Jesus.

Chapter Sixteen

The Christological Process Today

The christological task is to get Jesus into language. Words are needed to evoke his impact and convey his significance to people of every place and every time. Christians are charged to share the ongoing presence of Jesus, raised from the dead, as the one through whom the kingdom of God draws near, the one through whom, on the level of spontaneous felt meaning, ultimate reality is known as Abba, the one whose wildly impractical lifestyle, as Luke spells it out in the Sermon on the Plain, is the path through death in all its forms to the fullness of human living. That task impels the proclamation and worship that draw Christians together, it informs their life as a community, and it sends them forth with a mission to the larger world around them.

At the outset the christological task set in motion the process from which the documents of the New Testament emerged. Once formed, those documents and the community life of worship and discipleship out of which they grew generated questions about Jesus' relationship to the one he called Abba. Those questions sent the communities of Jesus' followers into a centuries-long process of trial and error that culminated in the classical dogmas of Nicea and Chalcedon.

Because Jesus' impact and significance are to be communicated to every place and every time, the christological task is never complete. Furthermore, since times and places differ significantly the christological process involves the Christian Church in a learning process. Each new time and each new place provides a new perspective from which to bring Jesus into focus so that insights into Jesus that had not previously been available become possible. At the same time, as a learning process the christological process is always a self-correcting process of trial and error.

In this chapter we want to indicate some of the major directions in which the christological process is advancing at present. We shall note, first, how the past half century has seen a corrective movement in the recovery of Jesus' full humanity. Second, while historical-Jesus research has played a key role in that movement it is important to note as well the limits of every historical portrait of Jesus. Third, new developments within a culture set up new perspectives on Jesus' significance, enriching the tradition. We shall briefly sketch how this has been occurring in response to four such cultural developments: liberation movements among the poor of Latin America, the women's movement, environmental concern, and dialogue among world religions.

Recovering Jesus' Full Humanity

The christological process has continued over two millennia, and it continues today. The Council of Chalcedon may have clearly taught the full and complete humanity of Jesus but, as we saw in Chapter One, that doctrine got somewhat blurred in subsequent ages. There was a tendency to view Jesus' humanity as so special that at times a boundary was crossed. On the far side of that boundary it could no longer really be said with Chalcedon that Jesus, as people were actually imagining him and thinking of him, was "like us in all things except sin." Chalcedon's doctrine of Jesus' full humanity was somewhat compromised.

Four or five decades ago Catholic theologians began to ask whether the standard christology of the day had not crossed that line. Did, for example, someone who could read other people's minds and who could foretell the future really fully share the human condition? These questions came to the fore in the flurry of scholarship occasioned by the fifteen-hundredth anniversary of the Council of Chalcedon in 1951. They marked the beginning of a self-correcting movement whereby, in the intervening years, Catholic theologians have set about recovering the full humanity of Jesus. In this way the stream of christology began to shift its course and carve a new channel. The task of recovering Jesus' full humanity led Catholic scholars, beginning in the 1970's, to join the quest for the historical Jesus that, we saw, had been underway in its most recent phase among Protestant scholars since 1953. At present Catholic scholars like John P. Meier have not only caught up with their colleagues of other persuasions but also represent the leading edge of historical-Jesus research as well as of biblical studies in general.

Part One of our investigation in this book reflected the major role this corrective movement of recovering Jesus' full humanity plays in giving the christological process its present shape. We devoted the six chapters of

Part One to the question of the historical Jesus, a question that cannot be avoided in our present cultural situation. In those chapters we sketched a figure who proclaimed and, in his parables, healings, exorcisms, and the company he chose to keep, acted out the nearness of the kingdom of God. This Jesus brought into the world of his day the nearness of a God who is Abba, a mystery of boundless care and acceptance; if some people found in that nearness healing, liberation, and wholeness, others found it objectionable, a scandal to their piety and a threat to their security. Some people found Jesus to be of profound religious significance, while others reacted to him with ultimately murderous hostility.

The Historical Jesus: Some Limits

We should note very clearly that this sketch of the results of historical-Jesus research, like every answer to the question of the historical Jesus, has its limits. These limits have to do with the character of historical research, and they derive from two sources.

First, in order to create a historical portrait of Jesus a historian scrutinizes the available data in order to decide what the relevant facts about Jesus are. We saw, for instance, how form critics sift the New Testament accounts of Jesus' sayings and deeds to determine which of them actually go back to events in his ministry. In some cases historians arrive at very high probability, as good as certitude. Jesus' death by crucifixion at the Romans' hands is one example. On other matters, however, the historical evidence may be less compelling.

Historians deal in probabilities, and their judgments of probability are always in principle subject to revision; new evidence may surface, or a better explanation of the data may become clear. In recent years, for example, archeological projects in Israel and other parts of the Roman empire have provided new data on the world of Jesus' day, as has the discovery of texts like the famous Dead Sea scrolls.

The point is that when any scholar creates a historical portrait of Jesus, that scholar weaves together what he or she takes to be a set of facts about Jesus and his times. Under close examination, however, that set of facts turns out to consist in a number of variously probable judgments about the significance of available data. Some of these judgments will be more vulnerable to future revision than others, but as any of these judgments shifts in its level of probability, so do the components of one's portrait of Jesus. Remember, for example, what happened to Harnack's portrait when it was seen that he had effectively screened out some of the most important of Jesus' sayings, those in which the coming of the kingdom was an external future event.

Second, beyond determining what the relevant data about the past, the so-called facts of the matter, are, the historian also provides an account of what they add up to. Here, perhaps even more than in determining what data the historian will count as relevant facts, the historian's own perspective plays a role. It influences the kind of unitary image that he or she will use to pull those data together into a significant whole. Bruce Vawter highlighted the importance of this factor in our discussion of the historicity of Jesus' miracles when he pointed out the uselessness of discussing the issue for someone whose mind was already closed on the matter one way or the other.

This factor of the author's own perspective was also crucial to our interpretation of Jesus' central theme. According to that interpretation, when Jesus spoke about the nearness of the kingdom of God he was speaking about the nearness of the reality of God as God really is, the transcendent mystery that can nonetheless be addressed as Abba. This interpretation takes religious discourse to be about religious realities. That may sound obvious, but as a matter of fact a grasp of religious realities depends upon the interpreter's religious stance and development. Even as *metanoia* was important to how people thought of Jesus during his lifetime it continues to influence how they interpret him today, and this applies to historians when they ply their craft.

The importance of the historian's personal development is not confined to the case of religion. Historians of art, music, science, or mathematics all need to be well versed in their respective fields in order to write competent histories of them. A historian who believes that religion is really not about God and people in their relation to God but is only a disguise for the interplay of social, economic, and political factors will offer an interpretation of Jesus' central theme quite different from the one we worked out.

Hence historical-Jesus research has its limits. Every portrait of the historical Jesus rests on a set of more or less probable judgments of fact, and it reflects the perspective of its author. One author's perspective may complement another's, and sometimes they may be radically opposed. Furthermore, not only do perspectives differ from author to author, they also shift with the passing of time. Because each new generation looks back upon the past from a new place, as it were, history has to be rewritten in every generation.

In light of these reflections we might suggest that like the discipline of academic history in general, historical-Jesus research operates within definite limits. No portrait of the historical Jesus can claim to have the final word. If by the historical Jesus we mean Jesus insofar as his earthly life can be reconstructed by the methods of the discipline of history it is clear that the historical Jesus, understood in this precise sense, is not the basis or foundation of Christian faith. Christian faith got along quite well for the eighteen centuries or so before the modern discipline of history arrived on the scene and brought with it the question of the historical Jesus. For those eighteen centuries Christian liturgy, Scripture, and life in community worked together in carrying out the christological task of communicating Jesus' significance, of evoking and nourishing the *metanoia* by which one becomes a follower of Jesus, and they continue to do so today.

The limits of any portrait of Jesus constructed by the historian's methods have one important consequence. At the outset of the Old Quest, Reimarus appealed to his portrait of the historical Jesus in an effort to discredit the Christian religion. Toward the close of the Old Quest, Harnack sought to modernize Christianity by playing his portrait of the historical Jesus off against Christian traditions of dogma, worship, and moral teaching that struck Harnack as outmoded. Both authors rested their case on an appeal to what they took to be the historical facts about Jesus. With hindsight, however, it is clear that their appeal to the so-called facts was a naive and simplistic maneuver. It overlooked the limits of historical research. Subsequent research has revealed the portraits of Jesus that Reimarus and Harnack took to be definitive, the "real Jesus," to be improbable and rendered them obsolete.

To insist on the built-in limits of historical knowledge of Jesus is not to deny the value of such knowledge. Because we cannot possess the final word on Jesus from a historical perspective does not mean that we have made no progress in understanding Jesus as a historical phenomenon, nor does it mean that one historian's portrait is as good as another. It does mean, however, that Christians place their faith, not in historians' constructs, but in Jesus as he is known through the witness of Scripture and the life of the community of his followers.

Changing Perspectives, New Insights

All human knowing is conditioned by the knower's perspective, the place from which he or she knows. If it is important to keep this limit on human knowing in mind, it is no less important to note that changing perspectives offer an opportunity for enriched insight. This helps to explain why Christian faith is a dynamic reality. Christian faith does not consist in affirming a list of unchanging, eternally true propositions. Jesus' significance, what it means to follow Jesus as the way to the one he called Abba, must be discovered in each new situation, and each new situation offers a new perspective from which to explore his significance.

Jesus the Liberator

One area of ferment in recent years has been Latin America. If Jesus' proclamation of the nearness of the kingdom of God subverted the world of first-century Palestine, Latin American theologians began to notice specific parallels between that world and their own. They saw both worlds as dominated by the dynamics of colonial exploitation, as divided between a small, wealthy elite and an impoverished general population, and having an official religious establishment that tended to enjoy and serve the privileges of the few while counseling patience and docility to the many.

In this context liberation theologians raised questions about the traditional Catholicism that informed the culture of Latin America. Specifically they found it necessary to criticize a traditional image of Christ, divine and human, as heavenly ruler. Worship of Christ formed part of the lifestyle of many of the wealthy and powerful in many Latin American countries, but their belief in Christ as divine and human was apparently too abstract to make them self-critical about their lifestyle and the unjust social and political structures that supported it. Indeed the image of Christ as heavenly ruler seemed to have the subliminal effect of aligning Christ with the ruling segment of society. Far from inhibiting members of the elite from resorting to violence to maintain their position of privilege, an image that associated Jesus with the ruling segment of society could even help sanction repressive activity like that of the death squads as a necessary means of preserving good order and national security.

Hence Latin American liberation theologians focus not on dogma and sacraments but on Jesus as the gospels portray him. They highlight how, in the gospels, Jesus proclaims the nearness of God's kingdom as good news for the poor. From this vantage point they re-symbolize Jesus' story as the tale of a battle of the gods. In their retelling Jesus pits himself and his Abba-God against the false god Mammon and its anti-kingdom of oppression. This anti-kingdom is powerful; Jesus' story shows that overcoming the kingdom of the false god Mammon involves suffering its violence, and in Latin America this has been no abstract theological point. Besides well-known martyrs like Archbishop Oscar Romero, the four American churchwomen, and the Jesuits of El Salvador, scores of obscure catechists and pastoral workers have been murdered for their labors among and on behalf of the poor. Jesus' fate on the cross reveals a God in solidarity with the poor who form the crucified body of YHWH's suffering servant, while his resurrection offers hope that the persecutors do not have the last word. In Latin America a new image of Jesus Christ the Liberator has come to the fore.

Jesus in Feminist Perspective

Liberation theology has spread from Latin America to other regions of the Third World, taking on distinctive features in Africa and Asia. In an analogous development starting in the First World countries of Western Europe and North America and now also spreading worldwide the women's movement has given rise to feminist theology.

The dynamics of feminist theology resemble those of liberation theology. Women's place in society, like that of the poor, was formerly taken for granted and now has been called into question. "The way things are" is no longer self-evident. Systems that subordinate women to men are evoking resistance. Even as in Latin America the injustice of the disparity between rich and poor has become intolerable, so also the many ways in which women have been treated as inferior to men are now being perceived as unjustifiable.

In this situation the question arises to what extent the Christian tradition, and specifically its beliefs about Jesus, have contributed to keeping women in the place a male-dominated society would assign them. This question generates a hermeneutic of suspicion. Reviewing the Christian tradition from this perspective, feminists have woven long chains of quotations from major male Christian thinkers of all eras documenting their opinion of women as naturally inferior and morally dangerous creatures. Those chains can reach back even into Scripture. Genesis 3, for instance, which we examined when we were working out a biblical understanding of sin, has been invoked to justify male monarchic authority within the family: "he shall rule over you" (Gen 3:16). This text has been interpreted in some circles as God's will for the relation of husbands and wives rather than a curse consequent upon the Fall. In the New Testament, of course, the letter to the Ephesians can be quoted to the same effect: "Wives, be subject to your husbands as you are to the Lord" (Eph 6:22).

Some women, having judged the Christian tradition irredeemably sexist, have moved on to other spiritual traditions. For Christian feminists, however, the tradition is ambiguous, not unequivocally negative. Taking a step beyond criticism of the past, feminist theologians discover resources for transforming the tradition in the present. Their positive efforts thus far can be related in three steps.

First, feminists like Rosemary Radford Ruether have emphasized the prophetic dimension of Jesus' ministry. As the kingdom of God draws near it turns the existing order of things upside down. This reversal does not substitute a new system of domination for the old one. The coming of the kingdom creates a new community in which power and leadership function to empower and liberate the downtrodden and outcast. In this biblical vision of the iconoclastic prophetic Christ women are recognized as the most oppressed among the oppressed: widows are the poorest of the poor, prostitutes the most despised of the outcast. At the same time women prove particularly open to Jesus' ministry. It is a woman who evangelizes the Samaritans, bringing the good news of the Messiah's arrival to the men and women of her nation, and it is another woman, the Syro-Phoenician, who wins from Jesus a healing even for a non-Jew. If, as a saying of Jesus has it, with the coming of the kingdom the last shall be first, then women, the least of the last, can expect a special place.

The biblical image of Jesus the prophet allows Christian feminists to invoke Jesus' opposition to all forms of injustice as sanction for their efforts to overcome the injustices women experience in male-centered societies. This is not to say that Jesus was a feminist before his time, although his dealings with women often flew in the face of the customs of the day. It is to say that discipleship today, in an age of feminist consciousness, requires attention to feminist concerns.

Elizabeth Schüssler Fiorenza moves the matter a step farther. Not only is the memory of Jesus the prophet relevant to feminist concerns today, but careful examination of the historical data leads her to claim that in its beginnings the movement centered on Jesus was an egalitarian one in which women exercised leadership roles alongside men. Appreciating this claim requires, however, that historians overcome male biases. To give an example, only the assumption that all the apostles were male has prevented scholars from recognizing the apostle Junia, whom Paul mentions (Rom 16:7), as a woman. Instead scholars have taken for granted, gratuitously, that this clearly feminine name was a shortened form of the masculine equivalent.

In this reconstruction of Christian beginnings women are restored to the ranks of the apostles (remembering that these are a distinct group from the Twelve), prophets, missionaries, patrons, and leaders of communities. This kind of community is reflected in Paul's words:

> As many of you as were baptized into Christ have clothed yourselves with Christ. There is no longer Jew or Greek, there is no longer slave or free, there is no longer male and female; for all of you are one in Christ Jesus (Gal 3:27-28).

Yet the egalitarian thrust of the early Jesus movement stood in tension with the societal structures of the world about it, as Paul himself also witnesses in those passages where he enjoins women to be silent in the assembly of Christians (1 Cor 14:33-36) and in other texts of the Pauline tradition that enjoin wives to be submissive to their husbands (Col 4:8).

Eventually, as the Church accommodated itself to the Greco-Roman world women found themselves excluded from the hierarchic structure of bishop, presbyter, and deacon that emerged in the second and third centuries. Nonetheless, Schüssler Fiorenza concludes, Christian feminists can appeal to more than the contemporary relevance of the image of Jesus the prophet. In the egalitarian character of the early Jesus movement, women possess a usable past to be reclaimed in their effort to transform the present.

Third, Christian language for God has been predominantly masculine and this has conspired with Jesus' *de facto* maleness to make Christians forgetful of the divine incomprehensibility, the mystery of a God who exceeds all human categories. Instead, a tendency to image the divine as male (think, for example, of the Sign of the Cross) and to erect maleness as the norm for human beings leaves women second rate as both Christians and human beings. This tendency culminated, feminists contend, in the official document called *Inter insigniores* in which, in 1977, the Roman Catholic Church justified its unwillingness to extend presbyteral ordination to women because of their natural inability, by reason of their sex, to represent Christ fully. On this argument Jesus was male, and therefore only males can be Catholic priests.

To clarify this issue and to counter the distortions in the Christian imagination that underlie it Elizabeth A. Johnson recommends a recovery of Wisdom christology. As we saw in Chapter 14, this way of making sense of Jesus arose very early in the Christian tradition and it pervades much of the New Testament. In this biblical tradition *sophia* (the Greek word for wisdom) names God in God's gracious nearness and activity in the world, both in the great events of salvation history and in the details of everyday life. Retelling the story of Jesus as the story of Wisdom embodied among us enriches our imagery for the divine, allowing us to tap into the resources of women's experience as well as men's. It also allows us to acknowledge the fact that Jesus was male without turning his maleness into a barrier to women's full participation in the life of the community or a support for male superiority.

In dealing with both feminist and liberation theologies it is important to keep in mind their diversity. Liberation theologies are theologies "from below" attempting to articulate Jesus' saving significance in the concrete circumstances of their particular situation. Hence liberation theologies differ from country to country in Latin America and, with their spread into Africa and Asia, from continent to continent as well.

The same is true of feminist theologies. All seek to promote justice for women, but women's situations differ widely. White North Americans, for example, face a "glass ceiling" in the public sector and the extent to which they are subject to domestic violence is also becoming evident. In China different concerns come to the fore: with that country's severe restrictions on population growth girl babies are often aborted or left to die after birth. In India marital abuses are drawing attention. Not only have wives been expected to immolate themselves on their husband's funeral pyre in the past, but even today, especially in rural areas, brides who bring an inadequate dowry may be burned to death by their husband's family. Feminist theologies will differ according to the circumstances of the locality that they address.

Variety in theologies stems from another source as well. Besides differences in the circumstances of injustice to which they are responding, liberation theologies and feminist theologies also reflect differences on moral issues. Liberation theologians, for example, divided on the question of the place of violence and armed revolution in opposing unjust governments while feminist theologians in North America differ greatly among themselves in their response to the agenda of "reproductive rights" and its underlying philosophy of liberal individualism.

Diversity of this second kind indicates the importance of recalling that the christological process is a process of trial and error. New perspectives offer the possibility of rich new insights but not every insight proves valuable, and some can distort Jesus' significance and thus promote the dynamics of sin rather than salvation. The ambiguity of the Christian tradition extends from the past into the present, and there is no reason to expect liberation or feminist theologies to escape it.

"The whole creation is groaning in labor pains" (Rom 8:22)

Two developments in the understanding of the relationship between human beings and the natural universe are fostering new insights into Jesus' significance. Whereas in the creation story of Genesis 1 God set up a stable and fixed universe "in the beginning," modern science gives us a universe that is still coming to be. From biology we learn to imagine the earth as a mega-organism in which evolution continues apace; astronomers enable us to capture new stars as they are being born on film, while physicists are calculating how many billions of years are left before our expanding universe is likely to lose its energy, grow dark and cold, and collapse back in upon itself. In place of the relatively young and stable abode of the biblical story, science would have us imagine a dynamic universe that flared forth fifteen billion years ago, formed the sun that centers our solar system four and a half billion years ago, and saw the first human beings a mere two and a half million years ago.

Besides re-imagining the universe as an ongoing process of cosmogenesis we are beginning to understand and own our responsibility for the harm that human beings have wrought upon the natural environment, especially since the advent of modern industry. Heedless of the community of being that we share with the earth and all it contains, we reduce nature to an object to be exploited and, exercising the mastery that we claim over it, we have been squandering the earth's soil, poisoning its air and waters, and condemning to extinction myriad living species that evolution's long labors have gifted with existence. Sin, the dynamic, expanding process of dehumanization and alienation that wreaks havoc with human societies and their cultures, attacks as well the natural environment on which we depend for our sustenance and well-being.

These two developments, contemporary scientific cosmology and environmental awareness, open up new dimensions in our understanding of Jesus' significance. Take, for example, the doctrine of the incarnation, the insight that Jesus is the human embodiment of God's Word (*logos*) or God's Wisdom (*sophia*). This belief has been spelled out in the tradition by saying that in the incarnation God took on a human nature. At least today, however, the philosophical term "nature" can sound very abstract. Yet the scientific developments we are considering help us recognize more than ever that our humanity, the human nature that God made God's own in the incarnation, is anything but abstract.

For example, contemporary physics teaches us to think of both our consciousness and our bodies as energy existing in different states; there is no ultimate opposition between matter and spirit. This insight in turn links us to the universe in its dynamic process of becoming. The matter that composes our bodies derives from stardust, composed of elements that began forming in the first few minutes of the universe's primal explosion fifteen billion years ago. Billions of years later, on earth, that stardust underwent the further transformative combinations from which life and consciousness have issued. From this perspective we can view ourselves as unique moments in the ongoing fallout from the original burst of energy, the so-called Big Bang, with which the universe originated. Hence, in taking on our humanity in the incarnation, God embraced and made God's own in a special way the entire process of cosmogenesis and its earthly continuation, evolution.

In Jesus' life, death, and resurrection God has provided a solution to the problem of evil, salvation from sin. In Chapter 13 we suggested that salvation unfolds in two moments. There is a final moment, eschatological transformation, on the other side of death. But salvation does not just concern the afterlife; salvation is also a process that occurs now insofar as people live the law of the cross, following Jesus through death to the many forms of sin toward the fullness of authentically human living. Liberation theologians have helped us see that a life of discipleship sets one in opposition to the systems of injustice that oppress the poor, and feminists have sharpened our perception of the particular forms of injustice to which women have been subject. In addition we are becoming aware that sin also affects the non-human life systems of the planet in whose community of being and life we participate. Discipleship, we are learning, demands a new stance of care for the earth. In this context Paul's words to the Christian community at Rome acquire a new depth of meaning when he writes about Christian hope for the earth,

> that creation itself will be set free from its bondage to decay and will obtain the freedom of the glory of the children of God. We know that the whole creation has been groaning in labor pains until now . . . (Rom 8:20-22).

Jesus Christ and World Religions

At the Second Vatican Council, in its "Declaration on the Relationship of the Church to Non-Christian Religions," the Catholic Church officially adopted a new stance of appreciation and openness to other world religions. The document spoke of the genuine holiness and truth to be found in Hinduism and Buddhism, it expressed high esteem for Islamic belief and worship, and it recognized the special ties and common heritage that bind Christians to Jews. With respect to all, the Council called for dialogue and collaboration.

This stance differed markedly from an earlier attitude, expressed at the Fourth Lateran Council in 1215, that "outside the Church there is no salvation." Abandoning a view that saw non-European cultures as barbaric and their religions as superstitious, and recognizing as well the historical particularity of both Jesus and the Church, Christians are now prepared to discern in other religions the work of the Holy Spirit drawing people to God through the gift of God's love and to learn from the experience of these other traditions.

In dialogue Christians encounter interpretations of Jesus in conflict with their own. Jews of an earlier age, for instance, portrayed Jesus as the illegitimate son of Mary and a Roman soldier. Skilled in black magic, an ancient Jewish source goes on to say, Jesus was rightfully executed as a sorcerer. On the contemporary scene Jewish-Christian relations have become less antagonistic and some Jewish scholars are reclaiming Jesus as one of their own. They can emphasize his affinities with the classical prophetic tradition and with the Pharisaic movement of his own day.

Still, these Jews firmly reject any messianic title for Jesus. From their perspective Jesus' coming did not bring the day of salvation for his people; instead, Israel's sufferings only intensified at the hands of those who claim to follow Jesus.

Islam reveres Jesus as son of the Virgin Mary; a wonderworking prophet, he was raised up by God to confirm the Torah and to prepare for a yet greater prophet to come after him. Muslims believe that Jesus did not die on the cross. Having escaped the Romans, he died a natural death. When Christians confess Jesus as divine they crudely betray the utter transcendence of Allah, the one God.

Mohandas Gandhi discovered in Jesus' teaching strong affinities with the Hindu way of *bhakti*, loving devotion and surrender to God. Yet Hindus find it arbitrary to restrict the incarnation of the divine to Jesus alone. At the same time incarnation becomes less important since it occurs in the realm of history, and for Hindus that realm is illusory and ultimately unreal.

These points of conflict also point to areas of common conviction among the religions, and in addition they can impel Christians to clarify their own self-understanding. For example, Judaism and Islam share with Christianity the experience of prophecy while both Judaism and Islam challenge Christians to recall that the God whom they confess as Triune remains always incomprehensible mystery. Indeed, Buddhist conviction that ultimate reality is "no-thing" finds resonances in the Christian mystical tradition; God exceeds all human categories. Or again, the Jewish critique of Christian messianic claims can temper any complacency among Christians that they hold salvation as a possession; in light of the sorry history of Christian persecution of the Jews it becomes all the more urgent that Christians live out the opposition to the dynamics of sin that shows them to be followers of Jesus and that alone can redeem history.

Dialogue and collaboration with other world religions provide a rich new opportunity for Christians to better understand and more fully respond to the gift of *metanoia*, the transformative gift of God's love which they have received through Jesus Christ. Like all dialogue, the dialogue of Christians with members of other world religions may entail at times a change in the way they understand themselves; at the same time, if the dialogue is genuine, such change will signify a deepening, not a loss, of Christian identity.

Index